The Ford White House

The Ford White House

The Diary of a Speechwriter

John J. Casserly

Colorado Associated University Press
Boulder 1977

For
Kevin, Terry, Jeff and Lawrence

Contents

Foreword

GERALD R. FORD assumed the presidency on August 9, 1974. The American people were disillusioned and divided, some deeply distrustful. America's Age of Innocence, if it existed, had ended during the previous dark days and events.

Our national conscience had been stirred to the innermost by the American tragedy in Vietnam. The prolonged war proved more than a military quagmire; it was moral quicksand.

Our Vice President, Spiro T. Agnew, had left office in public disgrace. Many Americans viewed him as a common, petty criminal.

Our President, Richard M. Nixon, after extraordinary national acclaim at the polls, left office cursing fate and the crushing reasons for his fall, smashing the lives of lifetime friends and some of his closest aides. No president—perhaps no American in history—had been so personally humiliated, or had so humiliated this nation and its citizens. Nixon became a virtual exile in his own land.

A national sense of betrayal permeated the times. Distrust of government and our political leaders had become part of the American dialogue. Our people were infected with a new cynicism concerning many of our institutions. Americans were angry and frustrated by our national troubles. Declining employment amid increasing inflation confounded the country and compounded its lament.

This was the America that President Ford inherited.

I entered White House service in October of 1974, about two and one-half months after Mr. Ford took office. It was no longer a mark of high honor and trust to serve in the nation's symbolic home. The White House had become suspect; its staff, their motives, their actions were all under intense public scrutiny.

I began this diary as a father's counsel to his four sons—to record for them events as they actually occurred at this pinnacle of power. As the days lengthened into months, I became acutely aware of the uniqueness of the Ford White House—the uncommon nature of this administration and the unprecedented period it represented in the history of the American presidency.

I became convinced that someone with no political or personal partisanship should chronicle for the public record some of the central characteristics of the singular Ford administration. As a lifelong political Independent, (a career civil servant for most of my White House tenure, and twenty-five years as a news reporter and professional writer, I was among the few neutral observers on the scene.)

The issues and problems that confronted me made even more clear the singularity of what had occurred in the transfer of power from the Nixon to the Ford administration. People and power intertwined. This changed my purpose somewhat: to record not only events, but their reasons and their rightness.

This chronicle was carefully kept. I recorded virtually all events in the diary on the day they occurred. Occasionally, because of speechwriting and other editorial deadlines, I was unable to type a final copy on the same day. Several days sometimes passed before this final typing took place, but I retained my notes and my final draft adhered rigidly to their meaning. A clean copy of my typed draft was prepared by Mrs. Dorothy Olson and Mrs. Lucile McArten. I am grateful for their careful work.

The completed manuscript was edited by my wife Joy Ruth

Foreword

Casserly and her longtime colleague Bette M. Orr. Both are first-rate scholars, Smithsonian fellows, whose years in research and other historical pursuits made them ideal collaborators.

These editors shortened the manuscript by eliminating repetition and other extraneous detail, and provided the quotations at the beginning of each chapter. In only rare instances did I change their work, and then only for emphasis or clarity—not material substance. Therefore, the intellectual and emotional contents of the diary are preserved intact to the moment and the hour. No material was added later.

While I am indebted to my wife and Bette Orr for their deft editing of this text, I assume full responsibility for an accurate accounting of each day in the White House.

I finally decided to publish this diary in the spirit of triumph over human weakness and error. So often in recording this great crisis of the American presidency, the redeeming qualities of daily life became lost in its trial and torment. I recount torment but also triumph.

There are no state secrets in this book, no bombshells. A conniver cuts a swath here and there. Gerald R. Ford proves to be an imperfect president, but God has not created the perfect politician.

I found no heroes in the White House, no pillars of wisdom. The mighty—so called—proved to be individuals of ordinary limits. In essence, my colleagues were somewhat average Americans, without special grace or greatness.

By the time I left the White House, I had arrived at an unpretentious view of the Ford administration and of those who peopled it, because this was not a pretentious president. Following the diary entries I have offered some specific conclusions.

I owe a debt to the American people who allowed me to be of some small service for fifteen months in the White House. I offer them my gratitude and these reflections.

—John J. Casserly

Lakewood, Colorado
1977

The Diary

Chapter 1
November, 1974

"We must not expect, that a new government may be formed, as a game of chess may be played, by a skillful hand, without a fault. The players of our game are so many, their ideas so different, their prejudices so strong and so various, their particular interests, independent of the general, seeming so opposite, that not a move can be made that is not contested; the numerous objections confound the understanding; the wisest must agree to some unreasonable things, that reasonable ones of more consequence may be obtained; and thus chance has its share in many of the determinations, so that the play is more like . . . with a box of dice."

BENJAMIN FRANKLIN, *as a delegate from Pennsylvania to the Constitutional Convention.*

Thursday, November 14, 1974

ABOARD AIR FORCE ONE, November 14, 1974—Flying at some
30,000 feet—winging west to Washington from Las Vegas and
Phoenix—President Gerald R. Ford hires a new presidential
speechwriter about 10 P.M. EST. His name is John J. Casserly,
forty-seven, father of Joy Ruth's four feathers—Kevin, Terry,
Jeffrey and Lawrence. Mr. Ford said:

"I would like you to come down a long and maybe rough road
with me—but on one condition: that you really want to come."

I reply: "It would be an honor and a privilege."

There is no magic in the moment. No drama. It is
matter-of-fact.

The President has finished dinner in his cabin after a very long
day. Air Force One took off early that morning from Andrews Air
Force Base outside Washington for Las Vegas. Mr. Ford addressed
the National Association of Realtors on housing in Las Vegas and
we quickly took off again for Phoenix. At Luke Air Force Base,
Mr. Ford spoke briefly and witnessed the unveiling of the Air
Force's newest jet fighter—the F-15.

The past week was dominated by one word—leadership. I
spent the week, my second in the White House, working on the
address President Ford gave today in Las Vegas. It had provoked a
battle between the departments of Treasury and Housing and Urban
Development. In essence, HUD wished to offer some rays of
sunshine—and some federal pump-priming—to take some of the
shock out of the disaster-struck housing industry. Treasury wanted
to stress fiscal responsibility—no pump-priming. I went to my
superior, Paul Theis, for guidance.

Paul Theis, our executive editor, did not have the answer. His
advice was: balance off the two viewpoints and let's circulate a first
draft. The aim is to try to balance off the differences between the
two departments and then let the President's top advisers reconcile
the various viewpoints. Theis, fifty-one, was the long-time public
relations director of the GOP Congressional Campaign Committee.
He was a lifetime Republican loyalist.

The comments were dutifully returned from the offices of
Secretary William Simon at Treasury; Secretary James Lynn at
HUD; Alan Greenspan, chairman of the Council of Economic

2

Advisers; L. William Seidman, chairman of the Economic Policy Board; and others. The positions of the departments seem irreconcilable so I return to Theis for more advice. He said in effect:

"Make the best of it. See if you can word it so that we come down right in the middle."

Theis was showing early that he had two convictions: caution and compromise.

I rewrote the speech into what I call "pea soup," a bland concoction that should get no one into trouble. At the end, Jim Lynn and others talk the President into pumping some federal funds into housing loans but the amount is minimal. The audience of realtors loves it—anything positive. But their Las Vegas locale does not appear to be suffering recession.

The Air Force's new F-15 fighter was unveiled in the presence of the President at Phoenix's Luke Air Force Base. Theis had said to write about five minutes for the President; but we were not to say anything that might offend the Russians because the President would soon visit there. That was the total direction he gave me. So the F-15 became a "Pioneer for Peace" and a "Pilgrim for Peace" since November is the month of the Mayflower. The President told General Secretary Brezhnev if he was listening:

"I would rather walk a thousand miles for peace than take a single step toward war."

Theis was elated at the speeches. So was the President. I was sick.

Could I continue to write speeches like this? Could I hold up for more than two years with little or no direction? Where the hell were we all going?

The press is asking the same final question: Where is the country going?

No one with whom I speak within the White House will discuss leadership except in terms of: 1) reorganizing the White House staff and clearing out most of the Nixon holdovers, including the cabinet; and 2) the need for time to get organized and present a "realistic" program in January's State of the Union message.

From my early experiences, however, I feel that leadership is a real issue. Columnists and editorial writers begin to question Mr. Ford's ability to lead. This does not so much anger as dismay the White House staff. Their answer is: We inherited a "mess." Give us time.

3

Lines like these most nettle the staff:

"The country has not had presidential leadership in more than a year. When are we finally going to get it?"

"Nice guys (talking of Mr. Ford) finish last."

"One thing about the Russians and Chinese—they've got some leadership."

"We need Golda Meir."

There is a reasonable answer to this although I have misgivings about it:

Mr. Ford has set out to depersonalize the presidency. For example, the University of Michigan's fight song is played—not "Hail to the Chief." He calls his living quarters "the residence" not "the mansion" as Nixon had. The President tells his staff:

"Don't push people around. Treat them the way you want to be treated. Be courteous."

Mr. Ford asks for all points of view. In our case, he requests regular meetings with the speechwriters. If it is urgent, any one of a half dozen aides can walk in his office at any time.

The President's closest advisers, Hartmann, Rumsfeld, Marsh, Seidman, Buchen, all disclaim "power" with the President. Donald Rumsfeld attempts to shield himself so that he will not be compared with either Haldeman or Ehrlichman.

There is definitely no "personality cult" around Mr. Ford. The President's style is relaxed and direct. One man close to Mr. Ford is not cut from his style. Henry Kissinger, Secretary of State, talks and acts "power." He is not a team or an organization man. But Mr. Ford likes him. These are my first impressions of the Ford White House.

This evening, the President held a televised news conference in Phoenix. This conference precipitated the first real hassle that I witnessed from inside the White House. This afternoon I listened as Press Secretary Ron Nessen and Bob Hartmann, counselor to the President, griped about the pullout of the networks from the news conference. It would be covered by only Phoenix TV stations.

"I don't mind having my throat cut by all three networks," Nessen kept repeating, "because they are experts at it. But CBS—those bastards—kept me on the string until the last minute."

Nessen made several calls to CBS and finally spoke on the phone with Sandy Socolow, the network's Washington bureau chief. Nessen was irate:

"I don't give a shit what you say, you guys told me you were *in* and we played it that way. I know why you're getting out. The Waltons (a popular CBS show). That's it. The ratings."

Ten to fifteen seconds silence elapse as Socolow speaks. But Nessen is not about to be denied:

"Don't ever have your White House man pressure me again about the President having more news conferences. Yes, he did—yesterday. Don't you ever do that again. You're not interested in news. You're interested in ratings. And you can quote me to your New York brass."

Bang! Nessen hung up. Hartmann smiled. He looked at me and said:

"They're testing him. They're testing the President. They are saying among themselves: 'We got a nice, easy-going guy in the White House. Let's show him who's in charge.' "

After this exchange I took a walk. The air was cool and fresh in the Phoenix suburb of Scottsdale. The presidential party was headquartered at the scenic Camelback Inn. The nearby mountains stood majestic in the bright sun.

The name of Nessen's adversary, Sandy Socolow, takes me back more than twenty years. Sandy had taken my place with the old International News Service in Tokyo after the Korean conflict. The war was the Far East to me and I was lost when the front lines fell silent. I loved the drama, the pathos of it. I was to change that thinking drastically in Vietnam many years later, but in those younger days the smoke of battle seemed to purify the spirit.

Nessen and I had covered many stories together; he for NBC and I for ABC News. I did not get to know Nessen well until Vietnam. He had the reputation for being a loudmouth but that did not disturb me. The comment of John Lawrence, a sensitive, young correspondent for CBS News, did. Lawrence, Nessen and I covered several stories together. Lawrence and I sometimes traded off carrying each other's film to the nearest point where we could ship by plane to Saigon. Despite my pleas, Lawrence would not let Nessen enter the bargain. He simply said: "I do not trust him."

Late one afternoon in March of 1966, I was taking a nap on a bunk in a U.S. Navy support vessel heading down the Vietnamese coast into the Mekong Delta. We were to switch to landing ships just before daybreak the following morning and land with assaulting

U.S. Marines on a wild beach area in the Delta. I felt someone
shaking me and a voice swearing. It was Ron Nessen. He was
shouting:

"Goddamn you. You johnny-come-lately. Get outta that
bed."

"What's going on, Ron?" I asked him.

"You've taken my cameraman's bunk, Mr. come-lately," he
hollered. "You guys come over here from the States and think you
own the place. Get the hell out of our bed. It's NBC's."

I climbed down and walked away. But I thought about the
incident until going to sleep on deck that night. Nessen was right.
You cover wars much of your life in all parts of the world. But in
the next war, at the next battle, you are just a johnny-come-lately.

My walk ended. My mind returned to the present and I took a
chair near the outdoor pool of the Camelback Inn. Drinks and
sandwiches swayed on large trays as waitresses whisked between
the tables. The atmosphere was calm and confident. Wealth in the
West is sedate and sometimes secretive, unlike much of the flashy
veneer of New York and the East. The Camelback's patrons were a
study in sedateness as they waited quietly and calmly for the
President of the United States to come and swim in their beautiful
pool. Gerald R. Ford took a dip as the sun went down. They
pretended not to bat a false eyelash.

After dinner I took one last walk around the grounds. It has
been ten years since I have been at the Camelback. I came here
as a news correspondent covering Senator Barry Goldwater in
the 1964 political campaign. Try as I might, I could not pick out
his home among those halfway up the nearby mountains.

Barry Goldwater . . . Bill Miller . . . Nelson Rockefeller—I
had covered all of them in the '64 campaign. And Lyndon Johnson,
too.

My most vivid memory of President Johnson is the night he
backed me up against a wall at Washington's TV station WTOP
and poked me in the chest with his right index finger, saying
quietly to me:

"You son-of-a-bitch. Don't you ever ask a question like that
again. Remember when you come to a press conference in my
office it's a press conference—not a goddamn political lynchin'."

Johnson's words froze me. I was unable to move for ten to
twenty seconds.

Thursday, November 14, 1974

The question that I had asked President Johnson at one of his Oval Office stand-up news conferences was this: "Who is Bobby Baker?"

Bobby Baker had been Lyndon's long-time aide on Capitol Hill. He was then on trial involving various charges of wheeling and dealing around Washington. Johnson wanted no implications that he could have been involved in any way. This was an election year.

President Johnson adopted two attitudes as he took the high road in the 1964 political campaign:

The first was: "Who me—a wheeler-dealer?"

And the second: "Bobby Who?"

That is why I asked the question precisely as I had: "Who is Bobby Baker?"

It was the only time I had ever seen Lyndon Johnson choke. He was so angry that he was almost apoplectic. George Reedy, the White House press secretary at the time, later told me: "He knows your name now, Jack."

Nelson Rockefeller briefly became my idol that election year. It appeared to me that no one spoke more clearly or candidly on the issues in 1964 than Rockefeller. He was incisive, logical and direct.

I covered Rockefeller's entire campaign that year and spent most of my time thinking up tough questions for his almost daily news conferences. Some of my questions were deliberately provocative. But Rocky was cool and even kind. Most of all, he was dedicated.

When on that fateful morning about 3 A.M. in the San Francisco Cow Palace the GOP conservative right began booing Rockefeller off the platform, tears welled up in my eyes. Delegates to the Republican National Convention were standing on their chairs and I remember one woman vividly. She shouted continually as Rockefeller tried to speak:

"Rocky, go home! Rocky, go home!"

He looked down at her in one of the front rows and said:

"It's a free country, lady."

Rockefeller was too late. Barry Goldwater had wrapped everything up in his three years of lonesome traveling and speechmaking around the nation. The Arizona conservative had made a herculean effort. He was thought to deserve a shot at the grand prize.

7

His running mate, Bill Miller, was a card-playing, cussing, loveable candidate from Lockport, New York. I covered him for six weeks in '64 amid some of the wildest moments of my life. *Time* magazine gave Bill a line each week as Goldwater's vice presidential running mate which said: "Bill Miller did his mediocre best."

We traveled on his plane, the Niagara, named after the Falls near Miller's home in Lockport. We loved the name because—as all the newsmen openly told Miller—every day was like going over the Falls.

There were many hilarious moments but the best was saved for last. We were flying back to Washington from Lockport the day after the election. The Goldwater-Miller ticket had been buried in a Johnson-Humphrey landslide. Bill had champagne for breakfast. I was one of the first off the plane and John Meyer, a CBS reporter, rushed up. He asked whether I thought Miller would give an interview. I tried to dissuade him, saying that Miller did not feel well. But Meyer was insistent.

As Miller stepped off the plane, Meyer shoved a mike in Miller's startled face. Said Meyer:

"Congressman Miller, now that you and Senator Goldwater have gone down to such a resounding defeat, it is believed that the leadership of the Republican party will soon pass to new hands. What is your reaction?"

Miller, whose bluish eyes turned steel-gray when angered, looked coldly at Meyer and said: "Would you mind repeating that question?"

Meyer repeated the question. Miller growled: "That's a crock o' shit if I ever heard one!"

The campaign ended on that eloquent note.

My voyage into the past ended abruptly upon returning to the White House staff lounge at the Camelback. It was time to leave for President Ford's news conference. After that, we are airborne and the presidential aircraft wings toward Washington.

I ask myself, looking at the darkening sky across the country:

Would this be a tougher job than Korea, Algeria, Vietnam, the Dominican Republic? As difficult as covering the Impossible War—the Arab-Israeli conflict? Rougher than the racial stories in Grenada, Mississippi or Newark or the burnings in Washington, D.C.?

Who is Gerald Ford? What is the White House really like on the inside, not the outside I had known covering it as a newsman?

I look up from my reveries and see President Ford. He looks tired. It has been a long day. Bob Hartmann, sitting to my left, speaks to the President:

"Jack was with me in the Middle East. We go a long way back. I'll never forget. We were in Baghdad together after the revolution in 1962. A bunch of news guys just hired a plane and we flew into Baghdad without visas."

The President smiles and nods, apparently the sign for Hartmann to continue. Bob keeps rolling:

"When we landed, they shepherded us into an airport baggage room. And we sat there for hours. The kicker was this. A colonel shows up and his first words were: ''Gentlemen, welcome to the revolution!''"

Hartmann roars. Mr. Ford laughs.

The President stands and we shake hands. He says:

"You write simply. I like simple words and a simple style. Your stuff is damn good. You keep writing the way you do, and I promise that I will become a better speaker."

He smiles. This is a humble man. The President's humility touches me deeply.

At the beginning of the conversation, Hartmann had mentioned to Mr. Ford that I am "on detail" from the Commerce Department. I have been the director of public information for the Bureau of the Census, an agency of the Department, for about four and one-half years. It is a career Civil Service post. Commerce is still paying my salary during this time in the White House. No one had indicated that I would be hired until the President put the question to me directly. Thus, Mr. Ford truly hires me.

Somewhere in the vast records of the federal bureaucracy, there should be a piece of paper stating that I was "transferred" from the Commerce Department to the White House. That piece of paper represents the end of four and one-half years of my battling the field division of the Census Bureau. Their indifference and insensitivity were major factors in the massive undercount of blacks in the 1970 decennial census. My last hurrah came in the form of a bureaucratic memo I wrote when the census director did not appoint a black or other minority member in organizing the original

9

1980 Census Executive Planning Committee. My swan song pointed out to the two Nixon appointees who controlled the Bureau, Edward Failor and Vincent Barabba, that such an omission would inhibit the government's ability to take the 1980 census. Their decision placed the Public Information Office in an extremely difficult position, and was insensitive to the criticism fired at the Bureau on the black and Spanish origin undercounts in 1970.

The two political operatives—Barabba, a Nixon pollster who bragged to me that no one would ever catch him like Haldeman or Ehrlichman, and Failor, a member of Chuck Colson's 9:15 A.M. "Attack Group"—tried to terrorize the public information staff while I was on vacation. On return to work, they attempted more of the same on me, enlisting two scared-stiff bureaucrats, Deputy Census Director Robert Hagan and his swooning sidekick, Paul Taff. In the time-honored tradition of bureaucratic Washington, I was promoted to a post with a bigger title and fewer duties.

As a result, Barabba was nicknamed "Barabbas" by some bureau staffers, and Failor was later blistered in the press by Jack Anderson, Mary McGrory and others on various charges of political trickery and personal misconduct.

When I went to work on the thirty-day trial basis at the White House, our executive editor, Paul Theis, told me that Failor had telephoned him. Theis said:

"Failor said you are an ardent Democrat and a liberal activist. An *ardent* Democrat. A liberal."

I said to Theis:

"I have been an Independent all my life. I have voted for many Democrats and many Republicans. On civil rights, I believe the Supreme Court was correct. I thought Martin Luther King, whom I knew well and covered for years, was a great American of incredible personal courage."

Theis smiled. "There's only one question you have to answer here, Jack," he said, "and that is whether you can write."

Air Force One is coming in for its landing at Andrews Air Force Base. The sky is clear. I look out and can see the outlines of Washington in the distance. It is midnight but the sky is lit brightly by the moon and stars and appears immensely open.

I drive home and go to sleep still seeing that immensely open November sky.

Monday, November 18, 1974

THE TYPEWRITER REPAIR MAN talks with me about the last year of the Nixon administration:

"It was like a state of siege. Everyone was scared. They wouldn't really talk to you.

"Everybody knew me. I've been around for many years. But you know the guards started stopping me at the gates. This got to me. I felt like quitting my job. I was sick. What was the world coming to?"

He pauses and then begins to smile saying:

"Now, it's all different. People are friendly. Nobody stops me. And I'm glad to come to work."

President Ford is completing his first three months in office. And this is what is being said by his staff: The government is still partially paralyzed. It has been "inoperative" for a year.

Nixon had concluded that his first duty was to save his own skin. Only secondly would he govern the country. The paralysis proves that.

This was obvious but interesting to hear first-hand.

The rancor that Nixon leaves behind is tremendous everywhere. His own people are now quietly turning on him. They begin to relate stories of his seclusion and secretiveness. Some say he lacked decisiveness; it took him much longer to come to any decision than President Ford. His loyalists are deserting him because they hope to remain on the Ford team.

The decline in the economy is also attributed to Nixon; he wouldn't take an unpopular stand on anything if it would help him hold on a while longer. Nixon only forestalled and caused much worse inflation, which Mr. Ford now has to face, by his wage-price freeze. Nixon dallied on every single critical decision affecting the economy.

The welfare policies of both Nixon and Johnson (yes, some blamed Nixon for part of the "welfare mess") has left Mr. Ford with an increasingly difficult problem on how to clean it up.

The Ford staff takes a wait-and-see attitude on foreign policy. Henry Kissinger is admired but the top Ford insiders want to take a closer look at any "deals" Kissinger and Nixon might have made.

The Democrats are in difficulty. They have no real leadership, which is considered both a plus and a minus for the administration.

11

The plus obviously concerns the 1976 election. The minus is that they may become "an unruly mob" up on Capitol Hill with no leadership able to negotiate with the administration.

Everyone seems stung by two claims that appear to follow Mr. Ford's every move: that he is not too bright and his staff is not the best, and that he lacks leadership qualities, that Jerry Ford is a plodder.

I quickly determine in my meetings with Mr. Ford that he is indeed bright, but reserve judgment about the staff because one needs several months to evaluate it clearly. New members are being added all the time.

If the President projects any values, he gives the very clear impression of being an honest, decent and open man.

However, the President has yet to project a sense of "new beginning" for the nation. I am told that will come in his State of the Union message. Two months appear too long a time to wait. The economy is plunging faster than anyone expects. I make note of this.

Yet, Mr. Ford has made gains since assuming the presidency:

—most Americans genuinely like his open, honest manner.

—his economic summit with business, labor and other national leaders opens a new dialogue which had been closed under Nixon.

—he starts the battle against inflation and economic downturn while Nixon had permitted economic drift.

—his statements on the continuity of foreign policy buy him and the nation time to evaluate events.

—the Whip Inflation Now campaign was evaluated as a complete bust but the most interesting thing about it from the inside was that Ford men and women called it a bust. This would never have happened under Nixon. It gave me confidence that this administration was one that could profit from mistakes, not cover them up. A minus became a plus.

—the President met with virtually every group possible in these months. None was consciously omitted.

—one of the most important differences between the Nixon and Ford administrations was an entirely new attitude and working relationship with newsmen. Mr. Ford genuinely liked reporters. He felt that politics and the press had a lot more in common than their differences. Nixon believed precisely the opposite. I have yet to speak with anyone in the White House who is not pleased with Mr. Ford's press relations.

Monday, November 18, 1974

On the other hand, as of this date, the Ford administration does not have a strategy and set of priorities. No one is giving it a sense of real direction and emphasis.

The President cannot do it alone. He needs help. Thus far, no individual or group of individuals has emerged to assist in the very tough job of leading the United States of America.

Chapter 2
December, 1974

"To struggle with misfortune, to combat difficulties with intrepidity and finally surmount the obstacles which oppose us, are stronger proofs of merit and give a fairer title to reputation than the brightest scenes of tranquility or the sunshine of prosperity could ever have afforded."

GEORGE WASHINGTON

Tuesday, December 10, 1974

PAUL THEIS CAME TO MY OFFICE about noon last Friday. He says that Hartmann has tossed out a speech prepared for the Business Council, a prestigious organization of the nation's top business executives, and wants another writer to take a crack at it. Theis asks me for a new draft as quickly as possible. I give him one about seven hours later with a warning: "Paul, I have had no guidance on this speech."

Seidman sets up a meeting on the speech for Sunday, December 8, in his office. Theis tells me to attend. Present are Seidman, Treasury Secretary Simon, Paul McCracken, former economic adviser to President Nixon, and Max Fischer, Detroit industrialist. In summary, this is what they say:

Simon: Attack wage and price controls now being proposed by the Democrats.

McCracken: Hit controls but also stress the need for national confidence.

Seidman: Point out that Nixon left us in a mess. Then take it from there.

Fischer pulls out a recent speech given by Henry Ford II and says: Talk about confidence, the need to restore the public's confidence, and leadership. Show that the President will be a strong leader.

Fischer shoves the Henry Ford speech into my hands, but I won't take it. I am trying to give him a message. I never do accept it. I am trying to tell him I work for Gerald Ford not Henry Ford.

I write a new draft of the speech on Sunday and meet with Alan Greenspan on Monday for further guidance. Greenspan questions me closely about the Sunday meeting. He expresses concern about his views not getting across. He asks that I describe the entire clearance process of a speech and why he has not been consulted earlier. Greenspan goes on to say that he would have been pleased to assist on a first draft of the speech. I tell him first that I was under tremendous pressure to finish a first draft and did so. Second, the Sunday meeting had not been set up by the speechwriters. Finally, I will consult him on the takeoff of every speech dealing with the economy from that moment on, but he

should talk with Theis rather than me. Greenspan then stresses that the speech should not get into specifics ''or we are inviting trouble.''

Today, December 10, the Economic Policy Board meets under Seidman; I am there to see whether they have come any closer to agreement on precisely what the Business Council speech should say. In the meantime, I have written another draft.

Seidman, Simon and Greenspan are joined by Roy Ash, director of the Office of Management and Budget, and Sydney Jones, an economic assistant to Simon. Greenspan says the speech must stress inflation and what we must do to curtail it. Simon joins him. Ash and Seidman also agree. Seidman, however, cuts himself loose from the others. He wants to be less dogmatic, less firm about fiscal ideology and says: ''Remember this is a speech, not a lesson in economics.''

Coming out of the meeting, I meet Ron Nessen. Nessen then introduces me to Don Rumsfeld. Rumsfeld appears very interested in our meeting and says he plans to see Mr. Ford about the speech. In the meantime, Bill Seidman asks if I would stop by his office. Seidman questions me closely about the speech and I am candid with him. I say:

''I have now written this entire speech seven different ways—seven completely different versions. I see no prospect of agreement among the advisers. Therefore, if I were the President, I would not give the speech. The way things now stand, the speech could do more harm than good. That is, unless the President can break this impasse.''

Seidman surprises me by agreeing: ''We never should have put ourselves in this position.''

I continue:

''People will say that this speech is strictly a defensive retort by the President to his critics instead of coming up with needed answers. This is what really bothers me about the speech; it has no real answers. It's a put-off!''

In the meantime, Nessen tells the press that the Business Council speech is now in its eighth draft. I call Tom Jarriel of ABC News, with whom I had covered civil rights stories in the South for about two years, and he confirms the Nessen quote. Jarriel says: ''That big mouth of his is going to get him in trouble yet.''

Theis comes to me at that point and says:

"The President and Hartmann are going to work out the final draft together. So don't worry about it. Everyone is out of it now except those two."

There is, however, still another meeting on the speech which Theis, speechwriter Milton Friedman and I attend. Says Friedman: "They've got to get together." And Theis adds: "I never believed that policy was ever made this way in the White House. Live and learn."

I return to my office and meditate in silence. I ask myself two questions. Where was Hartmann while I wrote draft after draft of the speech? If he is the President's chief speechwriter, why didn't he sit in on at least some of the policy discussions so he could clearly understand the differences? Will Hartmann continue to operate aloof and alone in the future, only to second-guess the results without witnessing the give-and-take in the decision-making process?

Why is it that a speech is forcing the President and his chief economic advisers to come to grips with our economic problems? Why isn't economic policy being made first and the speech written second?

With so many different shades of economic opinion around the President, I find it difficult to perceive how he will come to conclusions. I already know that the Business Council speech cannot say much because the President's mind is being tossed and turned by the colliding views around him.

Does the President have the ability to sort out the right economic answers? Will he eventually turn to only one or two economic advisers instead of the crowd that now calls out an indistinguishable chorus of advice?

I conclude on a note of sympathy for Mr. Ford. He must formulate a clear economic policy in the midst of clashing opinion. Will he fight the recession first, or inflation, or both at the same time? Does a wage-price freeze have any chance? Will he increase or cut taxes? Where will he find the jobs—in the private sector or the public? What investment incentives can he offer to increase private sector employment? How many government jobs can he create without heating up inflation?

I close my eyes but see and hear no answer; nor will the answers be easy for President Ford.

Wednesday, December 18, 1974

No ONE BLOWS THE TRUMPETS which Nixon so wanted for his
imperial presidency. But this is a day to blow some kind of horn. It
is the day of the "clean break" with the Nixon administration.
Don Rumsfeld formally announces the reorganization of the White
House into the Ford team.

The *New York Times* describes it as "dispersed" authority.
Others say Rumsfeld has emerged as the "power," with Bob
Hartmann and Jack Marsh, counselors to the President, sharing that
authority but in lesser roles.

I see the reorganization as a critical mistake. No one emerges
with real responsibility for the coordination of domestic programs.
No one is to coordinate the critical choices on the economy and
energy. There is no Harry Hopkins or Sam Rosenman of the FDR
era, no Clark Clifford, Ted Sorensen or even Bill Moyers. Point
Two of the reorganization announcement highlights this weakness:

"To limit the White House staff function to those that must
necessarily be performed within the White House. The cabinet and
agency heads will be relied on to perform all appropriate functions
best performed by their organizations."

It is also announced that the President's schedule is being
arranged "to provide broad access to him by cabinet members,
agency heads, members of the House and Senate and the public on
matters in which he is personally involved."

Rumsfeld gives a briefing and, for me, this is a key sentence:
"The President feels that his approach and working style is
reflected in this organization."

Considerable friction is built into the system. In my judgment
the setup will make for considerable infighting and confusion. In
theory, personal contact with the President is ideal. In practice, it is
revolving-door policy-making. No one can conduct from a
half-dozen to a dozen different meetings a day—not even the
President of the United States—and expect to make coordinated
decisions without an organized, specific team to do the staff work.
No one really has such authority under this plan.

With Rumsfeld's disinclination to "make promises that cannot
be fulfilled," which I interpret as no aims or goals for the
administration, I see a White House seeking little more than the

status quo. I hope that events would prove me wrong because, in the final analysis, I am a member of the Ford team.

I do not talk with a single member of the staff who is not elated at the reorganization. A few wonder if releasing a White House telephone book to the press is carrying openness too far.

Whether this reorganization will give leadership depends upon three men, Rumsfeld, Marsh and Hartmann.

Donald Rumsfeld is forty-two, with two terms as Republican representative from Chicago's North Shore before joining the Nixon administration. Starting in 1969, he was director of the Office of Economic Opportunity, counselor to Nixon, director of the Cost of Living Council and ambassador to the North Atlantic Treaty Organization. Rumsfeld is articulate, decisive, and handsome. Most who know him well describe Rumsfeld as very ambitious.

Rumsfeld is in charge of White House operations, which means he has much to say about the President's schedule and, therefore, has access to Mr. Ford. That means he is at the center of policy-making. Rumsfeld is also in charge of hiring and there are many "Rumsfeld men" throughout the system.

Jack Marsh is forty-eight and a folksy, friendly man who, at times, seems somewhat out of place in the swift pace at the White House. A lawyer from the Virginia apple country, Marsh is a reflective, studious individual whose love of the calm countryside marks him as a stable individual.

Marsh runs congressional relations. He thus has a real voice in how Mr. Ford deals with the Congress. Marsh is also in charge of the Office of Public Liaison which relates to numerous private and public interest groups around the country.

There is a marked contrast between Rumsfeld and Marsh. The Virginian does not seem to seek power in any way, but Rumsfeld gives the impression that he wishes to wield it every moment of the day. Thus, one is forced to ask the question: What did Gerald Ford see in each man that caused him to choose such different individuals as Marsh and Rumsfeld for his staff?

Robert T. Hartmann is fifty-seven and not to be compared with anyone on the staff. Hartmann is gruff, tough and real. He could well have starred in *The Front Page* without missing a nuance. I had first met Hartmann in Rome and we covered stories together in the Middle East.

Hartmann was a reporter, editorial writer, foreign correspondent and Washington bureau chief of the *Los Angeles Times* before he became Gerald Ford's right-hand man. He served with Mr. Ford for about a decade before entering the White House with him.

The President relied on Hartmann as a realist, a man who called the shots objectively without major ideological or philosophical hangups. Hartmann always saw his own good as Gerald Ford's good. He was loyal. Cantankerous, yes. Irascible, yes. An infighter, yes. But loyal. Hartmann's strong suit was loyalty. I was once asked by a friend to sum up Hartmann in one single reporter's sentence. I unhesitatingly said:

"He's a guy who throws a lot of bullshit, but likes as little as possible in return."

Kissinger, Bill Seidman, Ron Nessen and others deserve attention. But at this stage of my tenure at the White House, I only want to open the deck of cards and wait before placing any bets on the future.

Monday, December 23, 1974

MILTON FRIEDMAN, one of the speechwriters, walks into my office about 4:30 P.M. The former reporter for the Jewish Telegraph Agency appears tired and distraught. I know he has been working on parts of the State of the Union message. Various federal departments and agencies as well as the Office of Management and Budget have outlined economic and other developments as they see them. In turn, Theis and Friedman meet to review these drafts with the President's top economic advisers: Greenspan, Seidman, Simon, Ash, Frank Zarb (Federal Energy administrator), Arthur Burns (Federal Reserve Board chairman) and a few others on an intermittent basis.

In deliberate, disturbed tones, Friedman begins pouring out his woes:

"Remember all the troubles the economists gave you on the Business Council speech? They couldn't agree. Well, I have that now in spades.

"It's absurd. It's a debate in there, not a dialogue. And it's doubletalk. I don't understand half of what they're saying. It's become an ideological fight.

"Jack, it's doom and gloom all the way. If we wrote what they are saying, the State of the Union message would be one of utter futility. The country would wind up in awful shape."

Friedman goes on and on. Outside on 17th Street, the Christmas shoppers and those leaving early from work are caught in a traffic jam. Friedman is saying:

"This is ridiculous. If the country ever knew of all the division in here, I think it would collapse. I think these guys are giving the President a lot of bad advice. They are so confused and confusing. How can he make a judgment? This is crazy!"

There is a deep sense of frustration among the President's closest advisers. Their inability to decide whether to fight inflation or recession—or somehow both at the same time—is causing the President acute difficulty.

The newspapers are filled with comment that Mr. Ford doesn't understand what is going on in the economy. Pundits question the President's decisiveness and mental capacity. The economy itself is going from bad to worse.

From my observations at these meetings, President Ford is being victimized by some of his own experts. Seidman seeks practical answers—simple solutions. He keeps demanding proof and answers instead of what he sees as Simon's and Greenspan's conservative ideology. Yet these two are offering some answers although Seidman cannot cut through their jargon. Mr. Ford takes a beating in the press while trying to get his advisers to speak the same language.

Criticism of the President increases throughout the month of December. Rumsfeld feels it, too, because he begins passing the word it is part of his job to "defuse expectations." Too many promises have been made the American people. Too much is expected of the presidency. The new staff is unprepared for the mess left them by the Nixon administration. Summing everything up, Rumsfeld is saying: "The answer is not to do things right now, it is to do what is right."

In mid-December, James Reston writes in his *New York Times* column some thoughts which strengthen the entire White House, including the President. I doubt that Reston could ever have guessed how much this particular column meant to all of us inside the White House.

Reston concludes that the President is unable to make up his mind on whether inflation or recession is the nation's number-one problem. He explains that Mr. Ford is under severe if not savage criticism. The President has left questions unanswered on foreign policy. Yet he praises the President on these points:

— Gerald Ford has restored integrity to debate.
— He is giving the nation an "honest pitch."
— He is beginning to restore belief in the office of the presidency.
He knows the difference between right and wrong.
He is a man of trust and is worthy of confidence.
To most of us, the best conclusion of all is that . . . it is probably too early to count him out.

The Reston column is important for another reason. This White House staff listens to the press. It never tunes out and, to my knowledge, no one hates the press. Newsmen genuinely influence thinking within the Ford administration. I describe the relationship as a "friendly rivalry." To enhance the dialogue with the press, I begin efforts so that the *New York Times* will devote its entire Sunday magazine section to the President.*

*John Hersey wrote the section, which appeared on April 23, 1975.

Chapter 3
January, 1975

". . . Still one thing more fellow citizens—a wise and frugal government, which shall restrain men from injuring one another, shall leave them otherwise free to regulate their pursuits of industry and improvement, and shall not take from the mouth of labor the bread it has earned. This is the sum of good government, and this is necessary to close the circle of our felicities."

THOMAS JEFFERSON, *from his first inaugural address, March 4, 1801*

Thursday, January 2, 1975

IT'S A NEW YEAR. The President changes his mind. He will fight recession, then inflation. The press is calling it a 180-degree turn. Bill Seidman tells me it does not mean a change of policy, it is rather a shift of emphasis. He maintains the policy is the same. I say: Uh huh! Only it wasn't so convincing on my part and Seidman repeats his words slowly and carefully. The message is clear.

Simon is still talking inflation. Greenspan is on the fence—one day emphasizing inflation, the next day stressing the recession. I have the impression that Greenspan is genuinely frightened by what is happening in the country. He is less sure of himself. But he is extremely adept on his feet. No staffer knows the general subject of economics better than Greenspan—and he is quick to criticize anyone who misuses a phrase or term. Yet, in my conversations with him, Greenspan continually probes on who is giving the President what advice. He knows that the speechwriters are aware of who is making what changes on what Mr. Ford says in public. This disturbs him. It annoys him so much that he sometimes becomes curt and sharp. There is no reason to do so because I am not challenging his economic wisdom. I come to Greenspan looking for answers, for guidance. He senses that I am very uneasy with the contradictory guidance that I am receiving from different presidential advisers. He wonders whether I have the brains to balance the arguments well, and if not well, then in his favor.

The mood inside the White House changes each day. One day it is believed the President has made some definite decisions. The next day, somebody mentions WIN buttons to him—Whip Inflation Now—and he asks: How are we doing?

WIN buttons are the first big mistake I see Hartmann make. He is a WIN button man. I have told Theis quietly on several occasions that WIN is a disaster and we ought to dump it from our speeches. However, Theis is cautious, saying: Let's wait and see.

The *Wall Street Journal* does a nice column on the President in early January. It says he has grasped the office of the presidency. Then, the column destroys itself by saying:

"Of course all this could change by cherry blossom time since the moods of Washington are always mercurial."

Friday, January 3, 1975

I TALK WITH JACK RAFUSE, an aide to Frank Zarb, at the Federal Energy Administration. Rafuse tells me that Zarb will hand directly to the President at 3 P.M. today in an Oval Office meeting his version of the energy section of the State of the Union message.

I tell Rafuse that most of the President's energy message is on the front page of this morning's *Washington Post*. On returning to the office, I mention to Theis that Zarb is dealing directly with the President on what the State of the Union message will say about energy. Theis, calm as usual, says that we must be better organized. Zarb should be going through him so that all of us are on the same wavelength. If everyone went directly to the President with his part of the State of the Union message, nothing would make sense.

Late in the day, Friedman comes into my office and is extremely upset. He wants my latest draft on energy. I tell him about Zarb and the President. Friedman shows me the front page of the afternoon *Washington Star-News*. Much of the President's State of the Union message is in print—and it's accurate. Friedman is bitter:

"How many guys are leaking this stuff? What's the purpose in having a State of the Union message if we are going to hand it out page by page day after day?"

I see Theis late in the day and he tells me that Zarb has made a strong pitch to the President for a separate energy message—to be given a week before the State of the Union message. I say to Theis:

"In other words, he wants to scoop or not share the time with the rest of the State of the Union."

Theis winces.

Zarb strikes me now and has from our first meeting as a sharpshooter. I do not disagree with that. He fights for his own programs. However, as a speechwriter, I have to put a package together, not the views of one agency. I ask myself a bigger and more important question:

How many of these department and agency chiefs are trying to outsmart and outmaneuver the President himself?

The question shocks me but it represents a new dimension to my White House experience. I will watch for this in the months ahead.

Friedman tells me at the end of the day that the leaks are deliberate. I wonder what can be gained by these leaks. Surely, no one can be so unsure of the State of the Union message that the whole speech has to be floated as a trial balloon?

Saturday, January 11, 1975

ALL LAST WEEK, the State of the Union message leaked to the press as fast as it was written. Friedman completed seventy-two pages of the printed State of the Union message which is longer than the spoken address to Congress. Much of both is already in the newspapers.

Last Tuesday, more of the message filled column after column in the newspapers. Friedman was ill on Wednesday and Theis asked that I cut the seventy-two pages of the written address to twenty pages within three hours. No important details were to be left out. The length was definitely not to exceed twenty pages. I wondered about this. I put the twenty pages on Hartmann's desk at 6:55 P.M. that evening. No one knew why the summary was required.

On Thursday, Theis asked me to put a new lead on the State of the Union message. As it stood, the message was flat and portrayed a defeated and divided nation rather than one facing challenges.

I rewrote the lead calling on America, as a nation, to face challenges of the twenty-first century. At the same time, I heard rumors that the middle ranks of OMB were the source of most of the negativism. They portrayed the country in the most pessimistic terms. This is all well and good, as far as I am concerned, if it's accurate. However, it seems to me there must be some middle ground where we may say: Things are bad but America can and must strive to overcome its difficulties.

Nobody wants a sugar-coated State of the Union message but I feel the doom-sayers offer no answers. I am angry with American businessmen because they blame most of the country's troubles on government instead of putting their own houses in order. Why isn't Detroit getting into mass transit instead of building cars as if they were buses?

Sunday, January 12, 1975

Friedman returned to the office on Friday after his bout with
the flu. He startled me by attacking detente. I fail to see the
connection with the State of the Union. He attacks the
Communists, saying he saw their tanks trying to destroy Israel. I
still fail to see what this has to do with the State of the Union but
note his sensitivity about Israel.

Nothing seems to make sense these days.

Late Friday I learned from Theis why we cut the State of the
Union message to twenty pages. Hartmann is writing a final draft
of an advance State of the Union message that is to be televised
nationally on Monday night, January 13. Mr. Ford wants to beat
Congress to the punch on announcing where the country is going.
The new Congress, heavily Democratic, had attempted to preempt
the State of the Union message by scheduling to release their
program for the economy earlier.

Since the first of January, Mr. Ford and the Congress have
been jockeying for position. The President has already moved the
State of the Union message from the traditional date of January 20
to January 15. Carl Albert has scheduled a news conference for
January 13, the day before the 94th Congress convenes, to publish
the economic program drafted by the Democratic Party Study
Group. Mr. Ford and the White House cannot afford to let
Congress appear to be running the nation. Hartmann and the
President decide to get the jump on Congress with the twenty-page
speech on the eve of Congress's return.

Sunday, January 12, 1975

SUNDAY, JANUARY 12, dawns with the *Washington Post*
proclaiming in a banner headline: FORD ASKS SIX MONTHS TO
PROVE HIMSELF.

The *Post*, in its sometimes breathless style, has this key sentence:

"Gerald Ford, truly the accidental President, the first man
ever to serve without being elected by the people, is an optimist."

(However, Gerald Ford is about to give the most solemn, sad,
downbeat State of the Union "advance" address in the history of
the United States.)

The *Post* calls Mr. Ford "exceptionally disarming" and writes
of a "warmth and friendliness that are being beguiling."

29

The *Post* is almost ecstatic:

"Gone is the strained, tense atmosphere of the final months before Nixon's fall."

The final words are in a quote but clearly serve the *Post's* thinking. It's a mild warning to their newfound buddy, good ol' Jerry Ford, and the question is pointed:

Could he sacrifice his old ideas, old prejudices, to chart a new course for America? The *Post* concluded that it would take time to know the answer.

Bully!

Tuesday, January 14, 1975

IT IS THE COLDEST DAY OF WINTER. Theis phoned me at home last night asking me to come in early today to help Friedman edit the State of the Union message which President Ford will give tomorrow, January 15. The President delivered his economic and energy speech last night. Nessen, Bob Mead, the President's TV adviser, and Rumsfeld spent most of yesterday with Mr. Ford helping him practice his delivery. The idea was to enhance his "leadership" image, to convey the idea of a firm and direct President in charge of the nation's fate.

Mr. Ford practiced with a teleprompter and used it in his actual delivery. When the cameras switched off, Mr. Ford asked: "Did it sound as if I was reading?"

All agreed it had not. And the delivery was judged a success both inside and outside the White House.

During the afternoon, Friedman mentions to me that there has been a blowup between Hartmann and Rumsfeld. Rumsfeld apparently began editing Friedman's draft on the State of the Union. Hartmann blew up at some of Rumsfeld's proposed changes. Friedman also says Rumsfeld has been closing the door of the President's office to Hartmann more and more. Milt adds:

"This looks to me like an ocean liner heading for an iceberg. There is going to be a Titanic."

Late in the day, an FBI agent comes by to ask me questions about my background. He goes back to my teenage days. At times, I say to myself, it would be nice to be back in school.

Before going home, I send to the White House picture framers a certificate in regard to flying on Air Force One and a large Christmas card which we received from the President and Mrs. Ford. On the bus riding home, I read a newspaper article reporting that it costs the American taxpayers $92,000 a year for such framing. White House staffers have traditionally argued that, because of the long hours they put in without pay, they should have that small privilege. I do not agree, but it's too late now.

It didn't pay to get out of bed today.

Thursday, January 16, 1975

ONE THOUGHT overshadowed everything Mr. Ford said to the Congress. He said the state of the Union was not good. With remarkable unanimity, the nation's editorial writers and commentators agreed he had leveled with the American people. Gone was the Nixon rhetoric that the American people were the greatest and that the United States was the most powerful. Mr. Ford simply said we were in trouble.

Some historians say it was the most downbeat State of the Union message in our two centuries. If only they had seen it in the raw . . .

Friday, January 31, 1975

TODAY I COMPLETE my third month as a presidential speechwriter. Hartmann visits with the speechwriters for the first time since my arrival. He begins by saying Mr. Ford has a "pet peeve" in phraseology—the expression "am going to." Hartmann says we should never use it. We must always write "will" or "must."

Puffing a pipe, Hartmann adds that the President dislikes the "Nixon royal WE." He says we must always write the direct "I" except when "we" is really meant, such as "We, the people of the United States, etc."

In the hour which Hartmann spends with us, he volunteers virtually no insight into his or the President's thinking or planning. He speaks in generalities about Mr. Ford and himself and seems to say: "Refer any tough questions to me. Otherwise, just do what I tell you."

However, I press him on two questions: how to settle disputes in finalizing a speech and how to handle the policy-making aspects of speechwriting. In settling disputes, he says:

"When two or more people or departments disagree, buck the disagreement to me."

Under persistent questioning, Hartmann indirectly admits what is happening daily on our staff. He says that a speechwriter may sometimes find himself in a role for which he was never intended. He may be caught in the midst of an unresolved policy dispute; therefore, what he writes may affect or constitute policy.

I also ask about a speech becoming a catalyst for policy—when there is no policy and a speech deadline forces decisions. Hartmann avoids this question as well but admits that it happens. As a matter of fact, as the discussion bears out, it has become almost a rule in the Ford administration and in our work.

Disagreement after disagreement has been forced out into the open during the drafting of speeches. The deadline of the speech demands that policy be looked at closely if not actually set. The most recent example is the Business Council address, where a decision had to be made about the relative emphasis to be placed on inflation and recession.

It is clear from Hartmann's reserved comments that the speechwriters will not receive much hard and clear direction from him. We will find ourselves in the midst of many policy and other disputes in the future and will have to work them out ourselves before bucking them to Theis and Hartmann. Hartmann leaves me with the impression that he feels he is under tremendous pressure. I am not sure whether he is under that pressure or *thinks* that he is.

The entire policy effect of speechwriting and the role of speechwriters must yet be brought into focus. It is obvious that everything a President says constitutes policy. What he fails to say can also constitute policy. Because of Hartmann's vagueness, I conclude:

1) The new administration is still struggling to determine where it's going, and/or

2) No one in the White House has taken charge of any long-range policy thinking.

At 3 P.M., Theis and I meet with the President and Roy Ash to determine what the President will say at a coming budget briefing for 215 editors and other newsmen at the State Department.

The President stresses that the remarks should reject the popular notion of "uncontrollable" outlays such as Social Security, Public Assistance, Medicare, Medicaid, etc. He wishes to say that "transfer payments" *are* controllable if the Congress will help him control them. Mr. Ford says he is receiving unfair blame regarding the attempt to cut back on food stamps and other popular programs for the poor when the problem is much bigger. Federal spending, which is becoming astronomical, is the real problem.

The President wants to put the Democrats under pressure to start talking federal budget totals, not just individual items such as food stamps. He believes the Democrats could push through a $100 billion deficit spending program for fiscal 1976.

As the meeting ends, the President asks me what time that evening he may see a draft of the State Department remarks. Mr. Ford points out that he is seeing Britain's Prime Minister Wilson that evening but will be in his residence at 9:15 P.M. I promise him that the draft will be waiting for him.

After the meeting with the President, I work with Roy Ash and his assistants on the remarks. We agree to stress that so-called uncontrollable spending is not "uncontrollable."

To my astonishment, no one in the press picks up that statement in reporting later on Mr. Ford's remarks. This startles me. It also surprises Ash and his assistants.

Chapter 4
February, 1975

"1774, Monday, OCTR. 24."

"In Congress, nibbling and quibbling—as usual . . . There is no greater Mortification than to sit with a half a dozen Witts, deliberating upon a Petition, Address, or Memorial. These great Witts, these subtle Criticks, these refined Genius's, these learned Lawyers, these wise Statesmen, are so fond of shewing their Parts and Powers as to make their Consultations very tedious."

JOHN ADAMS

Saturday, February 1, 1975

THE CONGRESS is bombarding the President with criticism of his economic and energy programs. Yet, in seeing and speaking with Mr. Ford, he is calm, even relaxed. He keeps asking: "But what do they have to offer? What are their alternatives?"

It is obvious to me that President Ford trusts his staff work but is concerned about the conflicting advice given him. He considers each opinion as an honest one. Mr. Ford views criticism as necessary to politics and not personal, clearly separating the two in his mind. He knows, for example, that his promise of a 1974 tax rebate has stolen the headlines from the Democrats. They took too long in organizing themselves and now are arguing about details of the tax cut.

On energy, Mr. Ford knows that he can act rapidly and the Democrats cannot. His energy program is both controversial and complicated. He knows that any such program to be good must be complicated. Thus, in the long run, he feels he has the Democrats over a barrel.

The President tells us to keep reminding his listeners that he is the only person with a comprehensive plan on energy; no Democrat has one. He says:

"They are drifting and those freshmen up there may keep them drifting. At least, I can come to reasonable decisions."

One of the eventual pluses for Mr. Ford is the somewhat nasty jibe that he has a low IQ. People are beginning to see in his speeches, in news conferences, in personal conversations, in his general comportment, that whatever his limitations may be Mr. Ford is not a "dummy."

The President is forcing the American people to look at disagreeable prospects and distasteful remedies from the outset. Some have called this "political suicide." He has at least—compared to the Congress—some direction to offer the country, and he is doing so in a quiet, determined style. In my opinion, Mr. Ford is avoiding the biggest trap of all—promising sunshine and not being able to deliver it. Greenspan helped greatly in this. More than any other adviser to the President, Greenspan has consistently played down

36

creating what he calls "false expectations." Greenspan sees the most conservative principles as being the most promising for the country.

Monday, February 3, 1975

RIDING THE BUS into work today, I finish the *Washington Post* early on the trip. Some newspapers, such as the *Post*, have been assailing President Ford's economic and energy moves. Some attacks are personal. These claim that Mr. Ford simply doesn't understand either subject. In my many years as a reporter and writer, I have never seen anyone more immune to criticism than Gerald R. Ford.

I do not believe he is simply thickskinned, nor is he insensitive to criticism. He simply accepts it like water rolling off his back in a swimming pool; it is part of the action. I once heard him say:

"It just doesn't do any good to get mad. It never solves anything. You just have to move on."

Harry Truman, described by Mr. Ford as his model president in personal style, lambasted his critics in unprintable though not, for Mr. Truman, unspeakable language. Jack Kennedy would savor a rapier verbal thrust at a newsman who had sniped at him. Lyndon Johnson became so enraged at times that his emotions exploded. And Richard Nixon's hatred for the press is legendary. But not Gerald Ford:

"I like those fellas. They've got a job to do. I'll settle for the benefit of the doubt."

And the President underlines it: "I sleep every night."

I keep thinking back to remarks made to me by Bob Hartmann:

"We are not going to get into a pissing contest with those guys. That was Nixon's biggest mistake."

The President is an avid newspaper reader who covers a half dozen newspapers and magazines each day. In addition, he reads the extensive White House daily news summary. He sometimes clips articles and sends them to appropriate staff members to check out or for comment or followup action.

The President is, however, irritated by "news leaks" in his administration. Mr. Ford has asked aides not to slip stories to newsmen when he has made a decision. He desires to make his decision known personally. However, the leaks swell.

Inside the White House, three persons are considered "big leakers": Treasury Secretary Simon, Secretary Kissinger and Bob Hartmann. In the case of Simon and Kissinger, both desire at times to put some daylight between themselves and administration policy. In Hartmann's case, he appears to have two aims: to attack those in the administration who sway from the President's line and to protect his own role as a chief adviser to the President. It is nevertheless believed by some in the White House that when Hartmann initiates a leak, he is sometimes acting for President Ford. That may be true, although I have never seen any solid evidence or logical pattern to support such a conclusion.

In the final analysis, Mr. Ford has played the Washington game for so many years that little surprises him. He is a believer in journalistic predestination—that he will receive, no matter what he does, a degree of criticism and praise each day.

When all is said and done, the President feels, the "advice given him each day by the columnists and pundits is 'free.' " And he grins at that—grins and bears it—and sometimes accepts it.

Congress and Washington's bureaucrats escape much if not most of the direct attack to which President Ford is subject each day. A good example is a current one.

For some months now, several lawmakers such as Senator William Proxmire and a growing bandwagon of newsmen have been taking swings at the "good times" of Washington compared to the "bad times" around the nation. Proxmire complains that about 800 federal officials are being chauffeured around Washington "like potentates" in leased government cars while officials talk about an "energy crisis." Interior Secretary Rogers Morton (later Secretary of Commerce) is singled out as calling on Americans to sacrifice on energy while he is being chauffeured around town in a government-leased Mercury.

However, most public officials are not receiving direct fire as is the case with President Ford. There are numerous complaints that about 15,000 federal bureaucrats receive free or cut-rate parking space near their offices. It is estimated that such parking arrangements cost American taxpayers about $11 million a year. An attack on dining facilities is aimed at the Pentagon. About 500 of the Pentagon's top brass eat in five executive dining rooms—underwritten by the taxpayers to the tune of a million dollars a year.

Newsmen have also zeroed in on Capitol Hill where lawmakers get free haircuts, free parking, free tax-return preparations, free house plants and cut-rate prices in the House of Representatives stationery store. House members have raised their allowances for office expenses. The House and Senate plan to increase their staffs and build new buildings for themselves at multimillion dollar costs—all at a time of "national sacrifice."

Much of the criticism is biting, even fierce. But it is cloaked much of the time in the terms "bureaucrats" and "Congress."

The President gets it by name. Mr. Ford keeps his perspective, however.

I, for one, sleep better every night knowing Jerry Ford sleeps well every night. It sure makes life easier around the White House.

Monday, February 10, 1975

MR. FORD BECAME PRESIDENT six months ago yesterday. It seems a reasonable time to recount some impressions of his presidency.

My foremost impression is that Mr. Ford is remarkably calm in the job. This continues to make a deep impact on me. He exudes quiet confidence. I believe that Gerald R. Ford is a man who, some years ago, made peace with himself. He has long recognized his strengths and, more importantly, his limits.

President Ford has not yet asserted leadership of America. Perhaps he recognizes his leadership limits; he appears to be more comfortable seeking consensus. At the same time, the President has been torn by conflicting advice, causing him to appear indecisive as well. In his defense, it may be argued that he has sought to act prudently in the face of contradictory opinion.

Mr. Ford is a man of basics, not a devious individual. Contrary to what many assert, I am virtually convinced his pardon of Richard Nixon is more a proof of honesty than an indication of duplicity. No man with the President's long experience in politics could have escaped this conclusion: he would be severely criticized—his presidency castigated by many—for the pardon. Mr. Ford had to know he was running the risk of compromising his place in history and, indeed, might well compromise the possibility of election in his own right in 1976.

Time will probably prove Mr. Ford's assessment correct, namely: the "issue" or "problem" of Richard Nixon had to be removed from the American scene in order for our society to return to a sense of normalcy. The basic need for the pardon, combined with the President's awareness that such an action could only have a negative effect on his public life, will not place Gerald R. Ford amid the dark shadows of history. Rather, I judge, the historians of a hundred years from now will look upon the act as one of the President's more perceptive judgments in office. They may be far less kind to those who have impugned his motives so harshly.

The most significant and evident fault in the White House is lack of coordination and planning. One conclusion towers above all others: no one is really running the place. No significant planning is underway and no goals are evident, except solving immediate problems on a hit-and-run basis.

Contrary to what much of the press is writing, I evaluate Donald Rumsfeld as a weak team leader. True, he wishes to avoid being compared with either Haldeman or Ehrlichman. However, Rumsfeld's ability at conceptual analysis has never really been demonstrated. Many privately question whether "Rummy" sees through to the heart of problems, simplifying issues because of time constraints. It is certain that he is making little use of the Domestic Council where the combined brains exist. This appears to be a tremendous disservice to the President.

Aware of private reservations about him within the White House, Rumsfeld defends himself publicly. The staff coordinator says he offers Mr. Ford "all the options" on an issue or problem. Yet, the Rockefeller staff, if for no other reason than numbers, offers more depth in problem-solving. They brood bitterly that "Rummy" is short-stopping much of their thinking. Rumsfeld denies this but he has not convinced much of the White House staff for this primary reason: too many individuals privately express too many reservations about him. In a phrase, they don't completely trust him.

Rumsfeld fires back that he does not withhold information from the President so that Mr. Ford will never be "blindsided." The key, from where I sit, is use of the word "blindsided." This refers to immediate and direct issues. No one questions that he works with the President from problem to problem. The gut complaint is that

Rumsfeld demonstrates no real depth—the long-range direction of the White House on a host of unexplained issues.

The issues are too numerous to mention. One could select almost any one of the top twenty problems facing the country. To mention a few: health, education, crime or minorities' issues. On the two greatest issues, the economy and energy, the President's economic program is basically go-slow and don't tinker-with-the-free-enterprise-system. He adopted what had been the basic energy plan of Richard Nixon.

Those concerned with issues and policy, with root causes and ultimate effects, such as the speechwriting staff, receive no coordination or direction from Rumsfeld. Since Hartmann does not attend most policy meetings—and Rumsfeld is most aware of this—he knows it is all the more imperative that someone offer the speechwriters the latest guidance. Yet, Rumsfeld does nothing. This is partly because of his rivalry with Hartmann. But it is also a demonstration that Rumsfeld is a more secretive than substantive individual.

He is allowing administration officials to go off on different roads while the President pleads for ''new directions'' for the nation.

The President comes across as a man of basics, a middle-westerner of the old school, living the lexicon of past lessons. Terms like big spenders, deficit spending, the free enterprise system, and give government back to the people roll easily and repeatedly off his tongue. He is receiving precious few new ideas and plans about America's future.

In Rumsfeld's defense, it must be said that President Ford truly wished to decentralize White House as well as presidential authority. However, this never appeared to be an adequate excuse for lack of needed decisions on the country's aims.

The most striking sign of Mr. Ford's desire to decentralize presidential authority was his choice of Nelson Rockefeller as Vice President. Even now, Rocky's people wonder how and why Mr. Ford made such a decision.

Policy decisions by President Ford do not emanate from a single, sure, set system. They come from different directions: meetings with his aides; talks with cabinet members; a combination of cabinet members and presidential aides with an interplay involving the Office of Management and Budget; old friends in Congress; personal friends; and finally, his sixth sense on whether his decision will be acceptable to Congress. Mr. Ford has known well in advance that some of his policies would not fly on Capitol Hill, for example, his energy message, but he has also foreseen how to survive with the Congress and turn defeat to a compromise if not an advantage. This was the case with many of his vetoes. More significantly, it enabled him to take on the Congress as a do-nothing crowd.

Foreign policy, despite the rumors to the contrary, remains firmly in the hands of Henry Kissinger. Some Ford aides, such as Don Rumsfeld, are beginning an attempt to put some distance between the Secretary of State and the President, but Kissinger will not back off or down. He is a very tough infighter. He insists on taking over briefings. Kissinger insists on his full hour with the President every day, which no one else has, not even Rumsfeld. He insists on overruling White House aides who attempt to dabble in foreign policy speeches given by the President. For a Harvard professor, Henry Kissinger is a guy who knows how to hit you in the guts..

Other than Kissinger, and possibly Mr. Rockefeller, the President has not sought to bring stars into his administration. He talks of solid, basic people, not the flamboyant types. He believes in people. He believes that a lot of so-called ordinary Americans are intelligent. But don't forget that Jerry Ford is also smart enough to want real loyalty. You don't always get that from the big names.

There is a dogged tenacity in President Ford. Knowing that his untiring zeal is still not selling the energy package, Mr. Ford nevertheless persists.

I see a man who, over the years, has tasted defeat in his legislative life far more often than victory. As minority leader of the Republicans in the House, his deck of cards would collapse all over the House floor if he evidenced discouragement or defeat. So, to survive, Jerry Ford simply refused to be counted out. Psychologically, he chose to say that tomorrow is another day. He did this knowing that tomorrow would bring another defeat. The important thing about Jerry Ford was and is that he never confused discouragement and defeat with dishonor. The important thing was the next play. I see that characteristic in his presidency.

Mr. Ford is now down. On this date, six months into his presidency, I believe he will make a comeback if the economy gives him a break. He keeps trying, struggling, fighting. Mr. Ford is a living example of persistence leading to great things. George

Washington's greatest quality was, in my judgment, persistence. It's also Gerald Ford's.

At the moment, a number of congressmen taunt Mr. Ford from Capitol cloakrooms with the remark that they were elected and he wasn't. The fact is, however, that he was elected to twenty-five years of service in the Congress and would not now be in the White House had he not been elected all those years.

At this stage, this Congress is unpredictable. It is showing signs of coming unglued. It lacks leadership and it lacks direction. What appears predictable this February day with the Congress less than a month old is that it will continue to be unpredictable. Too many people are calling for a "new" this and that without a sense of direction. There is a tremendous sense of "rush" on Capitol Hill but nobody knows just where. Yet the heavily Democratic body says its partisan leaders will direct the new policies of the country. This is an astonishing prediction and may become a delusion because the Democrats already seem too divided to provide this direction.

Chapter 5
February, 1975

"Initiation of humanitarian programs did not deter us from our determination to reduce the federal budget. I told legislative leaders that balancing the budget was a cold phrase for an imperative necessity. And again and again I emphasized that our concern for fiscal responsibility was in the end a concern for people."

DWIGHT D. EISENHOWER

Tuesday, February 11, 1975

As I RETURN with the President on Air Force One from Houston and Topeka, the pressure of the past week ebbs. I had written speeches steadily all of last week and spent fifteen hours at the typewriter on Saturday.

The speech to the Energy and Economic Conference sponsored by the Houston Chamber of Commerce was written without direction from anyone. Theis had said: "Write an energy speech, about twenty minutes." The major thrust of the speech was that foes of the President's oil tax plan were taking a "reckless gamble" with the American economy by doing nothing.

The speech's main thrust was that "instead of betting on what foreign sources may do, we should put our money on what Americans can do and will do." The speech said that if the country offers private enterprise at home real incentives, it will solve our energy problems. On completing the first draft, Bill Seidman scrawled next to each mention of "free enterprise" the word "awful." Greenspan told me that someone had "gutted" the best parts of the speech, namely, about "free enterprise."

Seidman's point was that the Arabs were operating on a supply-and-demand or free enterprise basis but the President was not. He said Mr. Ford was placing taxes on imported oil and that was not the free enterprise method. Therefore, we were painting ourselves into a corner.

Greenspan rejected Seidman's view completely, saying he had created an artificial argument. I felt it best to stay out of the argument and suggested that Greenspan speak with Theis. Eventually, the speech was given and was well received.

Last night after the Houston speech, I was told to wait outside the President's suite to show him the speech which he would give tomorrow to the Kansas state legislature at Topeka. Mr. Ford was meeting with Texas Republicans. As the meeting broke up, I waited for the last guest to leave. I began to enter the President's suite to discuss the speech when someone pushed me aside. It was John Connally. He slammed the door in my face. Later, Dick Cheney, Rumsfeld's assistant, came out to tell me to let the Topeka speech ride; we might make some changes in it on the plane tomorrow.

At the time, Connally was facing trial, accused of taking a $10,000 bribe from a representative of the dairy industry, fellow-Texan Jake Jacobson. This episode makes me wonder about the nature of politics.

After the Connally incident, I went to the press room and Bob Hartmann was on the phone. He was furious. He wanted me to explain why I had not received written material which he had sent me over a White House signal line. I told him that I simply had not received the material. It had not arrived and that was the truth. Hartmann stressed how important it was that we put the material just as he had written it in the President's Topeka speech.

At that point, I mentioned to Hartmann that Cheney had told me he had received a message from Jerry Jones, staff secretary, about the Topeka speech. As we spoke, it became clear that this was the message intended for me. Cheney had said we would talk about it on the plane tomorrow. Hartmann blew up. He said he was being "sabotaged" in the White House: "Other peoples' messages get through but mine fall through the cracks."

Cheney finally showed me the message, the same message which Hartmann had intended for me, many hours after it arrived in Houston. I discussed the change with Greenspan, Paul O'Neill, deputy director of OMB, Cheney and the President on the plane to Topeka. The message proposed that federal highway trust funds be transferred to energy-efficient mass transportation. This transfer would give an immediate boost to the economy. Greenspan and O'Neill call the move inflationary but Hartmann had previously argued it was a good, tactical political move. The President rode with Hartmann.

That afternoon at the motel in Topeka, I marveled as Greenspan, Nessen, Cheney and many of the top White House aides stood around a television set and actually cheered as both CBS and NBC News carried stories attacking the Congress' inability to act on either energy or the economy. Greenspan was eating baked beans and potato salad, smiling as contentedly as a schoolboy, as he looked back at Washington and heard the Congress get roasted. I had witnessed no scene at the White House so vividly partisan. Nessen concluded: "Maybe *they* (the Congress) are the dumb bastards."

Friday, February 14, 1975

JERRY JONES, the staff secretary, gives the speechwriters a backgrounder. He says that it takes from two to three hours for a piece of paper to enter and leave Mr. Ford's office. Jones adds:

"The material comes out so fast I can hardly believe it. President Ford is much faster at making decisions than President Nixon, and I have served both. Also, President Ford sees a lot of people in making a decision, while President Nixon saw few or none."

Jones left no doubt. He had made the switch to the Ford administration.

Jones reports the President rarely watches television, including his own appearances.

The staff secretary openly laments that the President's advisers are fighting in print:

"They are leaking to influence events as well as the President. This would have turned Nixon off. Johnson would have double-crossed everyone and changed his decision. Johnson ranted about the press. Nixon hated it.

"Ford does not criticize it. He accepts or rejects what is written. He judges a story on its own merits."

Jones, obviously irritated by leaks to the press, gives us a lecture about talking with the press. He calls leaks a "disservice to the President" and intimates that if he were the captain of the ship a few heads would roll.

He repeats the Rumsfeld dictum about the necessity of giving the President all the options.

Jones, who apparently considers himself one of the President's closest working associates, reports that some staff members try to sidestep him and Rumsfeld in an effort to convince the President of their views. This startles me because I would surmise that Mr. Ford's naming of some men as his counselors indicates they need not necessarily go through either Rumsfeld or Jones to express their views. Nevertheless, Jones insists that he and Rumsfeld are quick to spot anyone trying to go around them.

Jones returns to the decision-making process in the White House. He explains that when it seems the President is taking a long time to make up his mind on a subject, one of the following is true: the President tells his aides he desires more information and they are seeking to find it; his aides are unable to form a consensus or, at times, agreement is not possible; or he wants to call a meeting on the subject.

Milt Friedman interjects. He wants to continue the discussion of leaks. Friedman says there have been many leaks in connection with speeches he has worked on, including the State of the Union message. Jones concludes that the "economic people" were doing this, trying to get their views across to everyone in town.

Jones resumes, saying that the President does "an incredible amount of reading—much more than President Nixon."

With all due respect to Mr. Ford, I find the latter difficult to believe. Whatever may be said of the former President, he studied his options, read all he could find on many subjects and appeared obviously better read than his successor. Thus, I concluded, Jones was a man to be weighed carefully and cautiously.

Wednesday, February 19, 1975

WE—HARTMANN, SEIDMAN, Theis, Kaye Pullen and Casserly—meet with the President in the Oval Office. The first topic is the Reserve Officers Association address to be given in two days. This speech has been agonizing. Theis had told me to make it a first-rate defense speech. I asked the Pentagon for input. It was a full-blown address scheduled for at least thirty minutes. But now the President asks: "I thought this was to be a drop-by?" No one speaks. Mr. Ford says: "Let's cut this speech to no more than ten minutes." Seidman attempts to kill a joke inserted by Bob Orben, our gag writer, which he says is "unpresidential." The President agrees.

Hartmann moans that the speech is "too eloquent," that it is not in the Ford style. The President says nothing.

We switch to the Hollywood, Florida, speech. Seidman wants it to be a major economic speech. Hartmann jumps in quickly and plugs for an idea I had mentioned a week ago, a forward-looking energy speech which tells where we hope to be in ten to twenty-five years. The President agrees on the latter, saying: "Something like how we are going to save America."

After the meeting, Theis tells me: "Keep writing with some eloquence. But be careful."

On the surface, the meeting appeared to be one of substance. In reality, the most critical decisions—what really went into the speeches—were made by the writers, not Hartmann or the President, the two who would or could veto but offered little direction or real vision.

I ask Theis to be relieved of the task of editing all the speeches and other copy because the constant interruptions for editing while I am trying to write speeches have become very distracting. I must interrupt a speech ten to twenty times a day to edit various papers, proclamations, letters, etc. The editing cuts down on the numbers of speeches that I am in a position to write. With the increasing number of speeches that the President is making, it might be good for all concerned if I did more such work since I write faster than anyone on the staff.

Theis agreed. Friedman was assigned to editing. (However, he soon said he was unable to handle the work for the same reasons I offered. We need a fulltime editor.)

I take the time today to reflect on Mr. Ford's speeches. I disagree with Hartmann, who maintains the President's speeches should strive for clarity, not eloquence. I do not believe the two are incompatible but Hartmann repeatedly insists they are. On many occasions, he blocks the turn of a phrase, anything that smacks of being "different." Several times he said to me that this or that sounded like John F. Kennedy. Since I did not live in America during Mr. Kennedy's presidency, it seemed unlikely that I would have been influenced by his writers. I came to believe, however, that Hartmann had been influenced by Kennedy's speeches and that he disliked both Kennedy and his "style."

Ideas, imagination, innovation—these appear to be the seeds of self-destruction in Hartmann's turf. Hartmann is a man who is at home with yesterday and uneasy and uncertain with tomorrow. He is comfortable with the trite and tired phrases of the past, the old political rhetoric of the "big spenders" when he refers to Democrats, and befuddled by the newer language of such writers as Kevin Phillips and Richard J. Whalen.

Hartmann is sour on much of life and the concept of public confidence does not come easily to his typewriter keys. At this stage in our relationship, Bob is less challenged by the presidency than by his own survival as an aide to Gerald R. Ford. This old Navy man wants no boat rocked. He is enamored of his swivel chair that allows him to live in the past as much as the present. Bob Hartmann wants his two legs on solid ground where life is safe and secure.

I read a different Gerald Ford than Bob Hartmann projects. While Mr. Ford likes simple writing, he seems to me to have untapped inner emotion and is willing to expend it. Hartmann is building an image in concrete, the homespun speaker. The President would comment at various times, however, that he liked this or that phrase, which seemed to contradict Hartmann's view. I must wonder why Hartmann and I are receiving such different signals. I believe Hartmann still sees Mr. Ford as a congressman and writes for him that way. I see Gerald R. Ford as President. It appears to be a forgone conclusion that I will lose.

Monday, February 24, 1975

IT IS A SUNNY, pleasant Monday evening—one of those golden days of the Washington winter when the temperature climbs near 60 degrees and burns away the wet, gray chill of Foggy Bottom. The Capital went on daylight-saving time yesterday and the skies are still clear when Paul Theis shouts through the door:

"Meeting with the President at 6 o'clock on the Florida speech."

Kathy Wooten, one of our secretaries, is still typing the fourth draft. The speech picks up downhill speed with each succeeding draft. A meeting that morning sent it plunging.

I met on the speech for three hours this mornng with representatives of the Office of Management and Budget, the Domestic Council and the newly created Energy Research and Development Administration. The White House staff had arranged a conference on the President's economic and energy proposals to be held in Hollywood, Florida. Mr. Ford is to deliver the speech tomorrow afternoon.

Glen Schleede of the Domestic Council is the first to arrive for the meeting. He presents me with a four and one-half page "insert" to "explain the President's immediate program better." The "insert" would consume half the speech's time and change its entire thrust. A skinny, small, bearded soul, who identifies himself as "Hugh" and "one of the bosses" at OMB, arrives with copious notes. Ray Walters, a quiet but direct man, represents ERDA. It does not take long for the barbs to start flying.

It soon becomes apparent that Schleede is not aiming at merely an "insert" but wants to revamp the entire speech in his image and likeness. I remind him that it is the President's speech. Mr. Ford wants to look as far ahead as the year 2000 in the entire energy field.

Hugh makes the point that government agencies always try to blow up their balloon when they get "this once in a lifetime chance" to have the President talk about their programs. Hugh assumes the role of the protector of the President.

Ray Walters is a soft-spoken, hit-and-run guy. He is a man with the facts but is not about to go to the wall for them. He defends his agency's projections across the board—on the use of coal, solar heating and cooling, geothermal, nuclear and other projects under its wing. But he is clearly not about to take on OMB or the Domestic Council. Schleede and Hugh challenge and try to compromise every ERDA statement in the speech.

I feel like a man watching an old tree being cut down. However weatherbeaten and battered, it seems to me that it has more integrity than the two men axing it down. Hugh and Schleede are chopping hither and yon. A buzz-saw would be quicker. But no, paragraph by paragraph they cut into ERDA's projections for America's future energy. And they substitute caveats and compromise "lest the President's policies be misunderstood."

Declarative sentences, filled with ifs, buts and maybes, become dishwater. The ringing pronunciations of a President become hollow sixty-word sentences, dangling with participles. Schleede and Hugh beam.

As bureaucrats, they have done their jobs—protected their rear ends. In service to their President and their country, they have failed to communicate. That is my job.

We are a few seconds late for the 6 P.M. meeting. Bob Hartmann has already entered the Oval Office. Paul Theis, Bob Orben, Kaye Pullen and I follow. The President appears relaxed and is already reading the Florida speech draft. On finishing, he is much kinder than the speech warrants: "This is a good start."

We go through the speech page by page and it is evident we need to do two things. We need to cut some of the extraneous language of the bureaucrats and we need to make the speech more hardhitting.

In the midst of the discussion, Jack Marsh suddenly walks into the room and announces in a loud voice: "Allen has done it again. He got control of the Senate floor."

Marsh is referring to Senator James B. Allen, an Alabama Democrat and diehard foe of Senate liberals who are attempting to change the fifty-eight-year-old filibuster rule. Reform advocates want to end filibusters by a three-fifths vote instead of the two-thirds margin required under Senate Rule 22. Allen and other traditionalists are using filibuster tactics to block an up-or-down vote on proposed rule changes.

With favorable rulings from Vice President Rockefeller, the Senate's presiding officer, that august legislative body had steamrollered nine consecutive roll calls through trying to establish this historic principle: The Senate, at the beginning of a congressional session, may shut off debate on proposed rules changes by a simple majority vote—rather than the two-thirds required for other matters.

Allen, an acknowledged master of Senate rules, repeatedly outmaneuvers his colleagues to block action on the proposal. President Ford, a man quick to pat another on the back, says of Allen to us: "He's a very smart fellow."

Mr. Ford is smiling. I read a lot into that smile.

The question strikes me, does President Ford see himself in Allen's plight? A man far outnumbered against the Congress. A man with a great burden on his mind—millions of Americans out of work; the Congress is "fiddling while the economy burns." That is one of the President's favorite phrases. He uses it constantly and credits the source, a headline writer on the *Christian Science Monitor*.

Senator Mike Mansfield, the usually unflappable majority leader, has come unglued by the Allen maneuver. He leaps to his feet, yelling uncharacteristically on the Senate floor, demanding to know:

"What's going on here?"

At the end of the long day, with Allen in control of the floor, Mansfield sums it all up: "Dillydallying—stalling and dillydallying."

That is an expression which Mr. Ford uses to describe the Congress's delay on his State of the Union proposals: "dawdling and dillydallying."

The meeting with the President ends with a discussion of a Bicentennial address that he was to give the following day and some jokes that Bob Orben has written in connection with the Florida trip. Mr. Ford is to golf with Bob Hope and Jackie Gleason after a morning news conference.

I work until 10:30 P.M. on revising the speech. I go home to bed and wake up with an earache. I attribute the earache to the Office of Management and Budget and the Domestic Council. They had pointed us in the wrong direction—dishwater—not the "new direction" of the President.

Friday, February 28, 1975

WE ARE CALLED to a briefing on the professional and ethical standards of White House employees. The first speaker, in the Old Executive Building auditorium, is Donald Rumsfeld. He begins by saying that the President must have all the necessary input to make the correct decisions. This necessitates thorough coordination. As an example, Rumsfeld refers to input on presidential speeches and concludes: "To the extent that the President speaks, it becomes policy."

I say to myself: "You are not writing a helluva lot of policy."

On the decision-making process, Rumsfeld sums up:

"It is our job to protect the President—to make sure he is not blindsided, surprised."

Switching to a new subject, Rumsfeld says that many activities of the federal government have been brought into the White House since the early 1960's, obviously referring to the Kennedy and Johnson eras. He explains that President Ford wants to reverse this trend and send many responsibilities back to the departments from which they came. He concludes:

"We should involve more agency people in decisions and restore balance to the executive branch."

Rumsfeld then describes the standard of conduct expected of White House employees as a "broad, gray area." He refers briefly to Mr. Ford's own statement that he will set a good example of personal conduct and others must follow. Rumsfeld advises all to read a White House employee manual carefully, especially regarding ethical conduct. He summarizes:

"We have a special obligation here in the White House. It would be OK for us to do certain things as private citizens, but not working here. Our behavior must be not only proper but perceived as proper."

He changes subjects again to the White House budget. Rumsfeld reports that the President's staff has been cut from 540 to 490 persons. He says the number of employees must be further reduced since "Congress watches the White House with close scrutiny." Rumsfeld explains that the White House could be in the red at the close of the fiscal year on June 30, 1975, describing the situation as "very tight."

The White House budget is in the red at the current time, most employees believe, because so many Nixon holdovers were kept on the payroll while they sought new jobs. In the meantime, new Ford staffers joined the White House payroll and salaries overlapped.

Rumsfeld concluded his part of the briefing with two general statements:

It is our job to serve the people. As he put it: "Our job is to help make government help the people."

Also, we should perform our tasks as we think the President would perform them if he were sitting in our chairs. We should remember this when we deal with any and all citizens.

It is a bland but studied performance. It is deliberately bland, as if to say: "I am no Haldeman or Ehrlichman."

To use Rumsfeld's own expression, he wishes to be "perceived" as a good guy. A good reporter might be left with a lingering doubt and ask: "Is he?"

White House attorneys Bill Casselman and Dudley Chapman take over the rostrum to discuss the "standard of conduct."

This lengthy briefing dealt with many aspects of standards and security. These same standards were on the books during the Nixon administration. But as Richard J. Whalen said so poignantly in the title of his book on the Nixon tenure, *Catch the Falling Flag*, the standards fell by the wayside and the troops marched straight into political hell with no one to stop them, and very few indeed were in a position to catch the colors as they came down.

Some work is slipped on my desk—to write a foreword for the new book of prayers by Dr. Edward G. Latch, chaplain for the House of Representatives. It is to be on the President's desk today for approval. I begin writing. And these are the opening words:

"This inspirational book of prayers opens the human heart to the love of God . . ."

Later in the day, one of my colleagues asks if I have a moment to discuss the Rockefeller "incident." I know little of what has occurred in the past two days and say so. Nevertheless, he wants to talk about the matter.

Vice President Rockefeller, flying back to Washington after delivering a speech on energy in Detroit, is being quizzed by reporters about his political future. Someone apparently needles him about his eventual presidential possibilities. The Vice President is quoted as replying:

"I don't think anyone gives a good goddamn, if you will excuse the expression, about 1980 politics."

Rockefeller says that President Ford is bound to be the GOP's candidate in 1976 and speculation about the 1980 race shows a "loss of focus" on current problems. The VP says he and everyone else should concentrate on solving the problems of today, not the future.

I am then told that Rockefeller phoned the President, advised him of the incident, and said he just wanted Mr. Ford to have the facts so that no misunderstanding could occur. The President is reported to have told Rocky not to worry and to forget the matter.

Then, the real reason for the meeting begins to emerge. This person has some "hot" information about an important White House staff man.

One of the black cleaning ladies, who works our floor in the evenings, has reported to her boss that twice within a week she was shocked by a man in one of the offices. He had allegedly taken off his pants while she was cleaning his office, walked across the room and put on a different pair of pants. She complained about it to him directly and he reportedly asked:

"Haven't you seen a man without his pants on before?"

"Yes," replied the woman, "some members of my family."

The gentleman did not take the hint, took off his trousers a second evening, and the good lady stormed into her boss saying:

"If that man does it one more time, I will not clean his room."

My colleague, who was then informed of the incident, asks me what he should do about it. He puts it this way:

"Can you imagine what people on the outside would say if they heard a man was walking around the White House without his pants on?"

I reply:

"They've heard and seen a lot worse in the White House in the past few years."

He admonishes me:

"You can't be serious. We've got to do something about this."

"Not me . . . you," I answer. "Count me out. I don't care what the guy does. That's his business. I don't want to become involved in any manner, shape or form."

My colleague responds:

"But what about the President? This could embarrass the President and the whole White House."

"The hell it could," I say. "I'm not calling the *Washington Post* and I don't think you are. And the cleaning lady isn't calling the *Star*. Forget it. She's just going to hit that guy with a mop and that will end everything."

But my colleague is pained. He wants action.

He keeps saying that this is the White House, that it has to be above reproach. I finally say:

"All I'm telling you is to put your money on the cleaning lady. She's going to bop the guy. But if you pop off, I can see it now: the Secret Service, the FBI, Rumsfeld, Buchen and a team of lawyers will hit this floor like a wave of Marines. It will be like dropping an A-bomb on an ant. I'll put ten bucks right now on the cleaning lady."

I leave his office with a feeling that he is putting his money on the official rule book.

At the time that I am discussing Rocky with my colleague, the President is addressing about 400 members of the Young Republican Leadership Conference in the East Room. Joined by Mrs. Ford and their daughter, Susan, the President says:

"We think this is a great home. It is a great home. And Betty does not like to move very often.

"I guess that leads to the conclusion that I am going undoubtedly, without any question of a doubt, at the proper time, to be a candidate for a political party that is devoted to the basic principles that have built this country from a small nation of some three million to a vigorous, effective nation of over 213 million people."

Fred Bird tells me that he wrote the President's remarks. And he explains:

''Nobody told me what to write. So I just decided to say that he was going to run.''

This surprises and bothers me. This is not the first time that a speechwriter has written, *on his own*, words of highest policy. These words, of course, had to be cleared by Hartmann and Theis, but the important factor to me is this: how and why are we speechwriters given so much latitude? What makes any of us presume that we can attempt to put such words in the President's mouth?

I am back to asking my favorite question: What the hell is going on here?

As speechwriters, we continue to lack direction from Hartmann and Theis on what to write. We are simply told to write a speech for this conference or that annual meeting. Some speeches are obvious—the economy or energy. But even there, we must choose our own thrust for the speech, what to stress and what not to. We desperately need more and clearer direction.

I conclude that perhaps survival is the name of the game. Hartmann offers no guidance to the speechwriters because he wants to be blamed for no mistakes. Hartmann will offer the country no ideas, except his ill-fated WIN buttons, but he will win the biggest victory of all. He will survive most of his White House contemporaries.

There is unspoken contempt for Hartmann among members of the speechwriting staff. Some is also reserved for Theis. However, Hartmann sets the tone for Theis and thus is blamed squarely for Mr. Ford's weak language and vapid thrust.

In the final analysis, Hartmann, and to a lesser extent the President, have adopted an outrageous position. Theirs is to do, to risk as little as possible, to make no enemies, and thus to hang onto power. This is the precise philosophy of the stereotyped bureaucrat whom they have used as a whipping boy for years, the big spender living off America's productive workers.

Chapter 6
March, 1975

"Our political setup is something unique in the history of the world and it is a matter with which the President must be entirely familiar. He must know where he is going and why he is going there and the manner in which he puts his policies into effect is a matter which he discusses with all his Cabinet and all his advisers. It really is a most interesting procedure that has to be followed by a President when he is trying his best to run the government in the interest of all the people."

HARRY S TRUMAN

Tuesday, March 4, 1975

AT 5 P.M. WE BEGIN a birthday party for Bob Orben, whose birthday it is, and Milt Friedman, whose birthday is due in about a week. The office girls present Orben with a laugh box. You push a button and the small battery-operated mechanism starts laughing, and continues. Orben can't get the box to stop laughing. The button is apparently stuck but Orben—after an heroic and hilarious effort—finally unwinds the laughter.

Friedman receives a crystal ball and he cracks:

"I hope this will tell me what Hartmann wants in the next speech."

Theis snaps: "And what Greenspan is thinking!!"

Friedman has just rewritten his first draft on a foreign policy speech after Hartmann rejected it saying:

"This is Kissinger's foreign policy. I want a speech with Ford's foreign policy. Give me a Ford foreign policy speech."

Thus was born President Ford's speech quoting Arthur Vandenberg, onetime Republican senator from the President's home state of Michigan, who called for a bipartisan foreign policy with Democratic President Harry S Truman.

Alan Greenspan, one of the President's chief economic advisers, is tough as nails on general principles but sometimes cloudy on hard-nosed specifics. When pressed on a point, Greenspan sometimes retorts with a tart tongue. He loves the general battleground, hurling big bombs, but avoids close combat. I concluded that Greenspan, the administration's towering intellect and colossus of conservatism, is also a romantic idealist in battle.

I am fascinated by the continuing confrontations between Greenspan and Bill Seidman, a Grand Rapids accountant and friend of the President, who is chairman of the Economic Policy Board. They clash to some degree in many economic meetings.

Seidman appears to be a feisty pragmatist with few firm economic convictions beyond making a buck. Greenspan is the eagle who soars above those in the room during economic discussions. His grasp of economic concepts is unequaled. Seidman does not concede this, publicly or privately. Greenspan is an imaginative economist. Seidman, who has a habit of shifting nervously in his seat when someone is getting the best of him, has an accountant's mentality. He doesn't know what Greenspan is talking about when the New Yorker's mind begins to pierce the upper atmosphere of economic theory. So Seidman becomes a part-time pragmatist and part-time skeptic, assuming the mantle of protecting the President. This dodge is an old and faithful ally of many past presidential aides.

Seidman makes one mistake, however. He assumes that he is politically pragmatic. In his attempt to be politically pragmatic, Seidman shoots from the hip on too many occasions. For example: no one attacks lines in the draft of a speech like Seidman. Next to sentences and paragraphs, he slashes at the copy with words like the following: "No . . . wrong . . . awful . . . terrible . . . lousy!" When pressed for an explanation, his real aim seems to be furthering a pet idea of his or thrusting a new thought into the speech which struck him only on reading the draft.

Today I found an article which Seidman himself had prepared on the economy, written for an Arizona bank by one of his assistants but edited by him. It is about as inspiring as an accountant's lecture on twenty years with the same firm. Some think: "The feisty rooster may be a mere clucking hen."

Friday, March 14, 1975

DICK KAISER, chief of the White House secret service detail, gives the speechwriters a briefing. He cops out immediately. Kaiser says he did not wish to become chief of the detail under the circumstances; Bob Haldeman had removed his predecessor without sufficient reason. He, Kaiser, was offered the post but turned it down. Later, he was told to take it or else. He took it. I sympathize with Kaiser, having worked under two Nixon loyalists, Barabba and Failor.

Kaiser is convinced that the Warren Commission report on President Kennedy is correct. Oswald was the assassin working alone. He says that each of his agents is instructed that a potential killer of a President has 2½ seconds to get off his first shot. In other words, each agent has only 2½ seconds to save a President's life.

There were seventy-five threats against the life of Gerald Ford as Vice President which the secret service took seriously. As

President, there are now, seven months after taking office, 400 threats against Mr. Ford's life which the agents have taken seriously. This is about the total expected.

Thursday, March 20, 1975

FOR A FEW WEEKS NOW, I have been listening to the speechwriting and speechmaking of others. The Republican Party is trying to find its soul, searching its innermost depths to determine its character and its mission. As a ticket-splitting Independent, I have always felt that the GOP has never done a good job of explaining itself and its aims. The Democrats are more for real. You see the black eyes and bloody noses after their fights while, in my mind, someone just disappears after a Republican shakeout.

I listen to the other speechwriters, other colleagues in the White House and various GOP public speakers. The Republicans seem to love theories. How are the hardhats and other middle-income Americans to be won? What are the main factors in winning more independents? Why the Wallace vote really is or can be a Republican vote. But I see no plans and certainly no action.

It is as if the Republicans believe they hold the Bible in their hands and people should come to them because they have the truth. The Democrats preach sin, hell and damnation; the joy of politics is their religion.

Thus, when President Ford told Republicans here in Washington that the GOP "must discard the attitude of exclusiveness," he was talking turkey. The broad-base concept was truly carried out, insofar as I know, only by Richard Nixon and only for election purposes. His cheers to the hardhats, incantations to the Catholics, sweetness to the Spanish, was strict pragmatism. The name of the game for Richard Nixon was victory. He never really had a plan to help the hurting Catholic school system. Nixon loved the hardhats on the tube when they were giving the "pinko media" fits decrying the liberal ethic. And the Spanish were to be used, to hang the GOP hat on "this minority thing." Nixon was a practical, expedient man of the day or the month. He proved not to be a disciple of the Republican right from which he sprang.

Mr. Ford told Republicans they "must erect a tent that is big enough" to cover a variety of new followers. He specifically cited

Independents and people under twenty-two years old. Less than 20 per cent of America's voters identify with the GOP. Only seven of every 100 Americans identify themselves as "strong Republicans." Yet, the Republicans continue to ignore "positive grassroots action." They make movies and give ballroom speeches while the Democrats make noise on streetcorners and give speeches in ballparks.

My complaint with the Republican party is that it has never demonstrated sufficient concern about the working man and woman. Business is not sold by the GOP in a way that makes sense to the man on the street or the housewife. The President himself has given few speeches to blacks. Also he has rarely mixed with them or with other workers suffering most from the recession.

Many workers, and I consider myself an average American worker by temperament, oppose huge government spending. They are critical of its many abuses and the crazy-quilt welfare system. They are fed up with the permissiveness of our society. The GOP has a chance among the working classes but will have to work to get it. President Ford must show he *cares* about them; instead, Americans repeatedly see him golfing with corporation lobbyists, the fattest cats in the country.

I sit here and listen to the bitching of Republicans about why the workers, "the producers," don't wake up and "do something" about the welfare mess . . . the spending debacle . . . the deficit doldrums . . . and the "runaway Congress" that doesn't know where it's going.

And I ask: Why aren't you in the streets? Why wasn't one Republican present at a recent Washington job rally to explain the GOP viewpoint? Why don't you show that you care?

The unspoken question in the White House is why do the American people appear to accept the most severe recession since World War II? Their acceptance is attributed to unemployment benefits from government, unions and employers. And, as the argument goes which I am coming to respect, more people are concerned about inflation than recession. In terms of numbers, that appears to be accurate.

Millions of Americans do not see these days as adverse ones, a time of trial and economic danger. They are not aroused. Therefore, I am told, my feeling about the "little guy" is exaggerated. I am not convinced.

As I sit here in my office, I am intellectually convinced that the honest course for the American voter is to be an Independent, as most are. To raise hell with both parties is a demonstrably good position since neither party appears to have the toughness of mind and spirit to discipline itself in the national interest. Neither has come out of these years of scandal with clean hands. Neither is able to win the trust of the people. There is something both sad and shocking about the ineptness of the two parties in their inability to offer better, stronger leadership to the country. And the old phrase of ABC's Bill Lawrence comes back to haunt my thoughts: "Jack, the only way to look at a politician is down."

Friday, March 21, 1975

WARREN RUSTAND, director of the White House scheduling office, briefs the speechwriting staff. He and his office have made some plans for Mr. Ford's entire term. They have already given thought to 1977. They must act on the assumption that the President will win the next election.

"Every minute, or literally nearly every minute, is accounted for about three weeks in advance," Rustand reports. "It is less so three months in advance but we keep a somewhat definitive schedule for that length of time. Of course, it changes."

The President receives about 300 requests per day to do something, from a public appearance to an autograph. About 175 of these requests come in by phone. Some thirty-five originate with the White House staff. And the rest are written requests, usually in the form of a letter. These requests come from anyone and anywhere. There is usually a heavy series of requests when the White House announces that the President is to visit a city or state.

Rustand quietly makes a few observations which startle me. "This is an impulsive President." He gives this in answer to a question about the acceptance of some speaking engagements.

Rustand questions the writers about the President's image. The consensus response is:

"He has no image or at least it is dimly perceived and perhaps negative."

"Why negative?" Rustand inquires. We reply:

"Because he does not project a program or goals. There is no Great Society or New Frontier or even New Federalism."

I say:

"Hartmann has told us he doesn't want this administration to have a theme or a label."

Friedman says: "The President wants to keep his options open."

Other writers say: "That's why he appears to be indecisive."

My private judgment is that the administration has few if any new ideas. I point this out quietly. I watch as many faces as I can while I say: "Some people may not like Harry Hopkins, but he gave Roosevelt an idea an hour."

Agnes Waldron, chief of the research section, replies: "Yes, and every one of them was wrong."

I respond:

"That doesn't mean the ideas President Ford receives will be wrong. Let's take our speeches as an example. We have very little direction from the top. I have been writing off the west wall."
(The "west wall" is an old newspaper term for looking up at the wall and dreaming up various details of a story.)

The speechwriters complain at great length about the lack of guidance on speeches. I suggest that a board be formed to review and define the content of speeches. This board could meet once or twice a month as necessary. It should be composed of the top White House personnel, perhaps ten people.

The meeting ends in agreement that we should have such a board. It is clear, however, that the White House speechwriters, as a group, feel they need more specific instruction to do their work. The long and short of it, by Hartmann's own definition, is that we are actually writing the policy of the United States with little or no guidance from the top.

Chapter 7
April, 1975

"A President cannot always be popular. He has to be able to say yes and no, and more often no to most of the propositions that are put up to him by partisan groups and special interests who are always pulling at the White House for one thing or another. If a President is easily influenced and interested in keeping in line with the press and the polls he is a complete washout. Every great President in our history had a policy of his own, which eventually won the people's support."

HARRY S TRUMAN

Friday, April 11, 1975

THE PRESIDENT delivered his State of the World message last night. Henry Kissinger had spent most of yesterday with him. There is no question inside the White House; Kissinger wrote the foreign policy speech. Kissinger's real motivation, the speech writers believe, is to prevent the President from using such words as "dissarray" or "mistakes" about any of our foreign policy. Kissinger is literally writing his own history. Of course, some foreign policy is in disarray. Of course, mistakes have been made. Kissinger will not admit that. Some say he wants to continue marching around the world as a "new Solomon."

Little new is revealed in the speech. The President requests $722 million for military aid. He asks for clear congressional authority to send American troops back into Vietnam to assist in the evacuation of some 6,000 Americans as well as several hundred thousand Vietnamese "friends" of the United States. There are no new concepts and no new ideas in the address. The media agree.

I put down the morning newspapers and my mind wanders into what is becoming my favorite question: Has Gerald Ford discovered the presidency yet?

Mr. Ford is genuinely searching for meaning, for a definition of what the presidency is. I do not believe that he has found it in Harry Truman. No man in that position can help but demand of himself an original contribution to the office, the country and the people. And Mr. Ford is talking the nation's ears off . . . dashing here and there around the country . . . in search of a job description he can live with.

How would Mr. Ford eventually define his job? I do not know.

It is argued that the President cannot be flooding the country with new ideas when he is trying to cut back federal spending. But many ideas do not cost money. A definition of the administration's goals or aims seems to me a low-cost necessity.

At that point, Paul Theis enters my office. He looks at me and asks: "Meditating?"

"Yes," I say, "on St. Thomas Aquinas."

"Who?" he questions.

"St. Thomas Aquinas," I say, "the man Chesterton called a dumb ox."

No wonder Theis thought some of us should take a few days off at times.

Saturday, April 12, 1975

THE SPEECHWRITERS meet with the President this morning for about forty-five minutes. Present are: Hartmann, Theis, Friedman, Orben and myself.

The President's mind is on Cambodia. He tells us that the evacuation of Pnom Penh has "come off without a hitch." He knocks on the wood of his chair. Mr. Ford continues:

"We were prepared to take out about 500 people but half of the Cambodians did not come. I mean some of the Cambodian government officials sent out their families but they did not come. I think that took a lot of guts—a lot of guts."

Secretary of State Kissinger suddenly enters. He and the President go next door to Mr. Ford's hideaway office. Hartmann says as Kissinger leaves the room with the President: "There goes our new speechwriter."

Hartmann confirms what all of us know. Kissinger wrote the President's State of the World speech delivered to a joint session of the Congress the previous Wednesday evening.

On return, the President tells us that he wants Kissinger to see his address to be given to the Daughters of the American Revolution. Mr. Ford wants the secretary's comments.

The President and Kissinger would both be addressing the American Society of Newspaper Editors shortly and Mr. Ford says:

"I don't want people to try to split us apart or to allow it to seem that we might be apart on anything. Our policy statements have to be the same. We have got to coordinate the two speeches."

The President says he has no ideas on what to say before the New Hampshire state legislature. Since I am writing his remarks he tells me to phone Norris Cotton, the retired Republican senator from that state, for subject matter.

Warren Rustand, who scheduled the New Hampshire speech with presidential approval, tells me the speech is to be a kickoff of Mr. Ford's campaign in New Hampshire in 1976. Rustand says:

"The President has got to win big and stop others in their tracks from challenging him."

Before the meeting breaks up, the President turns to Hartmann and asks that a joke about Kissinger be removed from his speech to the Senate and House Republican fund-raising dinner. The remark is:

"Trying to raise money on April 15 makes as much sense as Henry Kissinger saying: 'Nobody knows the troubles I've seen!' "

Monday, April 14, 1975

A FEW SENTENCES from a syndicated column by William F. Buckley sting the White House inner circle. Some privately agree with him. Rumors are everywhere. Buckley has written about "our shame, Ford's golf and decency." He says:

"There is only one thing that saves America from absolute obloquy: it is our essential innocence. There is a real innocence in the naivete of Gerald Ford. But the world has a right, in the face of our staggering diplomatic and military ineptitudes, to expect from the President a sense of decorum that harmonizes with what ought to be the national mood: shame, compassion, guilt."

Buckley argues that seventy million Americans get their news from television. They are watching acute misery in South Vietnam followed by film of President Ford playing golf in California. The columnist makes a case for creating wrong impressions and says, in effect, that the President is doing just that.

At least one presidential assistant has already advised Mr. Ford that he was making a mistake in going to Palm Springs, California, for an Easter vacation. He would be living in style at the home of a millionaire at a time of crisis in Vietnam and Cambodia and immediately after his signing of the tax-cut bill, a reminder that millions of Americans were not having life so good. News commentaries and cartoons in the press contrasted Mr. Ford's sojourn in the sun with hard times at home and human misery in Asia. One staffer says to me:

"How can the President be insensitive to the situation? My people are ordinary people and, believe me, they don't like it. My brother-in-law is having a helluva time and he's a Republican. He is saying: 'What the hell is going on with Ford? Doesn't he know what it's like in Ohio?' "

Tuesday, April 15, 1975

I ask myself, as others on the White House staff have already asked themselves, these questions about the President's trip. How could this kind, decent man be so insensitive? Why not go quietly to nearby Camp David? Did the President have a stubborn streak?

President Ford's decisions on food stamps and Social Security are interpreted by the public to mean he wants to cut both while his only intention is to curtail part of the increasing cost to the federal government. And if the decisions are not insensitive, then the language of his explanations falls far short of reasonable.

I am determined to correct that impression in an upcoming speech to the New Hampshire state legislature. Paul O'Neill, deputy director of the Office of Management and Budget, and I spend a long time in praising social progress in the United States while writing the New Hampshire speech. We stress, however, that some of these programs have proven worthless and they should be reexamined and cut by the Congress. The speech calls for a reassessment of domestic programs and spending.

I am stunned when Bill Seidman writes to Theis: "This is a good speech." All previous speeches spent little time on the "good" of social spending, emphasizing the "bad." And Seidman had approved them. This seems to be another example of unclear thinking at the top in the White House. I had literally switched gears and no one had objected.

O'Neill and I conclude that it is not only wrong but madness to write a speech attacking social programs. The thing that bothers both of us, and millions of Americans regardless of political affiliation, is the endless stream of promises to the American people that their problems can be solved by more government spending.

The President had told me in the Oval Office that he did not have any ideas for New Hampshire. Hartmann and Theis tell me the same thing. So I write the speech from the subject matter to the final period entirely on my own initiative.

(R.W. Apple later wrote in the *New York Times* that the speech was perfectly tailored to undercut Governor Meldrim Thompson of New Hampshire and his support of Ronald Reagan. Apple is saying that the President and the White House are attempting to show that Mr. Ford is as much a fiscal conservative as the New Hampshire governor, who publicly denounced Mr. Ford's fiscal budgets as excessive spending.

Apple suggests that the Ford White House has launched a grand political strategy. Paul O'Neill and I are hardly the usual picture of political theoreticians or strategists.)

Tuesday, April 15, 1975

ABOUT 600 PARTY FAITHFUL, paying $1,000 a plate, come to the annual Senate and House GOP fund-raising dinner to hear the President. The $600,000 "take" is disappointing to Mr. Ford and others. The same 1969 dinner, when President Nixon was riding high, took in some $3 million.

Fred Bird, who wrote this speech for the party faithful, puts it this way:

"I pounded the table so hard that I upset all the coffee cups. He gave a helluva speech."

Many do not agree. But that is not Bird's fault. Mr. Ford delivers the speech listlessly. His voice is barely audible at times. He seems, as some White House staffers put it, to be "going through the motions. He has no zip."

Bird confirms that he had been given no direction on whether the President will be a candidate in 1976. He simply wrote it. Obviously, the President would not make the public statement unless he was prepared to stand behind it. However, it bothers me that the President never once, at our staff meetings in the Oval Office this past week, said such a speech should contain a statement that he would run in 1976.

The President's speech is a subtle attack on Ronald Reagan and the Republican right, who defined the party only weeks earlier at a Washington meeting in narrow, ideological terms. The President told us earlier at a meeting in his Oval Office:

"This speech has got to say that we don't want a mob in the party—but we do want all those who truly accept our principles."

It is a compromise statement. The first part of the sentence is precisely what Reagan and the right are saying. The second part is Mr. Ford: "We need a broader-based party which appeals to all the American people."

At our meeting in the Oval Office, Mr. Ford was direct:

"We don't want people in the party just to pull a lever like the Democrats do. We want them in because they believe in the traditional Republican principles. That's why the Democrats always have so much trouble. They are always pulling themselves apart.''

In his speech, the President cites three principles as the bedrock of the GOP: 1) the free enterprise system and fiscal responsibility by the federal government; 2) belief in the need for a strong national defense posture as the only sure way to a peaceful world; and 3) freedom for local and state governments to make their own decisions and nongovernment intervention in business-labor relations and individual lives.

The President is to give sixteen speeches this week, April 13 through 19. This is an awesome schedule. These are sixteen- to eighteen-hour days. For several months now, the speechwriters keep asking themselves this question: Why is he giving so many speeches?

This morning, one of my colleagues on the first floor of the Old Executive Office Building whispers what I had detected in Kissinger's voice a few days ago: ''Nessen's in trouble.'' The rumor is everywhere; I hear it all day long.

White House Chief of Staff Donald Rumsfeld, Nessen and at least one other presidential aide are reported bad-mouthing Kissinger. They are zeroing in on Henry for apparently two reasons.

First, Kissinger wrote virtually every word of President Ford's State of the World speech of last week. Rumsfeld apparently believes Kissinger is doing no more than writing a defense of himself and his policies in the State of the World speech—the President be damned. Nessen always tries to follow Rumsfeld's lead.

Second, Rumsfeld allegedly wants Kissinger out as chief of the National Security Council. Rumsfeld feels Kissinger is not giving Mr. Ford a balanced and objective picture of world events. He wants someone who will.

At a federal fiscal budget meeting with the President, which I attended in December, Roy Ash bitterly criticized Kissinger to the President. He said in polite but clear terms that, in effect, Kissinger had lied to the President with regard to the budget, that Kissinger had slipped proposed appropriations into the budget which he had told Ash he would not do. I could not hear all of Ash's criticism but it was clear that the OMB director felt he had been outmaneuvered by Kissinger. President Ford, calm about it all, assured Ash he would look into the matter. The subject was quickly dropped when photographers and White House cameramen entered the Oval Office for a photo and film session on the budget.

Today, Kissinger is enraged over a CBS report that he is about to lose his National Security Council hat. He heard that Nessen is the source of the leak and phones the press secretary saying that 1) Nessen must stop it, and 2) he will go to the President about the matter if it is not cleared up. Nessen denies everything to Kissinger.

On becoming press secretary, Nessen told the White House press corps that he would never lie to them. He is about to break that promise. Nessen fired Louis Thompson, an assistant press secretary, and then solemnly denied that he had fired Thompson. Thompson and others not only confirm that he had been dumped, but Thompson charges that Nessen is the source of the leak about Kissinger's National Security Council position. It would appear that Kissinger believes Thompson, not Nessen. Nessen also denies that he is the source of the leak, but many, if not all, of the White House press corps do not believe him. Nessen, in the language of several presidential aides, begins a "massive coverup." As one says:

"This guy may not be a Ziegler but he is a Ron. And the son-of-a-bitch can lie just as fast as Ziegler. I wouldn't trust Ron Nessen after this episode. I think the President should wonder about keeping him."

Thus the rumors of Nessen's possible downfall permeate the White House. Some suggest that Rumsfeld may ultimately save him. For my part, I stay as far away from Nessen as I can. Many newsmen claim that Nessen has a fatal flaw. He is arrogant, they complain, and he shows this arrogance in his public as well as private conduct.

Bob Schieffer, the source of the CBS story, tells the Associated Press:

"I am not going to say who was the source of my story but I can state categorically that Thompson was not the source."

Nessen tries to shut off the rumors, saying:

"Secretary Kissinger and I have an excellent relationship."

William I. Greener, an Air Force officer for twenty years, is now named chief deputy White House press secretary to replace Thompson. Greener, it is noted, had worked as the chief press officer at the Cost of Living Council under Donald Rumsfeld. As one of my colleagues put it:

"Rummy is always ready. If the President dumps Nessen, he has his own man ready to step in at a moment's notice. That's show biz, baby. The show must go on!"

New rumors replace the old ones.

Presidential aides suggest that Kissinger is the source of rumors that he is on the way out. Every time Henry gets insecure, they say, he plants a rumor that powerful presidential aides are trying to push him out. And once again, the President must come out and say that Henry is doing a fantastic job.

Tonight, as the rain falls on the Potomac, Kissinger wears two hats. Donald Rumsfeld and Ron Nessen rarely wear hats. And I have a headache. However, one last question bothers me: Where do they get the time for all the intrigue?

Thursday, April 17, 1975

THEIS quietly slips into my office in midmorning and asks me to edit some copy and another writer's draft of a speech. He then hands me a memo from Orben to the President via Hartmann and says: "Read this, too."

The memo is show biz from start to finish. Orben praises Mr. Ford's performance as a speaker on a recent West Coast swing but is critical of the size of rooms where the President spoke, the microphone setups, the length of speeches at breakfast, lunch and dinner. What Orben says in effect is: I know show biz. Your staff doesn't know show biz. Let's operate on sound show biz principles.

I ask myself why Theis showed me such a memo. It has nothing to do with my work unless he wants me to be more show biz in approach. And Theis knows I am not about to go show biz. What is he trying to tell me?

I notice that Orben keeps stressing that the President's speeches should be shorter. I agree. At the same time, however, it also appears relevant that his jokes are becoming longer. Sometimes, they take up two pages of a fourteen-page address. This is fine for golf tournaments and football speeches. Theis once asked me about this and I said:

"We have too many people out of work in this country, Paul, for the President to be telling a lot of jokes at sports gatherings or, for that matter, to take two or three minutes of jokes in a serious speech on the economy. It is self-defeating."

Orben comes to my office to discuss the New Hampshire state legislature speech. He asks me to take a look at the joke he has written as an opener. The joke takes a full page of the eleven-page speech. Theis had requested in the morning that I trim the speech. I had cut three pages of the address.

I advise Orben that I think the joke is too long. Couldn't he shorten it? I had cut three pages of substance that morning because Theis said it was too long. Orben replies that he needs time to set the humor up. I respond that I also need room to discuss the President's fiscal philosophy but don't have it. Orben won't budge. Instead, he says:

"I'm busy right now. Would you check the facts in the joke to see if they are correct about the pay for legislators up there?"

Orben explains he has "an important meeting" in "the residence." Presumably, he is telling me that he is meeting with the President or a member of the Ford family. I say nothing but the message gets through. Orben picks up his joke and leaves.

For six months now, Orben has coached the President on how to read his jokes. Ambassadors, cabinet members and others see much less of the President than Orben. In addition, the President's delivery of the real content of his speeches—what I call the "meat and potatoes"—is not improving. I feel this is a mistake and politely say so to Dr. William Lukash, the President's personal physician. Following this talk with Lukash, I notice the President sets aside time before each address to practice it. Whether my comments have anything to do with this decision, I'll never know.

Friday, April 18, 1975

AIR FORCE ONE has just climbed to its cruising altitude on the way to New Hampshire. Politics is in the air. The New Hampshire primary of next spring is on everyone's mind. Hartmann is in a jolly mood as I discuss the state legislature speech in Concord, New Hampshire, with him.

The *Wall Street Journal* carried only two days earlier a long front-page piece saying: "Ford is restoring a sense of purpose to the Administration.'' It spoke of "solid if unspectacular accomplishments.'' The newspaper said the administration, once demoralized and nearly paralyzed by the scandal that drove President Nixon from office, had been revitalized by President Ford.

Russell Train, administrator of the Environmental Protection Agency, said: "It's been like coming in from the cold.''

He explained that Mr. Ford was getting better information by dealing directly with agency heads instead of having only a few assistants discuss problems and accomplishments.

Yet we on the staff are acutely aware that, while staff morale is good, the real make-or-break test for the administration is with the Congress. Spending, energy, foreign policy, credibility—these are the issues which will make or break Gerald R. Ford; the greatest of these issues is the economy. All of these issues hinge on how well the President and Congress can or will work together.

This question is an enigma to me. And this trip is to bring out some of the contradictions involved in the President's relationship with the Congress. I have written in Mr. Ford's Concord, Massachusetts, speech for tomorrow that "now is the time for reconciliation—not recrimination.'' But I am also aware that in a Monday night television interview with CBS News, he will probably blame Congress again for not voting immediately the funds he requested to aid Vietnam. (As a matter of fact, that is precisely what happened.)

This is contradictory. The country could not have "reconciliation'' at the 200th anniversary of the battle of Concord on Saturday and "recrimination'' on Monday.

It seems to me that we are a split personality. I favor reconciliation if we are to get anywhere with Congress, but obviously my boss does not entirely agree with that.

Monday, April 21, 1975

WE, HARTMANN, Theis, Bakshian, Pullen, Goldwin, Friedman and myself, meet with the President for more than an hour in the afternoon. Mr. Ford has spent most of the morning meeting in crisis sessions with Secretary Kissinger and others on the collapse of South Vietnam, the resignation of President Thieu, and evacuation plans to take most of the Americans and an undetermined number of Vietnamese out of South Vietnam. The President seems calm, even relaxed.

Dr. Robert Goldwin, the resident ''intellectual'' from the University of Pennsylvania, makes a strong pitch for a ''crime speech'' before Yale University's Law School. His argument is filled with the old rhetoric about the guilty going unpunished and the law-abiding doing the suffering. I decide to sit this one out while all talk respectfully of the ''crime issue.''

The President grasps the real issue quickly. Is a Yale Law School convocation the place to give a crime speech? Mr. Ford also remarks that he did not believe Yale taught criminal law. He recalls that, before graduating from Yale, he had to take criminal law during a summer session at the University of North Carolina.

No one joins Goldwin with any enthusiasm but he persists in telling us how he would write the speech. He laces the gut issue of crime with legal theory and lofty phrases which he reads from prepared notes. After the meeting with the President, I say to Friedman:

''A crime speech at Yale is a form of insanity. Everyone will ask: Why is he giving such a speech there? And worse, the President has no plan or program to offer on crime. People are going to see this as political—and weak politics.''

Friedman says little. He is keeping his options open.

At the close of the meeting, the President turns to me and says: ''Jack, that was a good speech you did at the Old North Church. That was a very good speech.''

Hartmann had cried as the President delivered the Old North Church speech. So did Senator Edward Brooke of Massachusetts, who was also present.

Agnes Waldron, chief of our research office, had left a note on my desk for my return. She wanted to know what occurred at the meeting. I told her and she said:

''Do you know that Goldwin, then a registered Democrat, was one of those asked to write the Republican Party platform in 1960? And it was finally decided that a Democrat should have no part in writing a Republican platform.''

Earlier in the day at the White House staff meeting, it was decided to organize a Bicentennial speaking program for the President, to give it a theme with his personal mark on it. I presume this flows from an article in today's *New York Times* by R.W. Apple in which he points out that the Bicentennial could offer a big political plus to Mr. Ford.

The day closes as I learn the President will discuss crime at Yale. I never learn why.

Tuesday, April 22, 1975

THIS MORNING, I pull out a memo which I had written to Theis on April 10 on another presidential address and reread it:

"The Old North Church address offers President Ford a logical opportunity to offer some goals·for the future of the country. That is why I placed five goals in the Old North Church speech. This was not to suggest that these are the President's goals, but to call attention to a most timely opportunity. The President could present his goals in general, historical terms if desired. I understand the opinion expressed in our last staff meeting about keeping options open. However, there are a good number of Americans who are not sure what the President stands for and what his goals may be. The historic nature of the occasion will allow the President to talk about America 100 years from now although he may wish to save that for a separate address. The conclusion that the administration should "keep its options open" only reinforces a much more serious conclusion on the part of some: that this is an interim or transitional government. I read the European press very carefully and that is their general conclusion. They see a power vacuum in Washington and attribute the adventures of the Vietcong and the intransigence in the Middle East to a lack of decisiveness here. A listing of goals will help establish 'who's in charge.' The U.S. press has made leadership an issue which readers cannot ignore. Thus, at home and abroad, it seems in the President's very best interests to present some solid views on where he and the nation must go. Bob Hartmann certainly could insert the goals in the Old North Church speech. I sincerely hope he may do so."

The President enunciated no goals in the Old North

Church speech.* Mr. Ford himself told me to eliminate the goals and discuss the future of the country in general, philosophical terms.

Later in the day, I discuss the subject of goals with Jim Cannon, Vice President Rockefeller's top assistant, who tells me he is charged with coming up with administration goals. We talk for about an hour. Cannon feels the administration needs clearer aims but his language is cautious. I find "caution" to be the word characterizing most of Rocky's staff.

Thursday, April 24, 1975

LAST EVENING AT Tulane University in New Orleans, President Ford took a page from veteran George Aiken, the retired Republican senator from Vermont, who had said a decade ago that America should simply announce that the Vietnam war is over . . . that we had won . . . and come home.

The President declares at Tulane to a tumultuous roar that, as far as America is concerned, Vietnam is "a war that is finished." Mr. Ford simply declares the war is over.

Kissinger has no part in writing the speech which, to me, appears to be a clear signal from the President that he accepts the advice of close aides to put some daylight between himself and Kissinger. The speech had been cleared by General Brent Scowcroft, Kissinger's top aide inside the White House. However, the most important passages of the address were not given to Scowcroft. They were decided later on the flight to New Orleans.

The President calls for a "great national reconciliation"—the idea that I had fought for in the Concord, Massachusetts, speech last Saturday. That speech was not cleared with Kissinger or Scowcroft.

In spite of the Tulane speech, Ron Nessen announces at the press briefing today that the President is still asking for $722 million in military aid for Vietnam.

As far as I ever determined, the end-of-the-war statement at Tulane was not planned or placed in the speech by any logical design. It simply evolved out of a conversation the President had

---

See Appendix, page 309.

with Hartmann and Friedman. I concluded that it was, to some extent, an accidental remark, and the conclusions to be drawn from it had not been clearly thought out. Otherwise, Nessen would never have made his apparently contradictory remark. This slipshod thinking and planning continues to bother me. Somehow, I feel, it is vital that we get away from day-to-day thinking and develop a pattern of conduct in foreign policy and another clear program on the domestic scene.

Friday, April 25, 1975

I DECIDE TO PUT ON PAPER in behalf of the "Kansas City milkman" my thoughts on President Ford in the White House after six months as one of his speechwriters. Reynolds Packard, an old friend of mine in Europe, wrote a book under that title many years ago and I like it. Simply put, each reporter is really writing for the Kansas City milkman—not the chairman of the local bank or the chess champion in town whose IQ makes most of us wonder why we're around.

It is a sunny morning and I feel renewed as the breath of spring sweeps Washington's air after such a rainy, miserable month.

What do I like best in President Ford?

He is candid. The man simply tells the truth when he speaks. He is good-natured, even-tempered and extraordinarily calm for a man with such responsibility. He is also predictable. I can generally guess what the President will do or say on any given subject.

Gerald Ford does not appear to me to be a man of great surprises, although he astonished much of America when he pardoned former President Nixon. I was not surprised. The President always leans toward what he believes to be the decent thing. If there appears to be a conflict between what is convenient and what is decent or honorable, Mr. Ford will inevitably choose what is decent.

He is a conservative of conventional wisdom. He thinks in terms of examples in his past life. In a word, he thinks from experience.

There is no "grand design" in the White House—no real strategy. The place is run from day to day; problems are met; but the President is not thinking in terms of a plan to achieve three, six or ten major goals. He is groping.

I am convinced that he does not yet understand the nature of the presidency itself, its history, its relative place in society. He is partially unaware of the power at his command—the power for change, the power to change minds as well as society, government as well as American life. Mr. Ford is not a deeply ideological man but simply a good, midwestern idealist who wishes others and his country well. He could easily have been a Democrat as well as a Republican.

I knew Pope John XXIII as well as any foreigner in Italy did. I saw a lot of him while he was Pope and had years of personal conversation with his secretary, Msgr. Loris Capovilla. Gerald Ford and Pope John have much in common as men.

Pope John never really left his hometown of *Sotto Il Monte* and I do not believe that Gerald Ford has really left Grand Rapids. As men, both based their philosophies on boyhood and youth. They retained their youthful innocence. But there is one difference and it is a mighty one. While Pope John disdained power, he had a man near him who knew what it was and how to use it. Gerald Ford does not. Loris Capovilla was a brilliant individual, the brains behind most of the changes made by Pope John. There is no such genius near President Ford. Perhaps the Roman Catholic Church needed Loris Capovilla, my friend to this day, and perhaps America does not need a man like him at this hour. Who is to say? But no one has taken charge of the White House and the presidency.

Looking at the White House from the inside, I see Mr. Ford's government as an interim or transitional government. There are really no ''new directions'' in it because it has no basic strategy. I believe that foreigners see and understand this more clearly. That is why the Arabs and Israelis have not come closer to peace in the Mideast despite protests that they have been closer to a major agreement than at any time since Israel was born. That is why the Vietcong and North Vietnam have been so adventuresome. They see a weak presidency.

Mr. Ford's ''nice guy'' attitude is good for the internal healing of America but, in my judgment, it is bad for foreign policy. I believe Kissinger is most astute in the conclusion that Mr. Ford must somehow show that he is in control.

Nevertheless, Kissinger tells the President only what he wants him to know—only what serves Kissinger. For the Secretary of

State sees himself as more important than Mr. Ford. He has come
to see himself in essence as the "President" of foreign policy and
Mr. Ford only as a possible obstacle. It is my prediction this day
that Kissinger may get America into trouble because of his massive
ego although the President's aides have seen through him.

Our chief researcher, Agnes Waldron, was wrong. She
knocked Harry Hopkins. But we need a Harry Hopkins today—a
strong man at the President's side who has his confidence, has guts
and will better organize the White House. This is my lament. This
is the tear I shed today.

As modest as my job is, I must give it my damndest. The
country needs hard work in the White House. It is calling us. We
must help this good man who is President. I must be a voice to the
Kansas City milkman, to write with honesty and humility, and
more guts.

Monday, April 28, 1975

RON NESSEN TALKS OF "sabotage" in the headlines. In briefing
reporters, the press secretary discusses Betty Ford's health:

"Whoever leaked that inaccurate story is not a friend of
Newsweek and is not a friend of the President, more importantly.
Mrs. Ford's health is good and there is no indication that it's not
going to be good."

Nessen quotes White House aides as suspecting "sabotage" of
the President's 1976 political campaign. He does not name the
aides making the charge.

Only this morning, I said to Agnes Waldron, "Agnes, what's
going on inside this place? Everything is leaked. The place is a
sieve."

She agrees. For example, the fact that the President will make
one Bicentennial speech a month was in print only one day after
the top White House staff had made that decision. Two things
appear to be happening: several staff members are trying to prove
to newsmen that they are in the "know" and a few don't know
how to handle power.

The May speechwriting schedule arrives from Paul Theis. The
President is scheduled to make fifteen public speeches. More will
be added routinely.

Last week at a meeting in his office, the President told us: "I thought we were going to cut down on the speeches."

Top presidential aides have been concerned about "overexposure" for several months now. In this month alone, Mr. Ford had some seventeen major public speaking engagements. Since assuming the office, he has given more than 200 speeches. The speechwriters are astonished that so many engagements are accepted by the White House. But Warren Rustand tells us his scheduling office agrees to the speeches only after Mr. Ford approves each and every one of them.

A few of the President's closest advisers, principally Bob Hartmann, have been suggesting to Mr. Ford that he must start the political ball rolling for 1976. On the recent trip to New Hampshire and Massachusetts, GOP political leaders there privately complained that the President was not acting like a candidate. Specifically, one advised me he was convinced that Mr. Ford was not a candidate because the President had not yet appointed a national finance chairman.

The President appears to be moving his campaign very hesitatingly and no one appears to know why. He has agreed to a Citizens for Ford committee but there is no indication when this organization may be formed. We have written that Mr. Ford will be a candidate without Mr. Ford's ever having told us to do so. President Ford has said these words from public platforms, but I recall not a single instance where he has asked or suggested that we write he will be a candidate next year.

Doubts about a Ford candidacy are causing anxiety among staff members. Obviously, most of them want him to run. I belong to those who feel he should not be pressured by anyone in any way but, whatever he does, he should do it with conviction. There should be no halfway measure about it. At this moment, I personally feel he has some doubts about running. This is not because of anything Mr. Ford has said. It is his failure to take concrete actions to seek the presidency in his own right that concerns me.

Chapter 8
May, 1975

John F. Kennedy, in one of his earliest press conferences after assuming the office of the President, responded to a reporter's question regarding his coverage in the news thusly:

"Well, I'm reading more, but enjoying it less."

Wednesday, May 7, 1975

THE PRESIDENT AND SOME of his top aides are stung by the
continuing chorus in the media that Mr. Ford may not be a
candidate in 1976. The same rumor persists on Capitol Hill and
among some of the party pros around the country.

I heard more than a month ago that the President felt
campaign organizing need not be started until early fall. At the
same time, I was told that Hartmann would run the campaign,
either from inside or outside the White House. Strong opposition
had developed inside the White House to Hartmann for the
following reasons: his abrasive personality had alienated some of
his colleagues and they had united against him; they were
convinced he had a serious health problem; they claimed his style
was undignified for the White House; considerable antagonism had
built up toward him among an increasing number of Republicans
on the Hill; and he was not qualified to direct the campaign.

"They are edging him out," I was told, "and he knows it.
He's trying to fight back but he has a personal problem."

Yet Hartman headed a top-level campaign strategy session
inside the White House only a week ago.

Two days ago, Theis asked the speechwriters to submit to him
questions they thought the President might be asked at a news
conference. I asked this question:

It has been reported in the press that Edward Failor, currently
administrator of the Social and Economic Statistics Administration,
attended the first White House planning session for the 1976
campaign about ten days ago. The press has accused Failor of
being a political "dirty trickster"—including association with
Charles Colson, G. Gordon Liddy and Jeb Magruder in the 1972
Nixon attack group. Why run this kind of risk when one of your
greatest strengths as President is your honesty and integrity?

Theis called me in on the question. He voiced concern about
it. I told him that Failor was considered "bad news" by the *New
York Times*, the *Washington Post*, Jack Anderson and others, that
many newsmen had extensive files on him.

Theis, obviously probing to see how much damage could
result from Failor, pressed the point. I simply said that the press
had written badly of Failor wherever he had gone in

government—with the Committee to Re-elect the President, the Bureau of Mines, and in his present position. As far as the Republican party was concerned, he obviously had better sources than I since I had no background in such political activities. On a professional basis, I found it prudent to check carefully anything Failor said. As administrator of SESA, his relations with the public information office of the Census Bureau, where I was director, could not have been worse. I indicated to Theis that to bring men like Failor into the Ford campaign seemed to me a form of insanity. My parting words to Theis were:

"If I were involved in the Republican campaign, I would rather lose honorably than win with men of questionable integrity. I happen to think that President Ford may win with honor."

As usual, Theis was super-cautious. He rarely offered an insight into his own thinking. So I had to ask myself if Paul Theis would accept the Failors to gain victory. Or would he accept defeat with honor?

I concluded that Theis would reject Failor because Paul was too much of a gentleman.

At his news conference last night, the President declared in the strongest words he has used thus far that he would be a candidate in 1976. He hinted that he would run on the twin themes of peace and prosperity, that the economy would be turned around in the right direction by election time.

The real convincer was Mr. Ford's announcement that an informal committee would meet to discuss his campaign plans "within the next few days."

I discover today that Hartmann will not call the shots in the campaign. Dean Burch, former White House political adviser and now a Washington attorney, will head the informal group. Others are former Defense Secretary Melvin Laird, ex-White House aide Bryce Harlow, Nebraska GOP leader Richard Herman, former Pennsylvania Governor William Scranton and Robert Douglass, a New York lawyer and close associate of Vice President Rockefeller.

The ticket that most concerns the Ford White House is not a Democratic one. It is the nightmare of a possible Reagan-Wallace ticket. This drives them nuts.

Ford is a President without a clear, conclusive ideology. The mere fact that we are writing speeches without direction indicates this. I find no one in the White House who is an ideologist: not Hartmann, the practical realist; not Rumsfeld, who is management-oriented and a middle-of-the-road Ivy Leaguer; not Seidman or Buchen, who are Ford friends with no political base and no political orientation other than being conservative. The list of advisers could be endless, but no one inside the White House stands for the farm belt, is a southern strategist, or is oriented toward bringing Middle America, including the blue-collar workers, into the Republican party. There is no ideological direction inside the White House and I note this today because it surely will become evident in the months ahead to millions of Americans.

As a lifelong Independent, I am attracted to independent-minded people around a President but this does not help to give direction to the country unless the President takes personal charge of the operation. Thus far, he has been running the country by consensus, more and more the consensus of his staff. I believe the President should direct the staff more instead of the staff directing him. It may be argued that he makes his own decision—and that is correct—but he is in virtually all cases greatly influenced by his staff. His signing of the tax reduction bill is a good example. Everything in Gerald Ford's background called for him to veto that bill, but he signed it after most of the staff suggested that he do so. Ford disregarded his traditional commitment to fiscal responsibility and followed the advice of his staff. Ideology was abandoned in hope of political gain.

Tuesday, May 13, 1975

IN THE LATE AFTERNOON, Theis phones me and asks that I come to his office. When I arrive, Fred Bird, a temporary member of the speechwriting staff, is in the room. He apparently is saying his farewell to Theis so I excuse myself.

I wait for about five minutes, sitting in the outer office, mulling over a magazine and the fate of Bird. The crusty old former Chicago newspaperman has been, as some say, "done in" by the staff. Kaye Pullen, one of the writers, has been particularly unappreciative of Bird. She claimed at various times that Bird was a loud mouth, ill-mannered and a braggart. Her most devastating thrust was that Bird's conduct in public reflects badly on the speechwriting staff. Finally, she refused to share an office with Bird, according to Theis, so I volunteered to do so. Theis turned that down because he wanted my office close enough so I could handle some editing.

I refused to take part in the criticism of Bird simply because I believed he deserved a fair trial as a writer, not a diplomat. He did rattle a few coffee cups around the place, literally. But Bird was for real. You knew where he stood and what he stood for.

Bird leaves and Theis calls me into his office. He hands me a speech I had prepared for Charlotte, North Carolina. The President is to give this address at the Charlotte-Mecklenburg Bicentennial Committee picnic in a week. Theis reads me comments which Bob Hartmann had written across the top of the first page:

"Junk it! Not Ford style. And don't quote Lincoln in North Carolina! Don't try to make every speech a Gettysburg Address. Just write a nice Bicentennial talk."

I ask Theis if he had time to discuss the speech and he says yes.

I remind him that I had asked for direction, any direction, when assigned the talk some two weeks previously. No direction was forthcoming. I also remind him that I had discussed the subject of "responsible leadership" with him at the time and he said I should proceed as I saw fit.

For the next ten minutes, I outline to Theis my understanding of general editorial comment about the President in newspapers across the country. The polls show only 39 per cent of the public favor the President and his policies. Presidential leadership, as well as leadership by Congress, unquestionably is a subject that we must address ourselves to at the appropriate time.

I tell Theis that I sincerely believe it is unrealistic to take the President all the way to North Carolina and spend the time "blowing smoke." Jimmy Breslin and other writers are describing the President's speeches as "Lions' Club rhetoric." The press and others will wonder why we are going to Charlotte for a few minutes of Bicentennial oratory. The President could wind up being criticized on the grounds the trip was not necessary. I mention that many scholars believe the basis of the event, the Mecklenburg Declaration of Independence, is a myth.

My basic contention is that we are not facing the issues before the country with substantive speeches and that we are very badly organized. Theis disagrees. The conversation closes on the understanding that I give Theis a new speech in "the simple Ford style" as soon as possible. It is a very polite conversation but I try to make one point clear: I am not raising a question of style, but of substance.

I return to my office and phone Agnes Waldron, our chief of research. I advise Agnes that my first version of the North Carolina speech has been killed and that she can stop checking it for accuracy. Agnes is in my office in a matter of minutes.

I relate the basics of the conversation with Theis and Agnes simmers. She is peeved about the Lincoln comment because she had suggested that quote. Primarily, however, Agnes laments the disorganization in the speechwriting department and the "wishy-washy speeches which the President is giving."

Agnes, a veteran, savvy political hand with a scholarly bent, suddenly pulls out seven legal-size, yellow pages which sum up her feelings on the President and his programs. It is a factual attack on the lack of leadership qualities and substance in the President's speeches. She refers only to speeches.

Her summary concludes that the President's actions are a maze of contradictions, from the economy through energy and into foreign policy. She says to me: "We walk up the mountain one day and down the next."

I advise her to sit on the memo, to let things cool. But Agnes is not to be denied on her Lincoln quote, which is from his Second Inaugural Address. She says:

"Don't they realize that Lincoln is also respected in the South? And that the quote "with malice toward none" has become part of the world's universal language? And besides, it could not be more appropriate for the context that it's in."

Agnes genuinely grieves that our North Carolina speech is not given, perhaps more than I, because she is a fighter.*

Friday, May 16, 1975

BANNER HEADLINES STREAM ACROSS the nation's newspapers. U.S. Marines dramatically recaptured the American merchant ship Mayaguez after it was seized by the Cambodian navy in

---

*For texts of the first draft and of the final speech, see Appendix, pages 329–337.

international waters. The entire forty-man American crew also was recovered. The last Marine was evacuated from Tang Island off Cambodia after a firefight with the Cambodian garrison. The White House staff is jubilant.

The Style section of the *Washington Post* notes that President Ford danced into the night after words of praise from the Shah of Iran. The Shah is on a state visit. Pearl Bailey drags the President out onto the dance floor at 1:15A.M. Pearl danced with Bob Hope as the President glided around the dance floor with Ann-Margaret, one of the evening's entertainers.

I am more intrigued with a story on the lower front page of the *Post*. It is about layoffs in the Detroit city government: 550 policemen, 300 firemen and about 800 other municipal employees. Coleman Young, the city's first black mayor, is quoted:

"Maybe if we renamed the city 'Saigon' and brought in a few Vietcong, we might get three or four billion dollars from Washington."

One of every four workers is unemployed in the Detroit area. I keep thinking that Detroit is, after all, part of the President's home state. Still, we have not gone there to see firsthand the difficulties of the men, women and children in trouble.

I am aware of the callousness of some who say that unemployment is the fastest and most effective way to kill inflation. One can rationalize economics, but one must also consider the human equation. Suffering can explode into violence—violence into death. Is there something different about dying in Cambodia and dying on the streets of Detroit? Where are the saviors of Detroit?

Monday, May 19, 1975

THEIS COMES TO MY OFFICE about 5:20 P.M. He inquires about my health since I was sick the previous workday with the flu. I tell him that I don't feel too well but the warmer weather should knock out the flu. He mentions that I might not be going to Charlotte, North Carolina, tomorrow "since Hartmann is thinking of going." In the past, a speechwriter, even if Hartmann did make the trip, always accompanied the President since the writer was familiar with details of the speech.

I advise Theis that I had already been told by Kathy Wooten, one of his secretaries, that I would definitely not be going to North Carolina, that "Mr. Hartmann had decided to go."

It seems clear to me that Theis and Hartmann are sending me a message: If you want to go on any trips, don't rock the boat. Don't question us about style or substance in the speeches, just do what we tell you.

I am not offended. The writer appears to be excess baggage on short trips anyway but probably should go on those longer than two days since writing assignments would probably arise. I could not help think back to last month's New England trip when Hartmann complained publicly that "Nessen has seventeen assistants on these trips and I have only one."

It is a beautiful evening in Washington—the nicest of a miserable, rainy spring. The temperature is about 80 degrees with a slight breeze. People are smiling on the streets as I walk to a bus. And I say to myself: "Hey, fella, your biggest job right now is to find your oldest son a job for the summer."

Friday, May 23, 1975

BOB HARTMANN BRIEFS the speechwriters today. He begins by saying that the speeches have been written "considerably better" in the past month or so. He wishes to continue a theme of "national unity" in the President's speeches. Hartmann says the President is a "unifier," although some perceive him as a "compromiser." He stresses that we must get out in front on the unity theme, to project the President as a "leader."

Hartmann explains that Mr. Ford's career has been one of "accommodating others' points of view. He has a talent for it."

He says the Congress does not appear ready to accommodate. That's their business. He implies that the President may renew his attack on the unwillingness or inability of the Congress to compromise.

Hartmann stresses the President wants national agreement on basic goals. He wants to put pressure on Congress to do this. As Hartmann puts it: "There will be a lot more vetoes in the coming months."

Theis asks if we should spell out the "agenda for the future" which the President has been mentioning in recent speeches. Hartmann replies:

"We can't create policy. It must be made before we express it."

Hartmann says that the President wants to ask everyone to help write a new agenda for the country. He adds that Congress has no agenda for the country. The President wants to project the image that he is open to ideas and innovations from everyone. He concludes:

"There will be no big bold programs expounded this year because we are not going to spend the money."

Hartmann says we should stress the unity theme again and again despite the fact that the President wants a "completely new speech" every time he talks.

He advises us not to forget energy. We should stress that energy makes the total economy go. Lack of it will cost jobs. The U.S. could be attacked if we lacked energy.

Hartmann is low-key. He speaks without apparent conviction or concern. He appears to be weary. But, above all, he appears to be telling some of us: Don't rock the boat! Be bland. Bland is good.

Chapter 9
June, 1975

"No government ought to be without censors; and where the press is free, no one ever will. If virtuous, it need not fear the fair operation of attack and defense. Nature has given to man no other means of sifting out the truth, either in religion, law or politics."

THOMAS JEFFERSON

Tuesday, June 17, 1975

POLITICAL FEVER IS BEGINNING to grip the place. Agnes Waldron shows me her research files on expected political issues in 1976. Jerry Popeo, our messenger, tells me he hopes to become an "advance man" for the President. Hartmann, Jim Connor and Theis stand in the hallway discussing space and how to juggle people and equipment so the writers will be ready for the campaign. But no subject matter is hotter than Vice President Rockefeller. His name and future are popping around the place like small firecrackers.

A few days ago President Ford endorsed Rocky as his running-mate next year. But the statement also left the door open for an exit. Mr. Ford said the final decision was in the hands of the delegates to the GOP convention. Reporters rushed to former California Governor Ronald Reagan with that. For the first time that I can recall, Reagan waffled. He has always clearly indicated he wanted the top spot or nothing. Now Reagan opens the door slightly by saying he hopes he is not asked to be the vice presidential nominee. Today such conjecture sweeps the White House.

Some insist Rocky will get the nod if he can defuse conservative opposition to him. The conservatives haven't trusted Rockefeller since he opposed Senator Barry Goldwater for the 1964 Republican presidential nomination. In addition to this longstanding antagonism, conservatives express worry on two current counts: the first, a controversial ruling by the Vice President while he presided over a stormy Senate debate. Conservatives screamed when Rocky appeared to side with the liberals in cutting off a Senate filibuster. Barry Goldwater was bitter, but Rocky later apologized.

Rockefeller is also under fire for his handling of the controversial report on the Central Intelligence Agency. Rocky announced all material would be made public. The President then reversed him by withholding part of the report concerning alleged CIA assassination plots against foreign leaders.

Mr. Ford decided to hand the assassination material over to the Senate intelligence committee now investigating the CIA and send a copy for possible prosecution to Attorney General Levi. The President believes a more thorough study and investigation should be made before the names of former American leaders are linked publicly to assassination attempts.

Clearly the latter is meant to embarrass Rockefeller because his committee investigation of the CIA was praised on all sides as a thorough and objective job. No one seriously believes it can reflect on his competence. Competence is Rocky's strong suit. Rumors persist that the precise intention was to reflect on Rockefeller's age. They suggested that the Vice President would be sixty-eight next year and the old vigor was slipping from his grasp. I found this reasoning very difficult to believe—and did not believe it—but it still made the rounds.

Barry Goldwater, reportedly warming to Rocky in recent months after their trip to Taiwan together, says: "I've always thought Nelson Rockefeller would make a good Secretary of State." Nevertheless, the statement has a double edge.

Mel Laird, former Defense secretary, one of the President's close political confidants, talks of an "open convention." This is interpreted as a canny move to concentrate conservative opposition on Rocky and not on Mr. Ford.

In the West Wing of the White House, some clearly imply Rocky should be dumped. They suggest he is a liability because the President needs more conservative support. Rocky symbolizes bringing Eastern Establishment liberal ideas into the Grand Old Party.

Others, however, claim the conservatives have no place to go. They must stay with the President. Hartmann has been saying this. Rocky is considered important in bringing middle-of-the-road and independent voters, who greatly outnumber the Republican conservatives, to support President Ford. Mr. Ford appeared to be supporting Rocky when he made a statement about the Republican party back in March. He said: "It is my feeling that the Republican party has to be a broad-based, wide-spectrum party if it is going to be a viable force in the political situation in the United States."

About the same time, at a meeting of conservatives in Washington, led by Senator James Buckley, there was serious talk of a new third party. This was to be a party of principle, they said, not an umbrella solely to win elections. Their purist oratory fired up conservatives across the country more than any event since the Nixon departure and the Ford ascendancy. But, as the days and weeks passed, the oratory died. However, the evangelism did not die.

"We've got to get the Independents," one of the top Republicans in town confides to me over lunch as if he is sharing a state secret. "That's why Rocky will be on the ticket."

He leans across the table, looks me straight in the eyes, and says: "You know, Rocky still has charisma!"

I wander back to the office in the muggy heat. The humidity is oppressive. And I keep thinking about that word "charisma"—a word apparently in search of a new Jack Kennedy, a new political personality to light up the television screens, a new image to enrapture the American romantic notion of leadership. And the spirit of an independent voter wells up from my soul:

"I think about half these professional polls are nuts. Lord, help and preserve us from these image-makers. These guys are crazy!"

Wednesday, June 18, 1975

POLITICAL LIGHTNING struck today. Ron Nessen, near the close of the morning news briefing, casually drops his flashing bolt of enlightenment. Howard "Bo" Callaway, a one-time Georgia congressman who headed Richard Nixon's 1968 campaign in the South, will become chairman of Mr. Ford's election committee. Callaway is resigning his current post as Secretary of the Army and will take up his new duties in a few weeks.

The announcement stuns some of the White House insiders. Everyone with whom I speak is surprised. Some typical comments:

"Didn't he lose to Lester Maddox in a governor's race there? What's his background? What's he long on? What's the advantage in Callaway? Do you know anything about him?"

The real news, to me, is that President Ford is being forced to show his hand this early. The complicated election laws and the implicit admission that he faces a tough race force President Ford to declare before he really wants to do so. The President will file papers setting up his campaign committee by Friday of this week—two days away. David Packard, a California industrialist, will become finance chairman of the committee. President Johnson had started much later in 1964 and in 1968. Richard Nixon let George Romney run out of steam before announcing his candidacy.

Nessen is hard pressed in the news briefing: What about Rocky? Will it be a Ford-Rockefeller campaign committee? "No," he says softly, "just Ford." The door is further opened for a switch to Ronald Reagan if necessary. The Rockefeller people are in hiding this afternoon, a friend says to me. This one hurts, he says.

I mark it down. The 1976 campaign begins today. Mr. Ford's hat is really in the ring. The delicate, ticklish questions have already begun inside the White House. Some of the staff talk of moving over to the campaign committee to get more "action" since Mr. Ford has stressed the campaign will really be run by the Republican National Committee, not from a back room in the White House.

The President does not appear in person to give the word on Callaway. Some suspect he did not want a hassle on the Rocky angle since anything he might say could offend Rockefeller. Mr. Ford is not a man to hurt anyone's sensitivities. He also doesn't want to answer questions about a "southern strategy" since Callaway's appointment clearly opens up that subject.

Alabama's George Wallace is speaking in town today. Governor Wallace has already raised more than $2 million for his campaign. And right now, he could whip Ford in every southern state.

"Bo" Callaway knows that better than most. If he does not concoct a real "southern strategy" for Mr. Ford in 1976, the President may find himself whistling "Dixie" all by his lonesome.

In my mind, George Wallace, a man in a wheelchair, has cast a long shadow across both the Republican and Democratic parties. Wallace has, in my view, correctly gauged where the election will be won or lost. It will be "in the great, gutsy middle class."

Wallace is again taking on "big government and the pointy-headed bureaucrats who can't park a bicycle straight" but he had an interesting new line today:

"The City of New York has taken the advice of the *New York Times* all these years, and has finally gone completely broke. The least thing you can say about Alabama is that we're not about to close down."

He received his loudest applause when he assailed Indian Prime Minister Indira Gandhi for hailing the victory of North Vietnam. Wallace said he would tell her:

"If I were the President, in view of the policy of your government, the next year you came to me to ask for more wheat, I'd tell you to go get it from North Vietnam and not the United States."

From now to November of 1976, the U.S. political scene promises to speak with more of a southern accent.

Friday, June 20, 1975

FROM TIME TO TIME, Theis would ask me to sit in on the 8:00 A.M. senior staff meeting in the White House Roosevelt Room. These morning conferences, chaired by either Don Rumsfeld or his assistant, Dick Cheney, usually consider developments of the previous day and look ahead to expected actions that day and the immediate future. Those usually attending were: Lynn, Greenspan, Cannon, Calkins for Hartmann (who sees the President early), Jones, Zarb, Simon, Seidman, Nessen, Friedersdorf, Baroody, Marsh, Theis, White, Buchen, Scowcroft, Greener and a changeable number of others.

Rumsfeld opened today's session by simply calling a name and asking if that individual had anything to report or comment on any future activity. Today Cannon says the Domestic Council is preparing an option paper for the President on auto emissions.

Lynn injects that the scientists disagree and urges a go-slow attitude before decision. Many nod agreement. Rumsfeld notes it on a pad.

Cannon notes his group is preparing more information on uranium enrichment for a presidential address to Congress. Rumsfeld says the address has been shelved.

Greenspan passes. Simon says he was on television this morning and chuckles that he said the Democrats' energy bill passed yesterday by the House should be called the Arabs' Redevelopment and Enrichment Act. Laughter.

Calkins notes that Congress will take another vacation in a week. Rumsfeld reacts to this quickly when Nessen says: "Can't we do something about that?" Rumsfeld asks Jones to look into what speaking prospects the President might have about that date.

An idea strikes Rumsfeld. He notes that the President's crime message "played well" on TV and in the press. He says Attorney General Levi did a good job. Someone whispers that Levi was "frightened as hell before facing the TV cameras."

Rumsfeld says that each presidential veto should have some backup by cabinet members "to give them more exposure." He suggests that HUD Secretary Carla Hills be prepared to appear when the President vetoes the housing bill. Nods of agreement.

Seidman, Friedersdorf and Baroody pass. Zarb, who has just come from a meeting with the President, says the Democrats' energy bill is "lousy" and "we've got to take the wraps off." He kids Simon about his TV appearance. The two banter and laugh.

White passes but Scowcroft reports that Mexico has discovered triple what it thought it had in oil reserves—about twenty billion barrels. He says "this is good for us."

Nessen asks Scowcroft what he should say in the press briefing about the meeting today between the President and the Syrian foreign minister. Scowcroft smiles and says "the same as last time, as little as possible."

Greener passes but Buchen notes the President has approved the concept of a federal appeals court, just below the U.S. Supreme Court. Rumsfeld jumps on this fast, saying: "I never liked attorneys and judges anyway." He is smiling. But he quickly notes that he has never seen any staff work on the project. Buchen says the matter has been approved. Rumsfeld insists he hasn't seen the staff work and goes around the table asking who has seen staff work. No one has. Rumsfeld asks to see the staff work.

Rumsfeld jokes. The former Navy pilot says: "They always tell you to give your exact position, and to say lost when you're lost."

Rumsfeld mentions the Chicago murder of gangster and Mafia chief Sam Giancanna. Simon breaks the place up with the crack: "Are we sending a rep to the funeral?" Obviously, the CIA assassination material is still on everyone's mind.

Rumsfeld leads a discussion about some of Nessen's recent troubles, particularly some heavy fire from the press on the fact that certain congressmen have asked for and received private, unannounced meetings with the President. Rumsfeld fights the idea of private meetings. He tells Marsh and Friedersdorf that such private meetings should not be agreed to. All meetings must be announced. Marsh answers that it doesn't help discussion at such meetings if the President reads on the front page of the *Washington Post* that he will meet that morning on a delicate subject with a group of congressmen and they are named. Rumsfeld insists that the meetings must be announced—perhaps after the meeting but formally noted. And he says the ground rules on what is said publicly of the meeting can be worked out when it takes place. Nessen nods agreement.

I and the others pass and the meeting is ended. Rumsfeld walks toward the President's office and Simon is telling a joke to Zarb.

Friday, June 27, 1975

AFTER EIGHT MONTHS on the job, it seems like a good time to examine the "selling of the President" aspects of the Ford administration. On the basis of my experience after two decades as a news reporter, including a stint of several years covering the White House, and nearly five years as a government public information director, it seems to me that Mr. Ford has the most extensive public affairs operation of any President in history. The big difference is the Office of Public Liaison, formed under Nixon but greatly expanded and used much more under Mr. Ford. Bill Baroody, Jr., sometimes called the White House Arab because he has a Lebanese background, heads the public liaison office and he runs a very sophisticated operation.

Baroody, whose father is a well-known, longtime conservative and great supporter of Barry Goldwater, is Mr. Ford's personal ambassador to the whole gamut of American private and public interest groups. The name of his game is "access," access of the President to certain groups and access of other groups and interests to the President. Baroody is the doorman, opening the door to business and labor groups, academics and professionals, farmers and veterans, youths and others. Bill arranges all types of meetings and conferences in and out of Washington for the "soft sell" of the President.

Baroody is magnificent in the job, soft-spoken yet direct and knowledgeable. He brings with his apparent easy-going manner a shrewdness and dedication to Republican principles that is matched by few in the White House. And Baroody is setting up a masterful network of future contacts and alliances that will make him one of the most important and powerful Republicans in the nation. Baroody may one day make the big leap forward from doorman to king-maker.

Before the Nixon administration, presidential speechwriters worked out of the counsel or legal offices. Now they are formally organized under Bob Hartmann, who is counselor to the President.

The staff of forty, five of whom are speechwriters, comes under the title of Editorial Office. We have a half-dozen researchers headed by the "old pro" Agnes Waldron, a veteran of the Nixon administration and the Republican National Committee. Agnes has worked all over town and knows more about research than many at the Library of Congress. Milt Friedman is our graybeard, in his fifties, who was the Washington correspondent for the Jewish Telegraph Agency for many years. Bob Orben was a Hollywood and New York gag writer for two decades. Kaye Pullen, the first woman speechwriter in White House history, came from the Republican National Committee and is a onetime Tennessee editorial writer and TV personality. Aram Bakshian, Jr., who plays classical music in his office on a tape recorder most of each day, is a veteran of the Nixon staff—the only speechwriter to survive. Pat Butler, in his late twenties, is on loan from a government agency at the moment. Pat, a former newspaper reporter, is a southerner. Fred Bird, the ex-newsman from Illinois, has left us to return to the Midwest.

We are described as wordsmiths who give Mr. Ford's speeches "a simple and commonplace style." After each speech is cleared by as many as a dozen or more White House aides, it is not difficult to emerge with a simple and commonplace style. Many aides actually axe up speeches to the detriment of Mr. Ford with overkill concerning their areas of responsibility. They think in legal and similar terms while the writers try to think in understandable and listenable terms. The wordchoppers win much of the time, although the wordsmiths sometimes secretly slip back a favorite word or phrase.

The Office of Communications, a Nixon innovation to get his message across to newspapers, radio and television stations, as well as other opinion-makers around the country, is now being turned over by departing Jerry Warren to Margita White. Warren, who worked under Ron Ziegler in the Nixon press office, returns to his old newspaper, the *San Diego Union,* as editor. Mrs. White, a gently groomed Swedish-born lady who once worked under Herb Klein at the White House, is starting to contact editors and broadcasters across the country.

The office of personal photographer to the President is not a one-man camera shop. Dave Kennerly, who holds the title, is assisted by five other photographers who take pictures of the Rockefellers as well as the Ford family. All of these are still pictures. In addition, the Army Signal Corps shoots movie film of presidential activities. Dave, who was a UPI photographer in Vietnam at the same time of my reporting there in 1966, has won the following accolade hands down: He has the foulest mouth in the White House and perhaps in Washington and maybe all the way to Moscow.

The press office, headed by Ron Nessen with a staff of about forty-five, is the lion's den. The briefing room is my favorite enclave in the White House. There are probably a fair number who would not trade it for the Oval Office of the President. As one whose heart still beats with the reporters for the most part, I nevertheless feel a need for greater civility among today's White House press corps. I am constantly told that things have changed from 1964 and 1965 when I covered the place for ABC News. Watergate changed it. Advocacy journalism changed it. Heated, hostile exchanges between Nessen and the newsmen raise the room temperature every day. It is rarely a dialogue, mostly a debate and sometimes a debacle.

Nessen has contended privately to me on several occasions that the press room is still permeated by Watergate. "It's a snake pit," he said. "It is going to take me six months to get the smell of Watergate out of the press room." It is now nearly ten months since Nessen took over the job and the hostility between newsmen and the press office is as great as ever.

Reporters react with a litany of complaints about Nessen. He has a "volatile temper" which sometimes becomes "personally vicious." He is "arrogant and vain." (These were two of the top complaints about Ziegler.) Many reporters say Nessen has lost much of his credibility. Several complain "he has completely switched and become a salesman for Ford."

On the other hand, Nessen receives high marks as well. The new procedure in news conferences allows a followup question to Mr. Ford when a correspondent feels the President has not sufficiently replied to the original query. More frequent private interviews and other exchanges between the President and the press are encouraged.

Nessen privately admits he has to work to control his temper but insists he's doing a better job of it. On the charges of arrogance and vanity, he believes it takes two to tango and hostility from the press requires him to try to hold his own. On credibility and salesmanship, Nessen says it's his job to reflect the President's thinking and it's difficult to draw a precise line between that and salesmanship.

Nessen may take a few extra lumps from reporters because he's working for one of the most congenial Presidents in White House history. Virtually all reporters like Mr. Ford personally and are slow to criticize him. Nessen is an easier mark.

I agree with Nessen that White House-press office relations are more open and candid today than any time in the past six years and perhaps the past ten. The trio of Bill Moyers, George Reedy and George Christian was no holy trinity of press secretaries under Lyndon

Johnson. Moyers was correct but canny and many times devious.
Reedy's only independent action under Johnson appeared to be
breathing. I believe that Christian was a more honest man with himself
than either Moyers or Reedy. He had an intuitive ability to be as
forthcoming as Lyndon's limitations would permit. Moyers appeared
to split theological hairs constantly, to equivocate and sometimes
deceive without religious scruple. Christian behaved instinctively;
Moyers had to think about it. Nessen also thinks about it.

The new factor that clouds the relationship between the press
secretary and the White House correspondents is "advocacy"
journalism. Many reporters are coming up the ladder with their minds
already made up that the press secretary and the President must of
necessity put the best possible face on everything. It is their job to take
the smirk off the press secretary's face and the smile off the
President's—whatever their names and party.

Some reporters still maintain detached "arm's length" reporting.
But their numbers diminish with each passing year. News is moving
toward opinion portrayed as reality, conjecture listed as facts and
personal anger displayed as public righteousness.

I would quarrel with Nessen on one count. He simply isn't
qualified to answer, nor would any press secretary be, some of the
questions he attempts to handle. In some areas of the economy and
energy, Nessen was far over his head in attempting to tell reporters
what administration policy was and is. He should have deferred to the
experts. To his credit, however, Nessen does his homework, much
more than some of the White House correspondents.

President Ford has returned the regular news conference to the
White House after Richard Nixon put it in the doghouse. Some claim
the entire Watergate mess would have been cleaned up earlier had
Nixon faced the press on a regular basis. Perhaps that is precisely the
reason why Nixon pigeonholed the news conference.

Nixon conducted thirty-seven news conferences in his entire five
and one-half years as President. Ford held ten press conferences in his
first seven months. Yet President Ford is now under fire. Reporters say
he doesn't give them enough news at these conferences. They complain
that they can't learn his next moves, that Mr. Ford's words and phrases
are cautious, and that he has pre-set answers on given subjects.

Reporters are correct on all three counts. When Mr. Ford wants to
make specific news, he asks us to write a statement for him. Only
rarely does he plan a deliberate bombshell. Gerald R. Ford is a very

cautious man. I have heard him say more than once: "Better safe than
sorry."

There is one thing that Mr. Ford does which few Presidents in our
history have done: put his arm on a reporter's shoulder. However, Mr.
Ford's policy of openness is not without its problems. The biggest such
problem is news leaks. I can assure those who will one day read books
about Ford administration "secrets" and assorted never-been-told
yarns that most had already been leaked.

Mel Laird, his old friend, gently lectured Mr. Ford about his
openness, saying in effect: People will say you're not in control of the
White House if the leaks continue. The President attempted to control the
leaks for a while, but the dike is leaking again, and as one reporter said to
me:

"I'm never going to complain about newsless press conferences if I
continue to get my share of the leaks."

Friday, June 27, 1975

I AM HAVING LUNCH with Ed Hymoff at the National Press Club. Ed
and I are friends these twenty-three years, a friendship forged while
covering the Korean War together for the old International News Service.

Helen Thomas, the veteran UPI White House correspondent, enters
the dining room with two women. I wave to her and she comes to our
table. And thereupon lies a story of honor.

I have known Helen more than ten years, from the days when I
covered the White House for ABC in the mid-60's. She is a reporter with
the old-time religion: don't take any crap. Helen is furious:

"That son-of-a-bitch, Nessen, said three times yesterday at the
news briefing that I didn't know what I was talking about. Three times,
he said, my question to the President at the news conference had a false
premise. But the United States has consistently disavowed the first use of
nuclear weapons. And everyone knows I asked that question. What was
he trying to prove?"

Nessen interrupted his regular briefing yesterday to charge that
"blind and irrational mistrust" and the "cynical thinking habits" of
reporters were undermining his news briefings. The flareup came after
weeks of sharp and sometimes bitter exchanges between Nessen and
newsmen. Nessen had been publicly called a "liar" and was accused of
covering up news—particularly the fact that John Connally had seen the
President and Nessen said he did not know of the meeting when, indeed,
he did. Nessen then claimed he had forgotten it.

Chapter 10
July, 1975

"The more I have studied American history and the more clearly I
have seen what the problems are, I do believe that the common
denominator of our great men in public life has not been mere
allegiance to one political party, but the disinterested devotion with
which they have tried to serve the whole country, and the relative
unimportance that they have ascribed to politics, compared with the
paramount importance of government."

FRANKLIN DELANO ROOSEVELT

Tuesday, July 1, 1975

MY EIGHT MONTHS' "DETAIL" to the White House from the Census Bureau is ending. That is the gist of government forms which I receive for signature. I am to move from my career civil service status to that of presidential appointment. One serves at the "pleasure of the President" and he serves at the pleasure of the American electorate.

I inform Theis that I have been officially notified that I become a White House staff member on July 6, 1975. He smiles and shakes hands.

Then I advise Theis that I am leaving sometime in 1976. I feel that the upcoming campaign will require speechwriters with a political bent.

We talk about the campaign. Theis says he thinks Mr. Ford will win. I agree, barring a Mideast war. Some might try to blame him for that. And there are always a lot of "ifs" in a war.

I leave because both of us have work to do. Back in my office, I recall a conversation of the evening before with an old friend, Kemp Devereaux. It had been a hot summer evening and we turned to philosophizing about the state of the world. I told Kemp:

"Today, looking back, I do not regard either the Vatican or the White House as places of greatness. Symbols, yes, but not places. Goodness, honor, decency—I have found these at odd times in sometimes strange places."

I saw more of Christ in the frail bodies of Buddhist monks in Vietnam than among many of the cardinals of the Vatican's Roman Curia. I felt more strength in the handshakes of poor peasants in southern Italy than among many diplomats of the world. I witnessed more truth in the faces of bleeding black children, caught in the civil rights struggle of the 1960's, than among the loudest voices arguing that tormented problem. I saw more serenity and peace in the eyes of soldiers dying in Korea and Vietnam than many of those who sent them there and those who cursed the whole, awful mess.

I was finally learning the wisdom of the centuries—that God and peace can be found only in one's own heart and love and honor can be found more easily among the poor and humble because life has offered them so much less in worldly goods and glories.

Wednesday, July 2, 1975

Bill Nicholson of the President's scheduling office and I eat lunch in the cafeteria. Nicholson says:

"They're getting on the bandwagon—two and three people a day. Big names. Coming out of the woodwork now that the polls show the President is looking good."

He speaks of Mr. Ford's dramatic gains in all polls following his handling of the Mayaguez incident and the upturn in the economy. He continues:

"We hear it from Republican congressmen and senators who had been sitting on the fence. They talk about the President speaking in their district. You see it in people reappearing after a year. We've never been so busy."

Only a day earlier Bob Hartmann had said to me in his office:

"They're coming back, the Nixonites. Slowly but surely they're coming back. They're working their way back into jobs around town, even here in the White House.

"I guess I didn't do a good enough job in getting rid of them!"

The word coming into the White House from around the country, however, indicates that many Nixonites have not returned to the so-called mainstream of politics. They are an embittered, although relatively small number.

They imply they will not support Mr. Ford, saying he is "too liberal." And they return to the harsh irony that Nixon was "hounded from office." They are bitter at Nixon, bitter at the press, bitter at the whole sorry spectacle. And they are spoiling for revenge, some of them, perhaps sufficiently so to "spoil" Gerald R. Ford in 1976.

The tourists flood Washington this hot, sunny day. Many gape through the fences surrounding the White House. Sailors from Spain take pictures of one another outside the fence, facing the main entrance of the residence. A father tries to lift his son above the fence so the boy can get a better look at the White House.

Wednesday, July 2, 1975

AGNES WALDRON SLIPS QUIETLY into my office in midmorning with some inside gossip. She has gotten wind of some of the talk at the Camp David meeting of Ron Nessen's staff. This is the meeting to improve the staff after Nessen's blowup at the press. Agnes is, in her calm way, upset.

Nessen and his staff, she confides, "excoriated" the way the speechwriting office is being run. Our texts get to them late. They want more flair in the writing. There's lack of coordination between their office and ours.

I say that I thought the meeting was to determine what was wrong with the press office. Agnes replies that other offices came in for much of the criticism.

I review with her my differences of opinion with Theis and Bob Hartmann about writing. Nessen has a legitimate complaint; the President's speeches do need more flair. But Hartmann and Theis have consistently edited eloquence from speeches. I remind her of Hartmann's written words to me: "Stop trying to make every speech a Gettysburg Address."

We continue talking. I ask why Nessen does not see Hartmann directly about the writing or "flair." That's Hartmann's territory.

Agnes points out that Nessen's remarks are all over the White House complex. And I say:

"The President trusts Hartmann and he likes Theis a great deal. Nessen may come in third in a three-horse race."

Ron Nessen has become a source of division inside the White House. Staff members are split on his continual bickering and several blowups with the newsmen. Those who are wary of the press side with Nessen, but many agree with the newsmen.

Nessen has overplayed the "adversary" relationship angle. He unnecessarily antagonizes newsmen with games of one-upmanship and arrogance. He takes tough questions personally, interpreting many of them as snide attacks on himself. The questions are tough because that is the name of the game at the White House. Anyone who doesn't recognize that is missing the heartbeat of reporters in Washington.

Any correspondent in town will admit the press got burned by Watergate. It was not just Nixon and his crowd. Every reporter held court with his or her conscience.

How and why did Ziegler think he could get away with lying to them? Couldn't they have exposed more of the Watergate mess earlier? How come the *Washington Post* consistently had the jump on them? But the angle that really burned them was the charade of lying. They will never permit that again.

Agnes has returned to work. Other intrigues around the White House come to mind. A few days ago, our United Nations ambassador, John Scali, came to my office. Scali and I had been friends through our years together with ABC News, perhaps closer friends because of our mutual love for Italy and most things Italian.

Scali was hurt and bitter. It takes a lot to hurt John Scali, but his deep pride and his Italian affinity for the concept of honor had been severely wounded.

"Moynihan (Pat Moynihan, who replaced Scali as our U.N. ambassador), that son-of-a-bitch, borrowed my apartment for three weeks. I befriended him. He drank my booze. He slept in my bed. He accepted my friendship. And then he screwed me."

Scali sat back on a couch and put his legs up on a small table. He continued:

"He comes into my turf—my turf, mind you. And he launches a speech telling us what U.S. policy should be in the U.N. He said nothing new. I said the same thing a helluva lot earlier about the tyranny of the majority at the U.N. He even stole my ideas. A real bastard."

John could not understand why he had been relieved as U.N. ambassador by the President. I asked John whether, indeed, it was the President who had removed him, or was it really Kissinger? Scali half smiled. He realized I was aware that he and the Secretary of State were in a mini-war. Scali asked:

"How did it happen? Why? Everybody said I was doing a good job, even Kissinger. What did I do wrong?"

I replied:

"John, I don't have the answers. But you might ask: What did Moynihan do right? People around here say he gave the President a personal pitch in a long meeting."

Scali's bitterness flowed in a long monologue about Moynihan's drinking in India. This was a John Scali I had never seen before. His charges stunned me and I tried to calm him by saying:

"Why don't you see Bob Hartmann? He likes you. Perhaps Bob may have a few words with the President and you'll get a good post."

Scali shot back:

"I've been offered a top post—Canada. I don't need Canada. I need money. Maybe I'll go back to ABC."

My recollection of Scali's plight is suddenly interrupted. One of Theis's secretaries, Judy Morton, rushes in and says it's time to leave for a meeting with the President. She hands me an "option paper," dated today, the first one directed to the President in my name.

The paper lists three options for Mr. Ford's coming address in Chicago before the Mid-America International Business organization: 1, a speech on energy; 2, the President's plan to continue economic recovery and provide for long-term growth; 3, stress on how decisions today will affect the economy in the next six to eighteen months. Seidman, Greenspan and I recommend the second option, with mention of the third alternative.

The three options cover more than three single-spaced typewritten pages. President Ford reads it and chooses option two within two minutes. This is not an indecisive man.

Milt Friedman discusses options on an address the President will give to a black college group in Chicago. Milt points out that the parents and students are poor people and the graduation ceremony marks a real achievement. The President picks up the hint quickly:

"Let's highlight the value and dignity of work. Let's say what can happen in America if people are given the opportunity."

The President stands and says:

"Fellows, I'm late. I've got to go and get a haircut. See you."

Somehow, the presidency is more human for me today, a higher office than yesterday, because Gerald R. Ford imparts in his soft manner a grace and class to common occurrences.

Wednesday, July 2, 1975

SOME OF ROCKY'S CROWD are unhappy. Several have leaked the story to reporters that Don Rumsfeld is undercutting Rockefeller. Rumsfeld says in his own defense that there is a "mischief-maker, either in the press or on the White House staff."

The story revolves around the Vice President's handling of the release of the CIA Commission report. Simply put, the President had some reservations about release of certain information. The two staffs did not coordinate well.

The story given Rocky was that Rumsfeld leaked a comment through Ron Nessen that Rockefeller blew handling the CIA report's release. Rockefeller was quoted: "Why would he cut me up like that? I'm a team player."

Rocky later reads a newspaper leak from a "long-time aide to Ford" who is quoted:

"Rumsfeld is trying to ease Rockefeller off the 1976 ticket so it can become a Ford-Rumsfeld ticket."

Rumsfeld says: "It's absolutely, outrageously false."

Another leak regarding the Rockefeller staff is also attributed to Rumsfeld. President Ford decided that James Cannon, a longtime Rocky aide, should be executive director of the Domestic Council. Rumsfeld had favored a friend, Harvard professor Philip Areeta. As Mr. Ford was deciding the matter, a story was leaked to a Washington columnist criticizing Cannon and praising Areeta. Rocky's men blamed Rumsfeld for the story.

Historically, the vice presidential staff has distrusted the top aides of any President. Rumsfeld and his assistant, Dick Cheney, are not exceptions. Rockefeller is said not to be angry. The "old pro" knows that it's a year to convention time.

Saturday, July 5, 1975

IT IS A HOT AND MUGGY MORNING in Washington. I draw the holiday duty. The atmosphere in the White House these days is bullish. The President's dramatic turnaround in the polls, a 23 per cent lead over Ronald Reagan in the latest Harris survey, is stunning in its magnitude.

The Ripon Society's latest poll shows Mr. Ford beating Reagan almost 2 to 1 if the Republican National Convention were held today. But the same survey indicates Rockefeller is vulnerable to a conservative challenge.

The White House is besieged with requests for presidential meetings and appearances, from a small-town stumper to a big-town bash.

The Congress fails to override four straight presidential vetoes. House Speaker Albert confesses that the Congress isn't cutting it. Albert is under fire from his own rank and file for lack of tough leadership. The Democrats are in disarray and the President is preparing to announce his candidacy for 1976.

There are now seventeen presidential contenders—President Ford, Reagan, Percy, Bentsen, Jackson, Udall, Shapp, Wallace, Humphrey, Shriver, McCarthy, McGovern, Harris, Carter, Sanford,

Anderson and Muskie—with a possible draft choice in Teddy Kennedy.

This time federal campaign aid is available. The airplanes, the limousines, the airport crowds, the exhausting evenings—the impulse of combat is bringing back life to old bones and the hurried heartbeat of hope to younger starters.

President Ford believes that Alabama Governor Wallace's greatest asset is his continual and consistent campaign against government, all government. Mr. Ford plans to run hard on that as a major theme. He believes that Middle America wants to hear fiscal responsibility and freedom of the individual as they have never heard it before. And he is about to give it to them.

The latest example of disorganization in the speechwriting department is the President's address this week here in Washington to the convention of the National Association for the Advancement of Colored People.

My office is next to Kaye Pullen's, who has been writing the speech. She has been swearing a blue streak all week. Several times, she has come into my office, slumped in a chair and said:

"They don't know what the hell they're doing. I am rewriting this thing because no one can make up his mind what we're supposed to say.

"The President says not to be defensive about the economy and minorities. But what have we done for blacks? Goddamn little.

"I was called in at 5 P.M. the other evening. Theis said to start all over. But where? With what? They know what they don't want but they never know what they want.

"I wonder if the goddamn campaign will be like this—or worse."

"Probably so, Kaye," I say, "remember last Thursday."

An hour and a half before meeting with the President on Thursday, July 3, Theis had rushed into my office and said that Jack Marsh's draft for the President's July Fourth speech didn't measure up. Would I edit it, "clean it up," and put a new ending on the address?

I read the speech quickly. It needed real work. Theis rang me. There was urgency in his voice. Could I finish in time? Would we make it? I assured him that we would, but I needed to cut the speech and rewrite parts of it. He gave his blessing.

It was a fast cut, paste and rewrite job. We completed the draft in time for the meeting with Mr. Ford. I had noted that Marsh's draft had been sitting around for at least a day and perhaps longer.

I tell Kaye that Theis needs to hire an editor to handle the routine and that he should concentrate on the important. Theis is allowing himself to be swamped in trivia.

One of the writers is pulling out. Aram Bakshian accepts a fellowship to the John Fitzgerald Kennedy School of Government at Harvard. Aram has put it to me this way several times:

"I'm the only holdover from the Nixon days so I can't rock the boat. But we can't continue on our own like this. That's for sure."

Wednesday, July 9, 1975

PRESIDENT FORD ANNOUNCED FORMALLY yesterday that he would seek election to the presidency in 1976. Once in a while, someone makes the mistake of saying "reelection." Few correct the error but everyone recognizes it immediately. They are all too aware of how Mr. Ford came into office.

The President spoke from the same desk in the Oval Office where Nixon announced his resignation eleven months ago. Mr. Ford entered the White House beneath clouds of gloom and stormy economic weather ahead. And the consensus was:

"Good Ol' Jerry Ford—a nice guy. But he's way over his head in the White House. And as President, forget it. Let's just hope he can hold things together until the 1976 elections. Then, the Republicans and Democrats will get themselves candidates."

The *New York Times*, on the President's announcement of candidacy, established him as the "clear favorite" to win the 1976 election. What was Mr. Ford's secret? The *Times* had the answers: his "easy, open, Midwestern style," in contrast to Nixon; the Mayaguez incident reassuring the nation, weary of foreign setbacks; and an apparent lack of the political manipulation found in recent Presidents.

President Ford's declaration was simple: "Duty, decency and constructive debate." That would be his campaign theme.

There are now four key men in the President's campaign, and they stood behind him in the Oval Office as he made his declaration

of candidacy. They are Campaign Manager Howard H. (Bo)
Callaway; David Packard, former deputy Secretary of Defense;
Robert Moot, former assistant secretary and comptroller at Defense,
as treasurer; and Dean Burch, former campaign manager, who will
stay on as head of a campaign advisory committee.

In the afternoon, we are called to the Oval Office to meet with
the President on the first speech he will give as a declared
candidate.

Meeting with the President are: Greenspan, Seidman, Theis,
Friedman and myself. It is an address before the Mid-America
Committee for International Business and Government Cooperation.
The President asks: "Who are they?"

I tell him that the group consists of wealthy businessmen
interested in international affairs.

Seidman interjects on another subject. He wants to eliminate
three pages of the speech. These pages outline Mr. Ford's economic
policies since he assumed the presidency.

Just hours earlier, Seidman requested that I insert just such
material into the address saying it was "absolutely necessary" as a
foundation. Shortly before conferring with the President, all of us
met outside the Oval Office. Greenspan attacked the idea of
reviewing the past.

"How many times do we have to beat our breast? Why do we
keep hanging out old laundry? This is crazy! I think we are making
a big mistake. Why don't we simply give a speech on where we are
today and where we are going tomorrow, period!"

Seidman spends several minutes defending the passage but
carefully not admitting that it was entirely his idea. But Greenspan
is adamant. He says:

"I can't agree. The rest of the speech is great. I like it fine.
But I am getting tired of resurrecting the past. It sounds as if we are
always apologizing."

In the midst of the meeting with the President, Seidman heads
off Greenspan by criticizing the section himself as "useless and
unnecessary." I say nothing but Greenspan's eyes widen at
Seidman's turnabout. Quietly, Greenspan concurs.

Terry O'Donnell, an office aide to the President, interrupts
saying that Mr. Ford's call to "Tip" O'Neill, the Democratic
majority leader, is ready. The President picks up the phone and
bellows into the receiver:

"Mister Leader! (It is a loud call like hailing a taxi!) How's your golf game? Great! You bet I'm ready for you.

"Listen, now you're going to follow through for me on Turkey (Congress is debating the resumption of some U.S. military aid to Turkey). I need your help. It's important. It's all set. Jimmy Jones is going to carry the ball. Just follow Jimmy!

"Great!

"Listen, Tip, I need your help, too, on this staffing business here (to increase the White House potential to hire personnel). We've got to take care of that.

"Great! Take care. See you. 'Bye."

The President is smiling.

Alan Greenspan questions a line about "social freedom." He wants to know what "social freedom" means. I kid him saying not all freedoms are economic. I point out freedoms involving health and education. He quickly realizes I am talking about "socialized medicine" and "busing." The President says:

"It can also mean freedom to associate with those whom you care to. I don't have any trouble with that line."

At the closing of the speech is this line:

"The greatest manifestation of power is its use with reason and restraint."

Reason and restraint are twin themes of the speech. Greenspan says he doesn't understand that. Again, I kid him:

"That's your old buddy, Aristotle, Alan. Straight from the man."

Around and around we go on Aristotle, since Greenspan can't recall the use. In the past, we have discussed Aristotle at length with great affection for that ancient scholar. But the President has the best line of all: "I'm not so sure I'm in good company."

All chuckle.

Greenspan, Seidman and I meet together to clear up a few final details on the speech. Both are rushing to other conferences but we manage a few minutes. Greenspan confides:"I think I go to about seventeen meetings a day."

Seidman never mentions to us his sudden reversal of opinion at the meeting with the President.

This first postannouncement speech from the President emphasizes jobs. I have tried to write in several sentences of compassion such as this one:

"Jobs mean individual dignity and I mean to restore that
dignity to all American workers."

I hope these words from the President will make a difference.

Thursday, July 10, 1975

FOR SIX MONTHS OR MORE, I have been trying to get Theis to
read several news articles written by Luiz R.J. Simmons on
employment policies. Mr. Simmons was a Republican candidate
for the Maryland State House of Delegates from Montgomery
County in 1974. I find on return to my office that Theis is
distributing a new article by Simmons entitled: "Why Ford Will
Lose in 1976."

"Thank goodness," I say to myself. "Maybe these guys are
finally discovering that we need a little compassion in what the
President is saying about unemployment. Maybe there's a change
of heart in Theis and Hartmann."

Simmons writes:

"At most doors where I was received, there was a presumption
working against Republican candidates—that they do not care about
the government worker, the mother with a retarded child, the
blue-collar worker, the working mother with children."

Mr. Simmons adds that people perceive Democrats as "people
who care—who care deeply." He adds that there is an absence of
"rudimentary political compassion" in President Ford's public
utterances. And he explains:

"Its roots lie in the sociology of Republicanism. Most of the
Republican leadership has never been unemployed . . . The
President's advisers are pursuing the Joe President strategy. Its
major premise is that a Nation repulsed by the moral menagerie that
was the Nixon White House will rush breathlessly to embrace a
good, decent, hard-working Middle American . . . "It isn't
working—nor will trendy efforts to cast Mr. Ford in the mold of
Harry Truman. . . . Truman was more than style. He was
substance, and it is the substance of the economic problem with
which Mr. Ford has yet to deal."

The article blasts the President and the Republican leadership
for not having been represented at a recent "job-in" at a
Washington stadium. It attacks Mr. Ford's veto of the jobs bill. He

insists that the issue of jobs must be addressed first. It is a question of priorities.

There is no comment from Theis, only FYI (For Your Information), as if that solves anything.

What the hell is he afraid of? Why not say: Let's address ourselves to the attached. But Theis is running awfully scared these days with Nessen attacking him behind his back and the Hartmann-Rumsfeld war continuing with Hartmann losing skirmish after skirmish from all accounts.

Why doesn't the President ask these questions, I ask myself. Why?

It is time to turn out the lights and go home.

Monday, July 14, 1975

A NEWS STORY OVER THE WEEKEND attests to the power of a presidential phone call—even to the opposition. Mr. Ford called House Democratic Leader Tip O'Neill several days ago in the midst of our discussion on speeches. O'Neill, rejecting a move by Democratic presidential candidate Morris K. Udall, of Arizona, delivered on his promise to President Ford. The overwhelmingly Democratic House granted, by about a seventy-five vote margin, President Ford the authority to double the size of his top-level policy staff. At the same time, there were reports that the House was thinking more positively of approving resumption of some U.S. military aid to Turkey. Mr. Ford had asked and received O'Neill's support for both.

But what do the Democrats get from this? I do not know. Presumably, Tip O'Neill has a telephone and he knows President Ford's number.

White House staffers are still figuratively picking up the pieces after two bombshell events of last week while I was deep in a speech. Only now are people getting a handle on them.

The first event was Bo Callaway's statements divorcing Nelson Rockefeller from the President. It was not so much that Callaway told newsmen the Vice President must win his way into the ticket with delegate support. It was the sharpness of Callaway's statements.

The President's campaign manager virtually called Rocky a liability to a Ford ticket. Callaway pointedly declared that Reagan

119

backers would not support Rocky and this would hurt Mr. Ford. Opening his campaign office, Callaway stressed: "I am asking no delegates to support Rockefeller."

No one inside the White House quarrels with Callaway's objective—the President's election. But most I knew were astonished at the length and sharpness of his comments on Rocky. Callaway was telling the GOP right: "Boys, don't worry. We may dump Rocky."

The President's campaign headquarters, located a few blocks from the White House on 18th Street, is a far cry from the Nixon days of the money mobs. A half-dozen volunteers, mostly women, and three paid staffers, including Callaway, work in the bare, seven-room office. It's expected the headquarters will eventually have about fifty-five staffers. That is one-fourth of what Nixon had in his last campaign.

The second bombshell came in the form of a news leak which suggested that Don Rumsfeld would be the liaison between President Ford and his campaign committee. Bob Hartmann, who heads the President's political affairs office, seemed the logical choice for the liaison post and was passed over.

Hartmann bruises the sensitivities of many persons with whom he comes in contact. Hartmann's attitude is: "I work for Jerry Ford, period." Brusque, caustic, critical, he uses to some degree the line about "working for Jerry Ford" as an excuse for some of his cynicism and bitterness. Although some are not enamored of Rumsfeld either, they enjoy the fact that Hartmann has been "cut down a peg."

Rumsfeld plays down the liaison role in chats with newsmen. "Just more coordinating," as he puts it. But inside the White House, it is different. The door of "access" for Hartmann has closed a few more inches and all know it.

I respect Hartmann because he has a savvy that is not evident in Rumsfeld—a savvy born of years of turmoil as a newspaperman and hard knocks that Rumsfeld has yet to experience. In a few words, Hartmann can smell a rat where Rumsfeld would be mousetrapped. Hartmann's face and, particularly, his hands show the years of tumult. Rumsfeld, to be sure his junior, shows none of that.

Over the weekend, the *New York Times* and *Washington Post* did interpretive stories on how the President would conduct his campaign. They used his trip to the Middle West, Illinois and Michigan, as an example. Both newspapers used the term "moderation."

Theis fought use of that word. He said it implied "softness." I defended it and, as a matter of fact, have consistently used such expressions since the Old North Church address in April. All my speeches stressed: "Reason and restraint . . . moderation . . . principles over passion . . . steadiness." They seemed to typify the conservative nature of the President.

Theis criticized many of these words, suggesting that we were "boxing in" the President. Any hint of stressing a theme in a speech caused Theis to pull out his pen and pencil. He appeared genuinely fearful of being pinned down on any issue—even of writing style. The *Washington Post* said:

"Indeed, the President appeared to present himself as a President and candidate of moderation and restraint; or as he said in his Chicago speech, as a steady long-distance runner."

Theis and Hartmann had knocked the phrase "long-distance runner" out of several earlier speeches that I wrote. Yet the description seems to fit Gerald R. Ford. Indeed, at the age of sixty-two today, he appears in extraordinary physical shape and everything about his life and career suggests that he is a long-distance runner.

Agnes Waldron knows of my writing differences with Hartmann and Theis. Just before closing last weekend, she came to my office and said: "What are you going to do?"

I reply:

"I am going to try to make Gerald R. Ford human in his speeches, Agnes. They will keep cutting the stuff out and I will keep trying to put it back in one way or another.

"I agree with those who say some of his actions appear to lack compassion. That is because his explanations of them do. They come off as lacking understanding and feeling. No one is trying to write the Gettysburg Address, as Hartmann keeps claiming about my speeches. I am just trying to write with some compassion.

"I've been hungry, Agnes. And I do feel deeply about unemployment. I don't know what the hell is wrong with Hartmann and Theis on this subject. But I an not going to argue with them directly. I'll write and they can cut it."

In coming into work this morning, an old friend of reporting days, Dan Rather, is broadcasting on CBS radio and he reports to this effect:

Gerald R. Ford has come a long way in eleven months. He is now considered by many Americans to be a good, competent President. But one thing that he needs in order to achieve greatness is "compassion."

Amen, Dan.

Tuesday, July 15, 1975

PRESIDENT FORD OBSERVED HIS sixty-second birthday yesterday with a thirty-five-minute physical examination. He was pronounced "fit" and said he feels forty. Most of the 2,200 White House staff members joined Mrs. Ford, with lemonade and spiked lemonade (very weak), to hear Flip Wilson salute the President in the East Room: "Hiya Tiger!"

The President roared with laughter.

To Mrs. Ford, the comedian quipped: "Hello, First Momma!"

Flip clowned as "Geraldine Jones" for about twenty minutes and the East Room rocked with laughter and a rock band.

Ted Marrs stood a few feet away from me. Marrs had just hit the headlines. He acknowledged that he was the flight surgeon for the CIA-organized B-26 squadron that bombed Cuba during the Bay of Pigs invasion. Marrs, a plump, genial gentleman, said his connection with the CIA ended after three months in 1961.

The Marrs story broke at the same time as another CIA headliner, the allegation that the CIA had planted "spies" in the White House in earlier administrations, specifically the Nixon tenure. Alexander Butterfield, who blew the whistle on the Nixon tape-recording process, was said to be the CIA man inside the Nixon White House. Butterfield denied it but speculation still streams across page one.

Marrs is now a special assistant to the President for human resources. He says he was recruited for the CIA invasion force through the Alabama Air Guard and served as a doctor at secret bases in Guatemala and Nicaragua. Marrs, a pediatrician, returned to his baby patients after the CIA venture.

The National Council of Scientology Ministers is calling for Marrs' removal as the President's liaison officer with religious groups. Marrs says he will resign if the past three-month stint is embarrassing to the White House.

In the eyes of many inside the White House, this is the first time that President Ford has come close to getting burned on a sensitive subject. Yet Mr. Ford is not one to quit easily on a man. He believes in a fair shake. A rumor that Marrs would resign quickly dissipated.

Forrest Boyd, of Mutual Broadcasting, suddenly says hello and we begin talking speeches. He ventures that Mr. Ford looked good as a "candidate" during the weekend visit to Illinois and Michigan. I smilingly suggest that the trip was billed as "nonpolitical." Boyd asks whether I believe Rockefeller will be on the 1976 GOP ticket. I reply in the affirmative without hesitation.

Boyd and I go back a decade together when we covered the White House as news correspondents. Thus he is not about to quote me or a "high White House official." But he asks why I believe Rocky will be on the ticket and I respond:

"First, Jerry Ford does not say one thing in public and something else in private. And he has made it clear privately that he wants Rocky. Second, Rocky is a class guy. He came in here at a time when Jerry Ford was down and he helped give the place class after the Nixon mess. Third, the President will not drop someone without serious reason. I don't believe Rocky has given him any personal or professional reason to drop him. In other words, Ford is loyal."

The rock band is blasting away. Jack Ford, the Ford's eldest son, walks through the crowd unnoticed. Jack Marsh is eating hot dogs. Don Rumsfeld, observing from the rear of the East Room, saunters out. And the band plays on.

Friday, July 18, 1975

I ATTEND THE 8 A.M. SENIOR STAFF MEETING for Theis today and yesterday. Jim Cannon, the signal-caller for the Domestic Council, has a headache and we listen. He explains that the administration must come up with a position on "equal athletic opportunity" by Monday. In simple language, the Department of

Health, Education and Welfare is trying to force all college coaches
to share their revenues with women. This is the latest bureaucratic
interpretation of new federal antidiscrimination rules.

Needless to say, the nation's football coaches are attempting to
punt that one out of the stadium. Some have even spoken with
President Ford on the subject. Cannon laments:

"That means the same number of college football scholarships
for boys and girls."

"Wow!" someone says.

"Wowee!" cracks another.

Cannon indicates that the President opposes any "quotas" in
sports. It's also suggested the President should favor an equal
number of college scholarships for each sex. Silence. Another
staffer says the President should support the concept of equality in
intercollegiate competition. A chorus of "yes." Rumsfeld favors a
national dialogue. Presumably, he means no voters will be
offended. And everyone in the room is thinking votes since the
President's announcement of candidacy. The subject is to be
brought to Mr. Ford's attention.

Jim Lynn, head of OMB, says the number of bureaucrats has
been cut by 18,000. Jim Connor notes the cut has not been
significant inside the White House. Rumsfeld disagrees mildly.
Lynn kids Alan Greenspan about the size of his staff. It has not
been cut despite Greenspan's many protestations about big
government. Greenspan brings down the room with this crack:

"I preach the intractability of government and I'm proving it!"

Greenspan then accuses some members of Congress of using
"scare" tactics and worse in attacking the President's plans to
decontrol domestic (old) oil prices. He lashes the Democrats and
concludes:

"I think some of them do not wish to see the economy
succeed. I think they would like to see it go back down."

It is a tough statement and all of us know it.

Rumsfeld says:

"I do not think we can afford to talk that way. That is not the
President's position. These are honorable men. They are the elected
representatives of the people. Let's be careful what we say."

Greenspan hedges on what he said but insists the Democrats
are trying to "scare" the American people with talk of
extraordinary oil and gasoline prices and other tactics.

That is yesterday's meeting. New problems are on the fire today.

Phil Buchen, counsel to the President, mentions that some members of the White House staff have received literature from Democratic presidential hopefuls. He suggests that all such material be turned over to him. Buchen simply wants to keep tabs on what the Democrats are doing.

Bill Seidman talks about the big three auto makers:

"The auto makers are after us because we are not pushing the five-year freeze (on auto-emission controls)."

I am stunned by this statement and others appear somewhat surprised. Since when is the White House carrying the ball for the auto makers on emission controls? Seidman clarifies:

"They say we are not doing enough for our recommendation for a delay in emission controls to ease the auto sales crunch and to get the industry back on its feet with more jobs."

Max Friedersdorf, chief for congressional affairs, interjects:

"Markley (Rod Markley, top Washington lobbyist for Ford Motor Company and frequent golfing companion of the President) wants it to go into full committee."

Frank Zarb agrees but he and others say that the White House should not be leading on this subject. The President has given his position. From now on, the matter should be handled by Congress.

Jack Marsh, counselor to the President, is next in line. As usual, he is direct and practical. Marsh warns that the Congress may try to "crunch" the President while he is in Helsinki. He would not be surprised if they were to try maneuvers on both an energy bill and the decontrol of oil prices, forcing quick, decisive action by the White House.

Zarb and Lynn agree with Marsh.

Jim Cannon reminds Dick Cheney, sitting in the chair for Rumsfeld, that a $3 million bill to kill coyotes is coming up. Ron Nessen, picking this up as a cue, cracks:

"I think those coyotes ought to eat up the women athletes and that would solve two problems!"

A few laughs. Zarb picks up the ball and says:

"Listen, Nessen, every day you leave here and quote us out there to the reporters. I think I ought to go out of here and quote you."

Jim Lynn discusses the pay of federal judges. Gwen Anderson, of the political affairs office, explains that Bo

Callaway's campaign committee office is "going beserk." She says
they have received "tons" of mail and need more volunteers. A
voice shouts: "Unpaid volunteers!"

Gwen says: "Of course!"

Cheney will report to Rumsfeld who will report to Mr. Ford.
The meeting ends.

The Solzhenitsyn affair has become a nightmare inside the
White House. The President declined to meet Alexander
Solzhenitsyn, the Russian Nobel laureate, on the advice of "staff."
Who? When? Why?

The President has been lambasted editorially from coast to
coast. The inside word here is that not a single letter received by
the White House defended Mr. Ford's action. The decision is out
of character for the President. Rumsfeld denies any part in this
decision emphatically but won't discuss the subject further.

I see the fine hand of Henry Kissinger in this affair. The State
Department quietly suggested that its officials not attend the
AFL-CIO dinner for Solzhenitsyn here in Washington. Kissinger
had to approve such a delicate move, particularly since George
Meany is not one to hide a grievance.

White House insiders know that Kissinger wrote at least one
(and perhaps more) memorandum to the President indicating that
detente might suffer if Mr. Ford were to attend the AFL-CIO
dinner honoring Solzhenitsyn. Apparently, it was suggested that the
President shake hands with the Russian author at a White House
reception. Yesterday, the whole mess took another downturn.
Solzhenitsyn was quietly invited to visit with the President at the
White House. He rejected the offer, insisting on a written
invitation. Caught by surprise, and unwilling or unable to agree,
the President's advisers sat on their hands. They bucked the
decision to Kissinger, and General Brent Scowcroft, his national
security deputy inside the White House. Then waited.

The Republican right and others are firing daily volleys against
the decision not to see Solzhenitsyn. The President is quietly
embarrassed and somewhat vexed. Others in the State Department
and on Capitol Hill are more vocal. In private they scorch
Kissinger with anger:

"He thinks Brezhnev might not be so nice to him next time."

"Kissinger has become one of the clique; he thinks he runs
the world with five or six other people."

Kissinger replies that Solzhenitsyn is preaching that the United States should overthrow the Soviet system. He says this is not acceptable to the American people and the world. Solzhenitsyn is a threat to world peace.

The reaction to Solzhenitsyn continues to be phenomenal. Requests for texts of his two American addresses swamp the AFL-CIO.

I do not find support for Kissinger's claims in Solzhenitsyn's texts. His words appear to have a much more analytical meaning than Kissinger suggests. He is really saying that the West is proving itself too cowardly and morally uncertain to defend its own civilized values and sacred rights. His message is a moral one, urging the West to defend its own principles.

I conclude that the Kissinger decision on Solzhenitsyn's not seeing the President is one of hypocrisy, political deceit and personal dishonesty. To suggest that Solzhenitsyn wishes America to go in and strangle Brezhnev and company is deceitful because the Russian author makes it abundantly clear he is asking the West to defend itself. Kissinger apparently is uncomfortable with the concepts of "good" and "evil," as enunciated by Solzhenitsyn. Deliberate nuances and diplomatic doubletalk have become so commonplace in his thought that Kissinger has descended to the role of a mere politician. Therein lies the sadness. The Russians have produced a Solzhenitsyn while all the opportunities offered by America have produced a Kissinger, pragmatist *par excellence*.

Wednesday, July 23, 1975

I ATTEND THE SENIOR STAFF MEETING and it is dreary until the close. Then two hot issues suddenly blaze: The President's gun-control legislation, clamping down on "Saturday-night specials," and Mr. Ford's decision to attend the European Security Conference in Helsinki shortly to sign a statement that virtually endorses Soviet control of Eastern Europe.

Bill Greener, Nessen's deputy, points out there is considerable opposition to the administration's gun-control measure from Republicans. As a matter of fact, no senior GOP senator will sponsor the bill. Senator Hruska, a veteran Nebraska Republican, has privately pressured his fellow Republicans to vote against the measure. He is sending his opposing comments to the White House this morning.

There is brief chatter around the table about saying "no comment" or a similar gesture until the administration can get its ducks in a row. That will not work, Nessen and Greener protest. A chorus of voices suggest various alternatives, all aimed at getting the President off the hook on the bill.

"But where's our credibility?" someone asks. Silence.

Jim Cannon insists that the best answer is the exact truth: there is disagreement within the Republican party and within the administration on the wording of the proposal. The implication is that they may have to go back to the drawing boards.

Nessen then brings up the Helsinki signing. He points out that "we" took it "in the neck" from the *New York Times* the previous day. Namely, the *Times* carried a story quoting Alexander Solzhenitsyn saying that President Ford would become involved in "the betrayal of Eastern Europe" if he signed the Helsinki document.

Nessen notes that the *Wall Street Journal* of today leads off its editorial page with a plea to the President on Helsinki: "Jerry, Don't Go." The *Journal*, in a bitter and biting condemnation of the entire affair, says there is no reason, domestic or international, for the President to go to Helsinki.

Jerry Jones says that the document is "worthless" since it is not legal and will not be registered with the United Nations. Nessen and Greener ask: "Then why are we going to Helsinki?"

Bob Goldwin, the so-called intellectual in the White House, calls for a PR campaign in the next few days to back the President's position. He says the agreement must be explained.

Nessen says he will try to get administration spokesmen on the "talk shows" in the next few days. He suggests that Mr. Ford personally speak about the matter before he leaves for Helsinki. Others demur. They see a possible loss of votes and perhaps trouble from the Republican right. No one says it outright. The feeling, however, is implicit that the President should let one or two underlings handle this hot potato.

Someone suggests that the President might speak on the subject when he meets with an "ethnic" group on Friday. Cannon and Nessen say the issue should be met head on by dealing with those who most oppose the signing. Others suggest that the President speak at the airport before he departs for Helsinki.

Jim Lynn repeats that the *Journal* editorial is one of the strongest against the President that he has seen. Jerry Jones insists that the signing is purely "symbolic" and in no way detracts from the true international rights of those nations in Eastern Europe that are Soviet satellites.

The agreement says, in effect, that the West recognizes Soviet dominance in Eastern Europe and receives in return "concessions" from the Russians such as less tension over West Berlin, prior notice on large troop movements, more humanitarian contacts, freer flow of information and the like.

The matter is left up in the air. Someone will take it up with the President. I am distressed at the equivocating in the meeting by those who want to get the President off the hook. Once again, a free press has made the White House sit up and listen and worry.

Wednesday, July 23, 1975

ONE OF THE MOST INTERESTING conversations I have had in the White House takes place in late morning. Jack Veneman, special assistant to Vice President Rockefeller, returns my phone call.

I tell him that I believe the President has been sounding too pro-business in his speeches. Mr. Ford may have put himself out on a limb. Some of his language is becoming repetitious in speeches—the old values and virtues. I want to know more about what Veneman is doing to draw up policy papers on various issues.

Veneman agrees Mr. Ford has been sounding too one-sided in many business speeches. He suggests the President do a speech on corporate social responsibility.

Veneman volunteers that he has just read a poll of Washington, D.C., Democrats on Mr. Ford. He gets good marks for being a positive person but bad marks for not having positive programs.

I say that I would like to know what is Mr. Ford's "agenda for the future." One of our speechwriters is writing on this subject now. I would like to know what Mr. Ford stands for. Where are the basic decision documents and discussion papers on policy that we have heard about?

Veneman drops a bombshell. He says:

"There are no plans. There are no programs. I wrote a social policy paper that has never cleared the White House."

Stunned, I ask: "What's going on?"

Veneman replies: "I showed some of my material to the Vice President before he went on a recent trip. When he came back, he said:

"Goddamn it, let's get moving on this. Let's get some action."

Veneman does not indicate whether the President himself or Rumsfeld is blocking decisions on policy. He says he can have the first discussion paper "with all the options" ready by September 22, 1975, two months away. He is beginning to develop papers on jobs, health and other subjects at Rockefeller's request, but he has no green light from the White House.

Our discussion ends with me saying:

"Jack, I can't write without knowing the policy. I've faced this for nine months now. We are heading into the '76 campaign and I don't know what the hell Gerald Ford thinks on a whole host of issues.

"We have to straighten out this 'agenda for the future' business. It has to be something substantial."

Veneman quips that maybe we ought to call it a "revised agenda." He explains that we are reacting, not acting, in policy matters.

I put down the receiver and sit in silence. I say to myself:

"My God, there is nothing thought out. There's not one blueprint. We are flying by the seat of our pants."

Obviously, that's an oversimplification. No one flies by the seat of his pants with all the experience there is in the White House. But it appears incredible to note that the White House and the nation, to a degree, are running on a day-to-day basis.

Thursday, July 24, 1975

FOR SEVERAL DAYS, the media have been heating up about the President's trip to Helsinki. The heat around the White House today is intense, much of it caused by Republican criticism from Capitol Hill. Congressman Ed Derwinski of Illinois and others rap Mr. Ford.

In essence, they say the U.S. is selling out Eastern Europe, blessing the Soviet domination, by signing the Helsinki accord. Some are calling it a "new Yalta."

Theis comes to my office about 11 A.M. and hands me the draft of a presidential statement written by Henry Kissinger. He asks me to put it in the President's style and to "fix up" any sections that leave the President open to criticism.

I read the statement and find many elements that are questionable. So I change Kissinger's draft.

Kissinger's wording implies that the President is going to Helsinki, among other reasons, because the results are "balanced." I find this tough to take. Do we send Presidents when we are lucky enough to break even with the Russians on a deal, and a Secretary of State or some other fall guy when we fall short? I ask this of Theis. He says, "Write it the way you think necessary."

Kissinger's draft takes little or no heed of critical concern about the Helsinki statement. How do we counteract this detente bliss if the Soviets don't live up to their side of the pact? So I write in the following:

"It is hoped that this dialogue will make a positive contribution to detente over time. It is a test of true intentions. If these intentions prove negative, detente cannot grow. There cannot be more meaningful progress with the Soviet Union and Eastern Europe if the spirit and principles of the dialogue are not adhered to clearly and concretely. Detente cannot advance without genuine commitment and proven progress along the way."

I add a phrase saying that the U.S. government will monitor the results of the Helsinki meeting.

Then I phone Dennis Clift, a National Security Council aide to Kissinger who helped write the secretary's draft along with State Department personnel. Clift is upset. He says that I am on "a soap box"—that the agreement and the Kissinger statement are exact and precise for reasons. I am not impressed and say so. I say that I cannot and will not send the statement to the President as written. Clift becomes angrier. He requests to see a copy of what I have written but agrees to furnish more specific rationale for the U.S. signing of the document.

I report back to Theis. He says that Hartmann is now in the act. Hartmann and the President have been meeting on the subject. He will send my draft to Hartmann, but, in the meantime, I should contact Derwinski on the Hill and read my draft to him. I should transmit these comments to Hartmann who, in turn, will see the President for final instructions. Derwinski later phones me but by this time Hartmann wants to speak with him directly. So Derwinski speaks with Hartmann and a new draft is born, incorporating some of my misgivings and adding many more, in select language, by the President, Hartmann and Derwinski.

Friday, July 25, 1975

THIS MORNING AT 9 A.M., Theis shows me the Hartmann draft. I read it. I point out three places where it will "send Kissinger up the wall." Theis smiles. Will they show it to Kissinger? Will it be like the end of the war statement by the President at Tulane University—declare the Vietnam war over and not tell Kissinger? At this writing, I do not know. But one thing is certain; the past twenty-four hours clearly indicate the President is taking a more independent line from "Superman." I have seen it firsthand. And Theis is smiling at me and saying:

"Hartmann liked the stuff you wrote. Don't worry about Clift and Kissinger. Hartmann isn't."

Was that the smile of President Ford's declaration of independence from his Secretary of State? I wondered.

Members of the staff are concerned about the President appearing too pro-business. Rod Hills, representing the legal viewpoint, Stan Morris of congressional relations, and Paul Leach, of the Domestic Council, meet with Theis and me.

Just before the meeting begins, I bump into Jim Cavanaugh, deputy director of the Domestic Council, outside Theis' office. He says he has found the prevalent feeling around the White House to be that there has been too much emphasis on business and not enough on consumers.

Hills, Morris and Leach emphasize that in our meeting.

Hills says:

"We've got to get away from the notion, for example, that regulatory reform (to lessen the "heavy hand" of the bureaucracy) is a ploy to avoid consumer advocacy."

Leach says:

Friday, July 25, 1975

"We should stress that regulatory reform is good for the consumer."

Morris explains that the President is taking "a lot of flack" from Capitol Hill because of his business emphasis in recent speeches, particularly the business approach to regulatory reform. He means flack from Republicans.

Leach adds:

"Regulatory reform benefits the customer through lower prices and less inflation."

Hills says it's essential that our various offices cooperate better, that all know our speechwriting schedule, and they will inform us on any particular ideas that should be incorporated in current presidential addresses.

As the meeting breaks up, Theis notes that their proposals will be presented to the President when the speechwriters meet with him this afternoon. I reflect on the emphasis of the trio, the concern in their voices. This administration must put business on the back burner for a while. I read it as a campaign measure. We can't win in '76 without the consumer. He has more votes than business.

As we walk through the White House this afternoon to the meeting with the President in the Oval Office, I whisper to Theis:

"What did Kissinger say about the President's remarks on the Helsinki conference?"

Theis replies:

"He's really teed off!"

"No kidding?" I ask.

"No kidding!" Theis says with a smile.

The President greets us:

"Hi ya, fellas!"

We chorus:

"Good afternoon, Mr. President."

We begin a discussion on the President's speeches for the next month. Those present are Hartmann, Cheney, Jerry Jones, Pat Butler, Bob Rousek, a new member of our office, Theis, and myself. Jones mentions that there are thirty-four occasions when the President will speak from three minutes to a fullblown twenty-minute address. The President speaks:

"That's a mighty full schedule (laughter). It seems to me that we should have three or four central themes and change them somewhat to suit the location and audience."

Hartmann:

"And we can stick in some news from time to time. But we've got to remember a lot of this stuff is going to bore the White House press corps. They will say that you are repeating yourself. But it has been done before and will be done again. We have to think about the local benefit to you—local and even statewide coverage."

Jones: "That's right. And it's also important that we get our message across before Reagan does."

Jack Marsh walks into the office and interrupts to say that Senator Clifford Case, a New Jersey Republican, has called him with a message for the President. The President's request for $350 million in arms for Jordan will not get out of his committee. It will lose by one or two votes. And it will not pass the Senate even if it does get out of committee. Therefore, would the President like to pull back his proposal and resubmit it when Congress returns in September?

Marsh then says he has spoken with General Scowcroft, Kissinger's deputy on the National Security Council, who told him that the financial figure cannot go down. The President tells Marsh to have all the details when he meets with Kissinger and Scowcroft in half an hour. Marsh leaves.

Suddenly turning to Jones, who is the new scheduling chief, the President asks if Jones has signed him up for the Danny Thomas affair in Memphis. Jones says he was not aware the President had decided to go to Memphis. The President, with a sly smile, says he told Thomas he would go to Memphis for a benefit in behalf of the hospital that the comedian is trying to help. Jones says he will arrange matters.

A few minor speeches are mentioned and quickly agreed on. We come to the Des Moines speech. I am writing that one, which will be the President's first major farm speech. The President speaks on his own:

"I like Governor Bob Ray's suggestion. We talk about the great job that the farmer is doing. Farmers are only about 6 per cent of the population and they feed the other 94 per cent of us as well as much of the rest of the world. They bring in about $22 billion in the balance of payments. Farmers are important not only in their fields but in our foreign policy.

"We don't need any big farm message or farm policy statement. It's simply this: high production, good prices and good farm income, and as little government interference as possible."

Friday, July 25, 1975

The President points out that crop reports will be announced about ten days before the speech. He says that if they are as good as expected the speech should emphasize more income for the farmer and lower prices for the consumer.

Jones interjects on the Russian wheat deal. That is a political hot potato. The President says that the speech can then compare our production with that of agricultural production in the Soviet Union. We should get precise figures on that.

We then discuss a GOP political fund-raiser in Des Moines the same night. Jones immediately suggests saying something about detente since Reagan is attacking Mr. Ford for going to Helsinki. Hartmann demurs. He says:

"Detente is not going to open their checkbooks and their hearts."

The President says the address should simply emphasize Republican principles, as in earlier fund-raisers.

Cheney and Jones zero in on Reagan. They insist that Reagan is making mileage in his attacks on detente, that detente is an issue. Both sound as if they are certain that Reagan will formally announce as a candidate. There is urgency in their voices. The President thinks out loud:

"A good theme is that detente depends on a strong national defense. If we don't have a strong national defense, we won't have detente. If we don't have detente, defense costs will rise greatly. It seems to me that we have the best of both worlds."

All agree. The President adds:

"Without SALT II, our defense bill will rise by three to five billion dollars. The United States can forget about cutting defense appropriations. Again, defense goes hand in hand with detente."

We return to fund-raisers and other speeches and the President says:

"I want to stay on the high road this year. We will not get into politics as such in any speeches. We may be partisan but we will be noncontroversial partisan. Next year, we go all out on politics."

Discussion switches to a Dirksen Library speech in Pekin, Illinois. The late Senator Everett Dirksen, a veteran Illinois Republican leader in the Senate, was a longtime friend of Mr. Ford while he was in the Congress. Hartmann hollers:

"I want to write that one. I can write it in my sleep. We'll put on an Ev and Abe Lincoln show."

135

"How about an Ev and Jerry (Ford) show like they used to do on the Hill?" someone asks. Hartmann says:

"We can do a little of that for humor but the real speech is an Ev and Lincoln show (comparing the two)."

We wind up on a speech before the hardware industry in Chicago. The President asks me about the audience and I tell him that it is a mix of retailers (small businessmen) and manufacturers (many big businessmen). Mr. Ford looks over various options offered him by members of the White House staff. He dismisses the proposals of our morning meeting and says:

"Call John Anderson. Ask him about a topic. He knows this group well. He got me to talk to them."

The meeting ends with the President saying: "So long, fellas."

Back in the office, I call Anderson's office and they promise to write up some thoughts. I mention to the Anderson aide that the President will probably thank him when he sees the congressman at the conference. The aide replies:

"Oh, the congressman is not going to the speech. He's going to China!"

Such is the game of politics.

Chapter 11
August, 1975

"A man who is influenced by the polls or is afraid to make decisions which may make him unpopular is not a man to represent the welfare of the country. If he is right, it makes no difference whether the press and the special interests like what he does, or what they have to say about him. I have always believed that the vast majority of people want to do what is right and that if the President is right and can get through to the people he can always persuade them."

HARRY S TRUMAN

Monday, August 11, 1975

WHITE HOUSE STAFFERS GREETED the anniversary of President Ford's first year in office with little or no outward interest. True, it was a Saturday, a nonwork day for many employees, August 9, 1975. But as I return today from vacation and talk with my colleagues, hardly anyone talks of the first year. Conversation is entirely about the future.

Mrs. Ford is in the headlines after telling CBS's *60 Minutes* her views on abortion and premarital sex. Many church people and others say she was "too frank" for them while some were far less charitable. The First Lady, who appeared to accept the possibility of both abortion and premarital sex, touched off a major storm.

Otherwise, Gerald R. Ford's first anniversary was just another day to those behind the scenes at the White House.

The President himself, talking with newsmen, says the job has gotten "progressively easier to handle, even though the problems have been tough." A political description of himself: "A middle-of-the-road conservative."

For me, the most important thing the President said was this:

"I think in the next State of the Union message we will point directions in the long run for the future of the country. We are going to develop an explanation of what we are doing, and how it fits into the long-range program, or we will come up with some long-range focus and answers."

My experience in the White House has led me to conclude that the President has sadly lacked in long-range direction for the country. With the one significant exception of his energy package, his aims and actions have been near-sighted. Only energy is a solid long-range program that hangs together logically. And that program actually belongs to the Nixon administration.

Speeches have become a catalyst for policy—policy that should be made more thoughtfully and not under the duress of a speech deadline. Someone says: "That's pretty good." And suddenly, it is policy.

Mr. Ford is a man of consensus. He is a compromiser. He is a man who works with people. He is, in the final analysis, a Republican who has seen so much defeat in his lifetime that he is unsure of the meaning and power of victory. Democrats understand power. They call it clout.

And yet, as everyone says: "Jerry Ford is a helluva nice guy. I wish him luck."

Monday, August 18, 1975

THIS MONDAY MORNING WAS a shocker inside the White House. President Ford had taken a nosedive in the polls. Harris had him at 60 per cent negative, 38 per cent positive. Gallup projected his approval at 45 per cent.

Mr. Ford had taken office with a high vote of confidence, 71 per cent in the polls. His fortune declined with the nation's economic slide and energy problems. But the President climbed up to 50 per cent approval with Harris and 51 per cent with Gallup after his handling of the Mayaguez incident.

We began to receive all types of encouraging news from the Democrats—mostly that the President would be a "genuine" and "tough" opponent. But the Democrats demurred with a truism: "It's still a year away." And they were, of course, right.

The latest polls prove it. Why the big slip? Is it more than the economy? Is it just a quirk?

No one seems to believe the latter. The uneasiness has always been here. But there was a euphoria bordering on ecstasy around the White House after the Mayaguez incident. People began to say: "We're going to win."

Even Paul Theis said that. And Theis is an extremely cautious man.

As an Independent, I felt Mr. Ford still had to make and prove his case. More and more, I came to believe that this election would be dominated by three things: the campaign of George Wallace; events that no one could control; and the economy in the last month of the campaign.

The second point was a perennial sleeper but I felt it should be listed because Ford has had an element of luck riding with him, from his selection and entry to the White House to Mayaguez and some breaks in the economy. As a "hunch" bettor, I would tend to count this second possibility in the President's corner. The first and third were impossible to call.

Wallace's health is a factor. So is the manner in which the Democrats let him down at their convention. If Wallace interprets his failure as an unfair fight, he could cause incalculable trouble for the Democrats.

The economy is highly problematical. If unemployment is not down to 7 per cent and inflation to 6 per cent, those two numbers alone may defeat Mr. Ford. I believe the American people may well conclude: a plague on both your houses. And they may vote out a great number in the Congress as well as the President. In other words, both the Congress and the President will suffer because of their inability to act affirmatively on the economy, energy and other issues.

So much for musing on a late mid-August day in the nation's capital.

Wednesday, August 20, 1975

THE DOG DAYS OF AUGUST are upon us. I returned from a two-week vacation to write a business speech for the President before the Hardware Industry Conference in Chicago. And this speech proved to be a real dog. I feel bitten in the arm, chewed in the seat of the pants and limping with a chunk out of my leg.

I have not listed details of some troubles of the past but this speech has become typical of the birth pangs of presidential addresses. The headaches began about a month ago when I presented the President five options on what he might say to the hardware people. Mr. Ford did not reject the options. He simply told me:

"Call John Anderson of Illinois. He knows these people. Let's go with his advice."

Anderson said the hardware folk would want to hear about the need for capital investment and the free enterprise system, coupled with remarks on governmental regulatory reform.

On my return, Theis and the President were in Vail, Colorado, but Theis had left me terse instructions to prepare a speech along Anderson's outlines. Three people were soon in the act—Ed Clarke of OMB, Paul Leach of the Domestic Council, and Rod Hills who was braintrusting the administration position on regulatory reform. Leach and Hills had participated in the July meeting that formulated the original option on regulatory reform which President Ford had previously dismissed.

Wednesday, August 20, 1975

Clarke provided me with an extensive background paper on the administration's antitrust position. Leach and Hills said it would make a perfect balance to the earlier part of the speech, a call for tax incentives for needed capital investment. They reasoned that the President's pro-business tilt had caused his image to drop. Political heat was coming from some Republicans on the Hill. Republicans were passing the word that Mr. Ford's unequivocal and conservative language on business was becoming embarrassing. There must be more balance. The answer was to be the traditional Republican response—hit 'em with antitrust . . . more competition . . . the free market place . . . get the government out of business with its sanction of cartels.

So I wrote the speech. That was the easy part.

Bob Rousek, a new man whom Theis brought in to handle his overflow work and do some editing, called me. He wanted to discuss the speech. Rousek had sent the speech around for clearance by various White House officials. I suggested that he also send it to Attorney General Levi, since part of the address concerned antitrust.

Rousek sat with the various comments before him. Some of these comments were conflicting if not contradictory. Others questioned certain facts and figures, valid responses. But some wanted to change the tone and content of the speech to suit their own tastes. And these were sometimes tough to deal with—especially if any one of them could get to the President with their views. Bill Seidman was particularly good at making these end runs.

I accommodated the views expressed as best I could within the aim of the speech. Paul Leach said to me, "It's a great speech. Just what's needed."

Agnes Waldron smiled and shot, "It's tough. I like the toughies."

After pulling and tugging with some fifteen different people on the speech, it was sent to Bob Hartmann. He exploded.

Milt Friedman, acting chief of the office while Theis was in Vail, went to see Hartmann and returned to see me. Our conversation went something like this:

He: "Hartmann says this speech is a radical departure from what the President has ever said in his entire career."

Me: "It's my understanding that it's standard Republican antitrust."

He: "That's not what Hartmann thinks."

Me: "Let's start at the beginning. Hills, Leach and Clarke say this is what should be said on antitrust. It's their baby."

He: "Have they said this to the President?"

Me: "You got me, Milt. But I presume that the backgrounder which they gave me to write reflects the administration's and the President's views."

He: "Hartmann says it doesn't."

Me: "Let's call Hills."

He: "Hartmann wants to know why you mentioned President Kennedy in the speech."

Me: "Because Kennedy's quotation makes a case for the President. Kennedy gave a speech saying precisely what the President is saying on capital formation. The President is under fire from the Democrats and the press for being too strong on capital formation. JFK was just as strong. The President is politely saying: 'OK, eat your own words.' "

He: "Hartmann says this speech will cause more business news than any speech the President has ever given."

Me: "Maybe. But let me ask this: Is the President for antitrust or not?"

He: "I don't know."

Me: "But he has spoken about it. He has talked about strong antitrust measures. Hills and company are talking tough."

He: "I'll talk to Hills."

Briefly, the speech said this: No nation has experimented or taken greater risks for progress than the U.S. No people has invested more in humanity and science. Today, America is called on to experiment, to risk as much as ever before. Economic progress depends on capital investment. All studies point to the increased need for capital.

America must avoid a longrun problem of inadequate industrial capacity. We must not condemn citizens to unemployment because we have run out of the modern tools with which to work.

The administration has proposed a tax incentive program to encourage capital investment. If the Congress does not like it, let it come up with a reasonable plan of its own. But let it do something. We must start somewhere.

On antitrust, the speech said that economic regulation must no longer be considered a substitute for competition. Where effective competition is possible, antitrust, rather than price and entry regulation, should promote order in the marketplace. Competition will drive costs down to their minimum and assure prices based on these costs.

America must look at the whole range of government-sanctioned monopoly. The monopolies range from the small franchise, protected by government regulations which prohibit competitors from opening their doors, to government-endorsed cartels controlling entire industries. We must recognize that the government has done as much to create and perpetuate monopoly as to control or eliminate it.

Back to the difficult birth of the hardware speech. Back to some fancy footwork. I phoned Ed Clarke to pose the question which Friedman had:

Did the background paper he gave me represent the views of the President?

Clarke could not have been clearer. He said Rod Hills had told him after meeting with Mr. Ford that the President wanted a speech making this strong case for antitrust.

Fine, I said to myself.

Unfortunately, in my call to Hills, he denied that he had ever spoken with the President on antitrust in connection with a speech. Beautiful.

The swirl of contradictions began to churn up feelings. Why did Clarke prepare the backgrounder? Because Theis asked for it. Why did Theis ask for it? Because he had discussed the matter with Hills. What did John Anderson think? Anderson was in Illinois and could not be reached for comment.

Finally, a fifth draft appeared on my desk with my name on it. About one-third of the antitrust material was divided into options for the President. He could choose his own way out of the dilemma. I could not help thinking of Harry Truman's old bromide: "The buck stops here."

As of this writing, the President has still not seen the speech. Hartmann has flown to Vail presumably to discuss this and other speeches with Mr. Ford.

Bill Seidman's office is asking Commerce Secretary Morton what the President should say in the next speech I am to write, a White House Domestic Conference address in Seattle. What Seidman's role is in asking this question of Morton is unclear, but his office has sent me a copy of Morton's reply. Of course, Morton and the governor's office in the state of Washington do not agree on what the President might best discuss.

But that is all in a day here in the White House on the Potomac, here at the apex of American and world power, here at the chair of leadership. This is a view from the summit.

Thursday, August 21, 1975

KAYE PULLEN WANDERS INTO MY office about 10 A.M. She laughs:

"Did you note in the news summary today that Mrs. Ford gave Hartmann an elbow? She said she didn't 'jibe' with him and that he was trying to run her husband's life."

Kaye is just warming up. She continues:

"We could use a little Hartmann around here, to run our lives a little more. I'm tired of writing from a blank sheet of paper."

I tell Kaye that she should start reading the *Wall Street Journal* and the *Congressional Quarterly*. In mock amusement, I say:

"They are giving us our directions. It's all in type, little girl. Just read the papers and magazines."

Kaye laughs again but it's no joke. She wants to be filled in. So I tell her about the *Wall Street Journal* article.

Vice President Rockefeller is about to "sell an ambitious domestic program to President Ford." The crux of the program is to be a new public financing and development corporation. And I add:

"You know, just like New York's Big MAC."

Kaye asks: "Are you kidding?"

"No," I say. "It gets bigger and better."

I explain that Rocky and company are talking about $30 billion or more for the construction of utilities and similar projects over the next decade. This new government corporation would speed up such construction. The assumption is that utilities, pipelines and others will not be able to raise the great amounts of capital needed to provide enough energy from domestic sources in the future.

In some cases, Rocky's giant dreamhouse would guarantee loans for private industry. It also would sell its own government-guaranteed bonds.

The article suggests that the proposal is already running into opposition among the President's advisers. And it surely will not rally the liberals, except in opposition.

Kaye listens in silence but finally says:

"It's good to get your guidance from the front page of the *Journal*."

I continue. Rocky's people say they are going to consolidate the country's labyrinth of social welfare programs. They will simplify regulations, weed out ineligible recipients, and slash the number of bureaucrats running the programs. The welfare system will be based as much as possible on cash grants. Food stamps will be the first to catch the eagle's eye.

Other programs under scrutiny are drug control, state and local freedom in spending federal grants, and streamlined federal regulatory activities.

Kaye's eyes blink when I say the *Journal* reports "tension" between Rocky and Rumsfeld. This reached a height with Bo Callaway's remarks about Rocky not being a help to the President in the South and elsewhere.

I shift gears to the *Congressional Quarterly* and quote it to the effect that these "sweeping proposals" will not be made public until late this year or early 1976. They will be a keystone of his domestic policy when the President campaigns next year.

The magazine indicates that the President has been "hinting" at the broad outlines of the plan in recent speeches. It says that Mr. Ford has been calling for the return to the "old" American virtues of thrift and self-reliance.

I begin to kid Kaye:

"Since I'm the one who began this 'old American virtues' theme back in the New Hampshire and Old North Church speeches, you can quote me, kid. Nobody told me a damn thing about restructuring social programs."

In a nutshell, the *Congressional Quarterly* reports that Mr. Ford's proposals will revamp social programs across the board. The plan could cut billions of dollars from the federal budget.

A review of all social programs is now under way. The White House task force is headed by John G. Veneman, former under secretary of HEW in the Nixon years. Not more than a month ago, Veneman told me that there were no position papers in existence. The group is concentrating in two major areas, health programs (such as Medicare and Medicaid) and "income transfer" programs, such as food stamps, welfare, unemployment insurance, aid to dependent children and housing subsidies. The aim of the task force is to get more productivity out of what is spent.

Kaye blurts:

"I still ask: Why aren't they telling us? We're the speechwriters. We're not going to leak it to the *Washington Post*."

I report:

"The *Washington Post* has already had much of this on its front page."

Kaye begins to describe some of the memos which she has written to Theis about receiving more input on the speeches assigned her. She says that she never receives an answer.

The clock swings around to 10:30 A.M. and it's time to write. Kaye has the last word:

"I think I ought to be writing cookbooks."

Friday, August 22, 1975

THE WHITE HOUSE IS GETTING up tight on the economy again. The first drift of it has come in the staff's nervous comments and petty bickering on the hardware industry speech. Yesterday, the Labor Department reported a 1.2 per cent rise in the July Consumer Price Index. That is at an annual rate of 14.4 per cent, and is the first double-digit rise in living costs since September. The numbers hit this place like a bombshell. No one expected it.

One of the top experts confides to me: "We have no real, long-term inflation policy except principles. Principles aren't enough. I just don't think we are being innovative. We should look at more options."

There are rumors of a power shift among the economic advisers. Greenspan, who long ago told me that Seidman was "out" insofar as policy-making is concerned, opposes Simon's current emphasis on tax breaks for business. Others say Simon's executive committee of the President's economic policy board is "ineffective." Simon is accused of spending too much time carrying his ideas to the public instead of thinking out answers for the President.

Seidman is criticized for being just a "moderator" at meetings, not an "innovator or thinker." One critic says:

"That guy just attends meetings, gets as much information as he can from OMB, and then tries to tell the President what's right while playing tennis. He's way over his head but he knows the President."

Budge Director Lynn and Energy Chief Zarb are moving to the apex of power with Greenspan. Both are clear and will take a stand. In the current crisis, Ford wants his advisers to take a stand.

Although the President has just told Iowa farmers the U.S. plans to continue grain sales to the Russians, everyone in the White House knows that Treasury has developed no further policy on grain sales. Treasury was caught flat-footed by the uproar about the grain-sale effect on the American consumer.

The Agriculture Department is now admitting that 1975 food prices will average about 9 per cent above last year. (Note: the estimate did not hit the double-digit 10 figure.) Butz just clashed again in public with consumer groups. He is traveling the country with a loaf of bread, pointing out the cost of wheat. He blames the middleman for big profit-taking.

Labor's Dunlop and Simon are battling. The labor secretary wants to postpone the decision on grain sales. Dunlop hangs tough and is moving up with Greenspan, Zarb and Lynn as the real power brokers.

This much is certain: recovery is not moving fast enough. There's genuine alarm about food prices. Butz is written off as a PR man for agriculture instead of a needed innovator of administration farm policy.

Saturday, August 23, 1975

WITH TWO POLLS, HARRIS AND GALLUP, against President Ford, the word now reaching the White House from California is that Ronald Reagan will challenge Mr. Ford for the GOP nomination. Reagan is said to have made up his mind after recent release of these polls. He feels that he has "a real chance to win." The new campaign reform laws make it necessary that he move this fall, not later.

In the White House, there are "inside" misgivings about President Ford's campaign. Bob Hartmann and others believe Bo Callaway has made some serious tactical bloopers. Rumsfeld is reported to have cast the vote of confidence that clinched the job for Callaway with Mr. Ford. He thus cut some of the campaign reins from Hartmann. This was formalized when the President named Rumsfeld to be his liaison with Callaway.

Callaway is criticized for "messing up" the Rockefeller situation. That is shorthand for saying Callaway was to placate conservatives by suggesting that Rocky would have to "prove" himself for a place on the ticket, as the President would have to win the nomination on his own. But Callaway went too far, saying Rocky was a "liability" to the President and sounding as if Mr. Ford wanted to "dump" the Vice President. Rocky got sore. Mr. Ford was forced to back him in clear terms. And the President was right back in the soup with conservatives who seriously want to dump Rocky.

The southerners are thus holding out for Reagan. Three recent developments strengthen their unity: the President's "snub" in not seeing Soviet author Alexander Solzhenitsyn; his trip to Helsinki and suggested "sellout" of Eastern European nations in behalf of a dubious detente; and Mrs. Ford's unfortunate television comments in which she appeared to adopt an easy attitude toward abortion and premarital sex.

Callaway's critics—and thus Rumsfeld's critics—complain that Bo is too much of a "salesman" and not enough of a "pro." For example, Callaway was quoted as saying that Ford trailed Reagan in New Hampshire. Apparently, even the President was irritated at this.

Yet no one wants to hurt the South's feelings by easing Callaway out of the job itself. So it is said Hartmann and others are suggesting to Mr. Ford that he place a "powerful pro" to work with Callaway in the campaign. The feeling now is that Callaway will be quietly sidelined after the primaries when the real campaign begins. Rockefeller has already indicated this to his staff.

Some of this is now being leaked discreetly to the press. It is discreet in the sense that the leaks are going to one or two reporters individually, not in any groups of three or four. Mel Laird, a confidant of the President and now an executive with *Reader's Digest*, and Hartmann are reported as being responsible.

The important point in my mind is that there is an effort to find a scapegoat for Mr. Ford's decline in the polls. Callaway, who has been talking too much, is readily available because he is not an "inside" member of the Ford team.

There is another consideration. The Callaway affair appears to be a clear instance of Rumsfeld not doing his homework. In pushing for Callaway, he apparently did not see Bo's weaknesses. Thus, some of the sharpshooters who do not cotton to Rumsfeld may be able to show Mr. Ford that his top coordinator has made a serious mistake. An attempt to downgrade Rumsfeld's influence with the President is being made.

Monday, August 25, 1975

I AM TALKING WITH ART QUERN, a new man on the Domestic Council, in his office about a speech the President is to make before the National (black) Baptist convention in St. Louis. I am trying to discover what the President is supposed to discuss, since no one knows. The White House scheduling office does not even know why the address was scheduled. Stan Scott and John Calhoun, black aides to the President, knew nothing about possible speech content; neither did anyone in our office.

I had suggested the general subject of education to Theis and he wanted to see several options. Scott asked for a day to think about it. Calhoun suggested a speech on the black contribution to America with emphasis on the "values" that have carried blacks forward.

Quern wonders aloud about education. He says that it will lead to discussion of busing and the administration has developed no position paper on the subject.

I take a straightforward approach with Quern, who was formerly on Rockefeller's staff in Albany. I tell him that I have just finished a speech, being delivered at that very moment, for the Hardware Industry Conference in Chicago. It had taken me seven drafts to arrive at agreement on what I considered two easy subjects, capital formation and antitrust. The administration had developed no real policy positions on these subjects. Quern candidly says, his honesty coming across with direct impact:

"There's virtually no administration policy on anything.

149

Maybe a bit on the economy and energy. But there is nothing on just about anything else. What I mean is that they have no plans on how to get from here to there. They don't know what is to be accomplished or how to accomplish it. And frankly, as you probably know, there is division in the White House. Some don't want any positions. They don't want any programs to accomplish anything. They want to stand pat and simply say: no new programs; no new spending.''

Quern then hits me with the punch lines:

"There has been a void in this administration for the past year. It has been living from day to day, from yesterday's newspaper to today's problems. The administration has taken leadership in practically nothing but the economy and energy.

"What does it stand for? What does it hope to accomplish?''

Quern's concern calls to mind a discussion with another Domestic Council staffer:

"We're up to our ass in coyotes. That's right, coyotes. It's a battle between the environmentalists and sheepmen—whether to resume poisoning them. We're stuck with that. Rumsfeld shuffles all his daily problems over to us. The result is that the Domestic Council doesn't have the time to do its own long-range planning.'' (The staff recommended that President Ford resume coyote poisoning.)

Quern's directness prompts me to say:

"We on the speechwriting staff need your help. Once the subject matter is finally decided on, we find ourselves with little or no guidance.''

We agree to stay in contact.

After meeting Quern, I see Pat Butler, a newer member of our staff, in the hall. He asks me about the hardware speech and I tell him I know nothing about the reaction.

I mention that the *New York Post* described the President's recent American Legion speech as "pedestrian.''

Butler relates that most of the "color'' and "punch lines'' in his speeches are taken out. He says it is no longer a speech but a dull mishmash.

Chapter 12
September, 1975

According to an incident reported in Washington in 1862, a senator once called at the White House and vehemently denounced the President for his "calm and moderate" views, ending with the words, "Sir you are within a mile of Hell!" To this Lincoln offered no dissent, but with a gentle nod of his head as if talking to himself replied: "Yes, yes it is just one mile to the Capitol!"

ABRAHAM LINCOLN

Wednesday, September 3, 1975

CONGRESS RETURNS TO WORK TODAY after a month's vacation. The President seeks a compromise on decontrolling oil prices, 1 previously rejected by the Congress. The administration hopes to phase in increased prices over approximately a three-year span. The economy is showing clear signs of recovery but whether or not the administration is demonstrating economic leadership is widely challenged.

The President's economic advisers are sniping at one another again. His economic policy board is in somewhat of a shambles.

Greenspan, Labor Secretary Dunlop, as well as Jim Lynn and his OMB staff, set all economic policy in consultation with the President outside the board structure. Other government officials, getting wind of the board's failures, are trying to bypass it by dealing more and more with Don Rumsfeld's office.

One of the board's insiders tells me in private:

"There's always a lot of chatter around the table. But we know the policy before we go in there and we affirm only what we know. We settle the secondary stuff—like speeches, testimony on the Hill, et cetera, but we don't set policy for tomorrow or next month."

One of the board's prime objectives is to lay down economic policy options for the President, to prepare for the future by heading off last-minute crisis decisions. With little staff help and disunity among its members, the board appears to be struggling just to hold itself together.

Presidents Kennedy, Johnson and Nixon had highly respected economic policy and advisory boards. These went under the names of "Troika" and "Quadriad." "Troika" included the secretary of the Treasury, the chairman of the Council of Economic Advisers and the director of the Office of Management and Budget. It was termed the "Quadriad" when the chairman of the Federal Reserve joined the group.

The current policy board has added the secretaries of Commerce, Labor and State, the Federal Energy administrator, and the directors of the Domestic Council and the Council on International Economic Policy. Most board members now regard the President's switch to the new, larger team as a mistake. And they are concerned. As one put it privately: "In the final analysis, Alan Greenspan is setting economic policy for the United States with Gerald Ford in general agreement. The rest of us are just reacting."

I see another example of reaction in today's *Washington Post*. David S. Broder, with whom I covered the 1964, 1966 and 1968 political campaigns and for whom I have the highest personal and professional respect, is writing on the Boston busing showdown. A Broder paragraph catches my eyes:

"But it (a hands-off policy by the White House regarding the coming Boston busing crisis) also suggests why there is a sense in Washington that the President is reacting to events—rather than trying to anticipate them and shape or control them."

Phil Buchen, the President's counsel, is reported by Broder as saying: ". . . the White House has had absolutely no input."

Broder says that it is "so astonishing that no one on the President's staff is involved with the planning for this confrontation" between blacks, whites and the Boston police.

When Boston schools open in five days, the federal government will have amassed on the scene the most powerful law-enforcement force that has ever been mobilized in behalf of school desegregation. The White House, however, will have had little say in its formation or use.

The White House response to such criticism is that the President has returned to various federal departments the power and responsibility that was originally theirs.

Leadership will be a legitimate issue in the 1976 campaign.

Thursday, September 4, 1975

PANICSVILLE, MAN. PANICSVILLE.

The secretaries are flying between their typewriters, the Xerox machine and the speech typewriter. A half-dozen different presidential speeches, additional airport statements and other White House comment sail across the room in various stages of midflight. Nothing is finished. The President leaves in less than two hours for a two-day trip to three West Coast states, Washington, Oregon and California.

The remarks which I wrote for Mr. Ford's appearance at the White House Conference in Seattle are out the window. All the material carefully culled from Governor Dan Evans's office on the state of Washington is up, up and away. So is the material Theis asked me to write on Henry Kissinger and the Mideast interim peace agreement between Egypt and Israel. So are all the figures on the economy. The new version, edited by Theis from an earlier Milwaukee visit, is bland. It says: It's great to be here and now let me have your questions.

The early version had sat on Theis' desk for nine days. On looking at it yesterday at 4 P.M., he rushed in and said: "Cut it to four minutes, put in a pat on the back for Kissinger and his Mideast accord, and get it back to me as fast as possible." I write it and he quickly dumps it.

The real crunch is the speech before the California state legislature. It's Bob Longood's introduction to White House panic. He's a new man, only a week on the job, writing his first speech for the President.

The Republicans in the California state legislature want a presidential crime speech. That's what they tell Longood about 5 P.M. Friday, the kickoff hour of the Labor Day weekend. Hartmann and Theis agree on the crime approach. Longood is given Mr. Ford's Yale speech on crime, a few general statements on the subject, and told to fly.

He works the weekend and submits a draft when the brass return to work on Tuesday. Theis adds material. However, the President was not available until yesterday and didn't like the speech when he saw it.

Hartmann steps in. He will write a new speech. Hartmann wrote last evening but no one knows the subject. Air Force One takes off and Cheryl Ford, a secretary who is making the trip, tells me:

"Mr. Hartmann's writing in the air. I understand that I will have plenty of work on the plane."

Bob Longood asks: "Is this par for the course?"

Silence. No one wants to discourage him. We need him. As Kaye Pullen puts it:

"With the amount of speeches coming up—better than one a day and no direction, baby—we need every able-bodied breathing soul we can get."

Since the panic is beyond my control, I turn for edification to the fourth estate. From the *New York Times* to *U.S. News &*

World Report and on across the country, the print media have zeroed in on the hardware industry speech which I wrote recently. All are saying this will be Mr. Ford's central theme of the 1976 political campaign—get government out of business and off the backs of the nation's producers and let the free enterprise system work.

The *Baltimore News-American* sums it up well:

"Economic enlightenment is one of the greatest needs in the nation today, and Mr. Ford has gone right to the jugular. If he can re-sell 'free enterprise' to Americans who have prospered more than any other peoples on earth because of that system, he will have accomplished a tremendous feat.

"As of now, what he says is pleasing to business leaders and knowledgeable economic students, but it cannot be regarded as a popular theme. Mr. Ford has chosen a tough road—but the right one."

U.S. News quotes presidential aides on the speech to the effect that Mr. Ford is "peaking" about fourteen months too early in the campaign.

This morning, newspapers across the country frontpage a story that "moderate" Republican members of the Senate have told the President that he must soften his conservative tone. A dozen GOP senators advised Mr. Ford in an hour meeting that his conservative base is secure and he should concentrate on wooing the Independents and the Democratic swing vote.

The real fact is, as I have been writing here, that there is no "conservative" plan whatsoever. I wrote the entire capital formation section on my own with no guidance from anyone. On checking into regulatory reform, the subject of antitrust came up. There wasn't any more *plan* to use it than a choose-up sandlot touch football game.

Friday, September 5, 1975

DAVID HUME KENNERLY, the presidential photographer, apparently has used that four-letter word once too often. With Mr. Ford on a West Coast swing, and Kennerly along, the rumors of young Dave's demise are everywhere. Dave has been irritating hell out of many senior staff members with his lifestyle of booze, broads and bitching.

Dave lets you know where he stands at all times. For example: "To hell with Nessen. I work for the President. Period."

Dave apparently has been irritating some of his Georgetown neighbors, drinking beer on his stoop, smart-aleking the girls walking by, and drinking much of the night with "the boys," keeping some of his neighbors awake.

White House guards are angered because Kennerly sometimes drives his sports car at high speeds in the complex and he virtually thumbs his nose at them.

Nessen's staff indicates that Kennerly has been requested to drop three of his seven-person staff. Nessen is known to dislike Kennerly and the feeling is mutual. But then, Nessen dislikes a lot of people.

Kennerly's conduct raises some basic questions about Gerald R. Ford. Is Mr. Ford aware of Kennerly's reputation? Does he believe he and the White House are immune from its consequences? Is Gerald Ford simply "too nice a guy" to fire anyone, even someone as inconsequential as Kennerly?

Amidst questions of national economic survival, the White House staff finds time to ponder the Kennerly matter.

Tuesday, September 9, 1975

KAYE PULLEN IS UPTIGHT and saying so:

"This is really a crock o' shit," she says standing above me in front of my desk. "They still haven't answered my request to join the White House Mess. I only want to use it once a month. I can't afford to eat there regularly."

I tell her to forget about the Mess. It's quicker to get a bite downstairs in the Old Executive Office Building cafeteria. She should concentrate on changing her White House parking sticker. Instead of parking a half-mile away along the Ellipse, she should try parking inside the White House complex or immediately adjacent. I say:

"Don Rumsfeld doesn't have that long walk in the dark at night and no woman should."

Kaye is fuming:

"That son-of-a-bitch is blocking everything. Anybody who works for Hartmann gets on Rumsfeld's shit list immediately. And he's supposed to be so fair in the President's best interests. Fair on what?''

The intense rivalry between Rumsfeld and Hartmann pervades the outlook of the speechwriting staff, even to questions of parking.

The ''Rumsfeld men'' in positions of power are well identified by everyone working inside the White House: Attorney General Levi, CAB Chairman John E. Robson, Cabinet Secretary Jim Connor, Bob Goldwin, White House liaison with the academic world, Rumsfeld's deputy, Dick Cheney, and Max Friedersdorf, assistant to the President for congressional relations. The White House personnel office has been completely dominated by Rumsfeld appointees.

The Rumsfeld-Hartmann feud exploded today in the waiting room adjoining the President's office. Rumsfeld was not present. He was issuing instructions to Terry O'Donnell, Mr. Ford's young immediate aide. O'Donnell had phoned Theis saying our 3:30 P.M. meeting with the President had been moved up. The speechwriters should come to the President's office as soon as possible. Theis, Butler, Rousek, Orben and myself rushed to the waiting room. Hartmann was waiting. Suddenly, O'Donnell told us, as he took telephone instructions from Rumsfeld, that the President would meet with a labor group instead. We should return at 6:30 P.M. Hartmann literally jumped out of his chair. He charged at O'Donnell shouting: ''What am I doing here then? Why was I called away?''

O'Donnell, clutching the phone, backed away. Hartmann bellowed:

''Everything is more important than the speeches. I mean everything!

''Why is it that the other subject is always more important? Why is it that we always get screwed?''

Hartmann walks out of the waiting room and the secret service agents appear flushed in the face. They are jittery, even inside the White House, since the recent attempt on the President's life in California.

Hartmann's voice may not have carried into the Oval Office but several other offices obviously picked up the roar. I noticed secretaries craning their necks to see who was shouting. Hartmann gives one final burst: ''We always get screwed!''

Kaye Pullen traipses into my office after we return and says:

''We had at least ten people in the Oval Office this morning, all editing what the President should say on decontrol of oil prices. Rumsfeld, Marsh, Hartmann, myself . . .''

I stop her and ask: "How did Rumsfeld and Hartmann get along?"

"Stern," Kaye reports. "Real stern. But they let the President get in a few words."

She exits laughing.

The speechwriting staff is not anti-Rumsfeld but we are aware it is his fine hand that blocks accreditation to the White House Mess for some, better parking for others. He is a person of detail but, it strikes us, a petty individual.

I ponder Rumsfeld's obvious jealousy of Henry Kissinger. He and Hartmann lead in leaking anti-Kissinger stories. This appears to be their only point of agreement. As one story goes, Kissinger agreed when Haldeman decided to "exile" Rumsfeld to NATO in Brussels. Rumsfeld, the untried ambassador, also felt that Kissinger deliberately kept him in the dark on various aspects of U.S. foreign policy; he therefore wasn't as "sharp" as he should have been in the post. "Sharp" is a Rumsfeld word.

In the final analysis, Rumsfeld is an image-maker—slick, smooth, professing proper deference to the President—but the image he is obviously trying to create is that of himself. And he doesn't know what it is, or should be. Hartmann, the tough, old, hardened realist, saw this and began exposing it in "defense" of himself and the man he served, Gerald R. Ford.

Friday, September 12, 1975

JOHN C. CALHOUN, a black aide to Bill Baroody, and I are talking about President Ford's speeches.

"Wooden," Calhoun is saying. "Seventeen people sometimes edit them."

I reply, "Like the speech I wrote for the hardware industry in Chicago."

"This is killing him," Calhoun says.

"Listen to this one," I answer. "Between Theis and everyone else who took a crack at the speech I just wrote for the black Baptists, this is what they tried to cut out of the President's remarks:

"Historical reference to slavery. Dropping a quote from Martin

Luther King on 'I have a dream' because he and Dr. Jackson, the Baptist leader, didn't always agree. That blacks also spilled blood in defense of America. Busing and blacks. Quality education. And some political references.''

''What happened?'' Calhoun asks.

''I begged,'' I reply. ''I literally begged saying it had to be an emotional speech or it would be a dead one.''

Calhoun emphasizes:

''They're killing the President all right. That girl in California missed but these guys are doing it slowly. They're afraid. They cut out the heart, the emotion, to be safe.''

I leave Calhoun's office and a colleague pulls me aside. He wants to know if I knew Stan Scott, a black aide to the President, planned to leave in a few months. I had heard the rumor. He confides:

''So Stan went over to see Rumsfeld as part of winding things up. And Rumsfeld tells him what a great guy he is and what a great job he has done. Listen, I know that Rumsfeld put the skids to Scott. That's Rumsfeld. That's what makes it tough to deal with him. And I have known him for years. You never know which Rumsfeld you are talking with. He likes to settle things privately—no noise.''

I say nothing. He continues:

''I know why Rumsfeld and Hartmann don't get along. It's a matter of turf. Hartmann wants to hold onto his turf. Rumsfeld wants it all but he's afraid that Hartmann will make noise.

''Hartmann doesn't attend meetings. Do you know that? Domestic Council meetings, other meetings. That's why the speechwriters are behind in policy changes. Hartmann isn't informed on them until later.

''That's why some people don't want to say too much to you speechwriters on policy. They don't want to seem too close to you. Rummy might not like it. That's bad, man, real bad.''

I leave him without saying much other than:

''It'd be nice to have everyone on the same team for the campaign next year.''

I wander on and Kathy Wooten, one of our secretaries, stops me. She is talking about the President's trip to New Hampshire yesterday. Mr. Ford motored about 120 miles through the state, stopping at various towns to give speeches in behalf of Louis Wyman, the Republican candidate in a runoff race for the U.S. Senate. Kathy enthuses:

"Don Rumsfeld just said it was tremendous—just tremendous. Big, warm crowds with a lot of applause."

This is the public Rumsfeld. He is projecting a different view privately. He and others seriously question the amount of traveling the President is doing. Mr. Ford is visiting a dozen or more states this month, delivering about thirty speeches that we have written and ad-libbing many more.

Warren Rustand insists this frenetic pace is entirely Mr. Ford's idea. Rumsfeld and others have stepped back to second-guess but no one goes forward to suggest to the President that he may be speaking politically more than a year too early.

I am surprised by one aspect of the President's travel, the assassination incident involving Lynnette Alice Fromme in Sacramento. There has been little or no discussion of it among White House staff members. It is almost as if the incident never took place. Perhaps the staff is reminded of how fast they, as well as a President, may exit the White House.

Among the first to go would be Rumsfeld. Rockefeller's staff distrusts him and that is a certain signal that the Vice President does, too. The Rumsfeld crowd is again bad-mouthing Rocky. They now say that he tried to make an endrun around Rumsfeld in an effort to sell a "bad program" to the President.

The plan envisages a $100-billion public corporation that would work on research and development in the field of energy. It's claimed that Rocky tried to get Mr. Ford to accept it without going through channels. The Vice President's men insist he has the right to go directly to the President on major legislation. Everyone accuses everyone else of leaking the story to the *New York Times* to further their own ends.

The bitterness between some in the White House West Wing and Rocky's people continues. Mr. Ford apparently is not inclined to do anything about it.

Monday, September 15, 1975

SENATOR HENRY BELLMON IS IRATE and telling me so. The Oklahoma Republican says:

"President Ford tricked the farmers of Oklahoma. He told us to plant and we planted. Then, George Meany stepped in and said his unions wouldn't load the grain on the ships to Russia. Now, Meany steps out and President Ford says we still can't sell to the Russians. He tricked us all right and, unless he says something about this whole grain deal, he will be booed off the platform in Oklahoma City.''

Mr. Ford is scheduled to address the Oklahoma state fair in four days. He wants to talk about energy. Bellmon says the President better talk about the grain deal with the Russians or "our people will be real sore.''

I carry this message to Theis, who asks the latest on the Russian grain deal. I tell him that the President met with the head of the American Farm Bureau Federation and other agricultural leaders in the Oval Office this morning. Mr. Ford turned down their request for an immediate lifting of his suspension of grain sales to the Soviet Union.

"What do you think?'' Theis asks.

"Bellmon's very irritated,'' I reply. "I think he wants something positive said at the state fair.''

"Call Butz. Call whomever you have to. Get some answers.''

I start with Paul Leach who handles agriculture on the Domestic Council. He asks me to hold off on Butz. He wants to speak with Seidman. I don't hear from Leach so I call him on Tuesday.

"I'm still working with Seidman,'' he reports. "Seidman is holding this one close to his vest. I'll get back to you.''

I tell Theis and he says Hartmann is anxious to get things settled by 2 P.M. I advise Leach of this.

I try to get other speech material typed but the secretaries can't handle it. The front office is a jangle of phones and clicking typewriters. I meet Pullen in the hall and she says she had to take a day off because she was "becoming hostile about the job, the whole business.'' Orben, who made the last road trip with the President, says the speech I wrote for the (black) National Baptist Convention was interrupted thirty times with applause. He adds that he hadn't thought much of the speech. On this occasion, our gag writer wasn't kidding. He thought it was a lousy speech.

There's now a defensive attitude in the White House about the President's travels. He has logged about 120,000 miles in his thirteen months in office and visited some forty states. The scheduling office says the President will step up his travel and speeches next year.

The deadline for Oklahoma state fair speech input has come and gone. I am left holding my pencil. I put some paper into the typewriter and say to myself for the hundredth time:

"Remember, you don't make policy. You only write it. Sit tight and wait for our leaders. But go ahead and write, since they need something to say."

Wednesday, September 17, 1975

I AM IN THE MIDST of writing the President's Oklahoma state fair speech. Theis is again cutting the color and emotion out of the speech, which is a sharp attack on Congress. Agnes Waldron, who urged me to leave the emotion in after I suggested Theis would cut it, maintains that Theis will be less willing to edit out emotion from the speeches that I write henceforth.

Theis had edited out most of the emotion from the speech I prepared for the President's appearance before the National Baptist Convention. The President asked us where the emotion was in the speech at a meeting last week. It was a delicate moment. I didn't want to say that Theis had cut it. I merely said the address needed it. After the meeting, Theis allowed me to put the emotion back into the speech. Bob Orben, who made the trip as our staff rep, reported back to Theis that the speech was well received. Theis then told me, "I guess you were right."

Nevertheless, he now edits out most of the color again and we are giving the President another wooden speech. Griping by individual staff members is increasing. Orben, for example, has been sounding off repeatedly in recent days. He tells the staff that outsiders think Hollywood or show biz is a crazy, mixed up world, but describes our speechwriting operation as "chaos" bordering on "insanity."

Today is no exception. Bill Seidman, with the assistance of his assistant Roger Porter, Paul Leach of the Domestic Council, and Paul MacAvoy of the Council of Economic Advisors, sends me an insert for the Oklahoma speech. This one tops anything Seidman has ever dreamed up. The following is Seidman's long insert:

"The immediate challenge which faces us is whether our abundant crop this year will be used wisely. Unfortunately, inventories of wheat and the expected inventories of corn are still far below our long-term average levels and below those considered safe in a period when the economy is beginning to grow rapidly. It is critical that we keep livestock to meet demands next year. Unless there are sufficient grain supplies available in the coming months, ranchers and feed-lot operators will reduce their livestock herds, pushing meat prices down in the near term but resulting in skyrocketing meat prices next year. In the absence of ample feed grain stocks both farmers and the economy as a whole will suffer.

"While our crops look good, and we expect a record harvest, it is still premature to predict with any confidence our final production. We do expect further purchases of grain by the Soviet Union. But we must not allow the reduction of American cattle and feed-lot production to return to the unacceptable low levels of early this year."

Theis scrawls across the top of the Seidman insert: *"Translate into English."*

Seidman emphasizes that the U.S. has achieved a record wheat crop and expects a record corn crop to be harvested by the end of the year. At the same time, he warns of below-level wheat and corn inventories. He frightens hell out of already worried ranchers by talking about a critical need to keep livestock in the face of possible depressed prices. This astonishing sentence would shake up the most rock-ribbed farmer: "In the absence of ample feed grain stocks, both agricultural producers and the economy as a whole will suffer." Seidman boasts of record crops on one hand and pushes the panic button on prices with the other.

I call Claude Gifford, an assistant to Secretary Butz at Agriculture, who listens while I read the Seidman statement. Gifford begins cautiously, "It's thoroughly confusing."

"That's all?" I ask.

"It pits the farmer against the rancher," says Gifford.

I ask Gifford for his opinion on the statement and he suggests that I quietly bury it. He suggests I write that the farmer will be able to plan with real certainty under a proposed long-term grain deal with the Soviet Union. He stresses there is nothing more important to the farmer at the moment than security when he is producing full crops. He doesn't want to be left without a market.

Instead of the Seidman insert, which I do bury with Theis's agreement, I write the following:

"Let me review events so there will be no misunderstanding on

163

the part of the farmer or anyone else about what is happening with respect to a possible grain agreement with the Soviet Union.

"First, it is essential to understand that Soviet grain purchases from the United States have fluctuated considerably in recent years. In 1971-72, for example, the United States exported 2.8 million metric tons of grain to the Soviet Union. In 1972-73, that figure soared to 13.8 million metric tons and it plummeted to 2.2 million metric tons in 1974-75.

"In this crop year we have already sold 10.2 million metric tons and the Soviets want to buy still more. These wide fluctuations, these peaks and valleys, have brought about serious repercussions in price and in marketing both here at home and around the world. They have caused serious international shipping complications. The United States wants a solid agreement from the Soviet Union on the future grain purchases. The American farmer would benefit tremendously from such an agreement . . .

"I am hopeful that the United States and the Soviet Union will soon come to an agreement that will benefit both our countries."

I meet Mary Weidner, a girl who simply showed up at the White House, asked for a job and got one in the scheduling office. Mary is a Marquette University Journalism School grad and, since I am also one, we are alma mater buddies.

I had quietly griped to Mary about the fact that the scheduling office had set 4 P.M. as the time of the presidential address in Oklahoma City. That would be 5 P.M. Eastern time, making it extremely difficult for the President to make the evening TV news.

I nudge Mary on the subject again because the Oklahoma speech is now shaping up as a big one. Suddenly, she opens up:

"Jack, Warren Rustand plays tennis three hours a day. What do you expect!"

Taken aback because Mary is a mild person, I ask: "Really?"

She replies: "He plays all the time and any time."

The scheduling office is another mess in the White House. Rustand is rarely able to explain the rationale behind a presidential appearance, his timing (as for the Oklahoma speech) is often questionable, and his combination of trips is erratic. On the latter, the President is making two trips to the West Coast in three weeks, mystifying just about everyone in the White House. The Rustand reply is typical: "That's the way it worked out."

We meet with the President in midafternoon. He shows us (Hartmann, Theis, Friedman and me) three color photos of his golden retriever, Liberty, and her nine new puppies. The President, chortling like a proud father, tells us:

"We had to take Liberty out of the room where the pups were so she could receive some shots. She started scratching the wall, trying to get back to the pups, until we let her go."

We discuss the Oklahoma speech. The President wants to be absolutely sure that the American farmer knows he's doing his best to come up with a long-term grain agreement with the Soviets. He also wants to make it plain that he didn't cave in to George Meany when the AFL-CIO walked off the docks, refusing to load grain bound for Russia. They later returned to work.

During most of our discussion, I notice that Hartmann has a cigarillo in his mouth but is unable to find a match to light it. Finally, the President opens a desk drawer and tosses Hartmann a book of matches, saying: "Here. Don't say I never gave you anything."

Hartmann laughs.

We conclude with the President in good spirits. He is smiling and laughing often. And yet, the press is roasting him today. Louis Wyman, for whom he campaigned long and hard in New Hampshire, has lost the special Senate race to John Durkin by a wide margin. The President has accepted it without complaint.

I attempt the same equanimity. I put aside grain sales. It is our twentieth wedding anniversary and I have an autographed "wedding anniversary" photo for Joy from the President. President and Mrs. Ford also sent my wife and me a warm telegram extending their best wishes.

Thursday, September 18, 1975

IT IS A LITTLE AFTER 9 P.M. in Bob Hartmann's office. We are reviewing, line by line, the Oklahoma speech. It is now in its fifth draft.

We have in effect three different versions of the speech. I wrote one; another includes a series of inserts favored by Agriculture Secretary Butz; and a third was written by General Scowcroft of the National Security Council. Butz wishes to say as little as possible about details of a pending grain deal with the

Soviet Union. He says he doesn't want to tip our bargaining
position to the Russians.

I have taken a middle-of-the-road position. The speech gives
sufficient detail so the President can stand before the nation's
farmers and say: I'm working in your interest by trying to get a
long-range agreement with the Russians, rather than a
year-by-year decision in which they may or may not buy after you
have planted a full crop. Scowcroft's version is somewhat tedious.

We are working on a fifth draft because of continued
differing views. In addition, Scowcroft has been working most of
the day on a meeting between Soviet Foreign Minister Gromyko,
Secretary Kissinger and the President on everything from the
nuclear talks to the Mideast. His draft is late. The scheduled
one-hour meeting between the President and Gromyko ran nearly
three hours.

Hartmann snaps:

"Where the hell has our staff coordinator (Rumsfeld) been all
day?"

Hartmann, coming to the end of the Oklahoma speech
review, is talking out loud:

"I haven't written the goddamn law speech for Stanford
(University) yet. Friedman is in there typing and he still hasn't
written his speech. Here we are with the President leaving
tomorrow and every goddamn thing is up in the air. Have a
drink, Jack, have a drink." I decline.

Hartmann is standing in front of a cabinet pouring himself a
drink as I leave. He is shouting, "Where the hell is Friedman
with his speech?"

Friedman is typing madly in a small room nearby. Kathy
Wooten, one of our secretaries, is coming across the street in the
rain from the old Executive Office Building. She will help out
with the late typing. It is nearly 10 P.M. The rest of the White
House's West Wing is quiet. It is raining outside as I run across
the parking lot to my office.

I pick up a copy of tomorrow's *Washington Post* on the way
home. It has the whole story on how we plan to approach the
Russians on the grain deal, quoting "two government sources."
Secretary Butz's secrecy is out the window—or maybe it's a trial
balloon to see what the Russians think. Who knows in all of this
confusion? It rains all the way home.

Tuesday, September 23, 1975

THE PRESIDENT, usually in his office at 7:45 A.M., is not there today. He does not arrive until well after 9 A.M. It is believed the President and Mrs. Ford had a long, heart-to-heart chat into the night on the second attempt to assassinate him in seventeen days.

Sara Jane Moore, described as both a radical and a former FBI informant, fired as Mr. Ford was leaving a hotel in downtown San Francisco. The President buckled momentarily as the shot was fired. Then he was grabbed and pushed into his limousine by secret service agents. The car sped directly to Air Force One.

Today, reaction inside the White House is this: the President should cut his furious travel schedule around the nation. (His family should try to talk him out of the frenetic pace of his travels.) He should no longer plunge into crowds. (He hadn't plunged into a crowd yesterday.)

The President is saying over and over privately what he has said publicly. He cannot, as President, buckle under to the "crazies" but has an obligation to the American people to get out and meet them. He must exchange views.

What happened to the Secret Service? Since they questioned Mrs. Moore before the attempt, why didn't they have her locked up until the President left San Francisco?

The word from both parties on the Hill is that Mr. Ford should cool it for a while. One crazy fires up the imagination of another, a new domino theory.

No one in the White House is suggesting the mandatory federal registration of handguns. Others are doing so on the Hill. The administration "handgun bill" is much weaker than anything proposed by the Democrats but the President is sticking by that proposal despite the latest events.

The President has told aides he will definitely return to California late this month for fund-raising events in Los Angeles and San Francisco. What is wrong with a scheduling office that has the President booked into California three times in a month?

By midmorning, the White House had counted about 200 telegrams and thirty-five telephone calls. Some 115 expressed "congratulations" at the escape. Twenty-three suggested tougher gun control measures; eight urged less travel by the President; and the rest were various suggestions, including five who advised the President to keep traveling at his current pace.

Beyond the furor over the latest assassination attempt is a furious fight inside the White House on another subject. I first got wind of it last week when Milt Friedman recounted to Hartmann with some glee that a "helluva fight" was taking place over the Rockefeller proposal that would create a government corporation to finance up to $100 billion in energy projects during the next decade.

Friedman, who attended some of the meetings, described the scene as an all-out battle, a "blockbuster," which would be "impossible to reconcile."

Alan Greenspan, Bill Simon and Jim Lynn, three of the President's closest advisers, strongly oppose the plan. Greenspan, in an internal memo that is beginning to leak to the press, argues that the new agency ERFCO (Energy-Related Facilities Corporation) would have a "large potential for real or perceived corrupt practices."

Vice President Rockefeller, Rogers Morton at Commerce, Arthur Burns at the Fed and John Dunlop at Labor support the plan in varying degrees. They see it as a major way to sustain economic recovery. All believe it will act as a public assurance that national growth will not be stymied by energy shortfall. They are telling the President that this "modified form" of government intervention is the only method to do the job.

Those who oppose the program do not say so directly but they make it clear that such a policy would be inconsistent with much of the President's rhetoric about getting government out of business and would not jibe with many of his policy positions. They imply that the public might interpret the formation of such an agency as essentially a "bail-out" device for big business. In other words, the President would be willing to bail out business, but not a big city like New York which continues in dire trouble.

Would this be further encouragement for business, especially those needing capital, to turn to government as an answer to their problems? Will this encourage massive federal handouts of capital in the future, with the federal government (the American taxpayer) taking all the risks while private industries walk away with the profits?

These are some of the arguments being batted back and forth. But suddenly, startlingly, with disagreement on all sides of him, President Ford decides to go with the Rockefeller plan. Why? Very few people, if any, know. Friedman, who wrote the speech outlining the plan, is as mystified as anyone. Hartmann, whom I watched edit it, was still trying to find out who disagreed with whom about the plan.

The entire speech staff is stunned. This does not represent the conservative, oldtime religion of Gerald Ford of the past year. This is what Gerald Ford has been denouncing for a full year as "expediency." What about the budget deficit? Will these loan guarantees be managed by smart, backdoor financing that will not technically increase the national debt?

One thing is certain. Never again will I write a speech for the President with the same conviction about getting government out of the businessman's hair.

Wednesday, September 24, 1975

THE DOMESTIC COUNCIL is quietly jubilant. They have defeated Rumsfeld. At least that is their interpretation. One of their leaders confides to me that President Ford's acceptance of Rockefeller's $100-billion energy project is the Vice President's greatest victory since assuming the post.

Mr. Ford will ask the Congress to authorize the Energy Independence Agency this year. The agency would underwrite the construction of coal-powered, geothermal and nuclear energy projects. Funds would be made available for research into new sources of energy.

A story is being leaked to the press that presidential acceptance of the plan represents a Rockefeller victory over Mr. Ford's top economic advisers. The Rocky men don't see it precisely that way. They see Alan Greenspan, Bill Simon and Jim Lynn as competent professionals who are expressing views based on long and tried experience. It's not considered a "victory" over the economic advisers. But it is seen as a "magnificent victory" over Don Rumsfeld, the President's staff coordinator. A Rocky man remarks:

"What does Rumsfeld know about economics? What does Rumsfeld know about the intricacies of long-range finance? What does he know about foreign policy or transportation or health or commerce for that matter?

"Rumsfeld says he's just a coordinator, just a traffic cop who gives advice or direction when asked. Forget it. He's what some people might call an 'influence peddler.'"

Rockefeller himself clearly believes Rumsfeld would like to see him dropped from the ticket so Rumsfeld might be in a position to take the VP spot on the 1976 ticket. Barry Goldwater's statement that Mr. Ford should have a young running mate who could step in and wage a winning campaign in 1980 has not fallen on entirely deaf ears at the White House. Rumsfeld has an extensive team, the nucleus of a shadow government, already operating for him inside the White House.

Mr. Ford's sudden decision to accept the Rockefeller plan, despite the division among his top advisers, is based on simple and direct reasoning. As Rocky's people put it:

"He simply said the time has come for action on energy independence. Someone must move."

Simon fought the plan as hard as he could, saying it was a political and economic mistake. Rocky phoned Simon, blistering him for leaking his views. One adviser put it this way in Greenspan's case, "Alan laid his body on the tracks on this and the train ran right over him."

Opposition still exists despite public announcement of the President's decision. And reasons for the disagreement are still leaking to newsmen. Some of the reasons are ideological. The program technically takes most of the cost out of the federal budget process by a technique known as "off-budget borrowing." This eliminates lower priority items in the regular budget and tilts toward the concealment of total spending. Guarantees to business would actually cover up large deficits in the federal budget. It violates the entire spirit of Mr. Ford's public statements on big government and continued increases in government spending.

The essence of the plan is that the federal government's virtually unlimited credit and fund-raising ability is being used to provide capital for energy-related projects for private business. The new corporation would float federally guaranteed bond issues in public markets. It would then re-lend the money to private energy development companies.

Thursday, September 25, 1975

Privately, I happen to agree with the Rockefeller proposal. I believe the President has made the right decision but for the wrong reasons. His decision contradicts both the spirit and substance of his speeches. I do not believe energy is only a national issue. It is, in my mind, an international issue. Internationally, United States business has suffered because of the cohesive forces working against it. These forces are the alliances between foreign governments and firms of their nations. The Japanese are the most notorious example of this. The Japanese government and its firms operate abroad as a single unit. U.S. embassies abroad, while sometimes cooperative, take a general hands-off position with respect to American companies operating in their areas.

The argument may be made that I have leapfrogged the real problem, the government getting involved in business. The facts of life are that the federal government is now up to its neck in American business in one form or another. This energy financing package is not a divergence from the norm but rather an example of it.

The central question being asked by the White House press corps is: Was the President's mentality changed by his "cronies" from the business world?

Rod Markley, for example, is the sixty-two-year-old chief lobbyist of Ford Motor Company in Washington. He has been a friend of the President's for some twenty-five years. Markley is synonymous with business chiefs like William G. Whyte of U.S. Steel and Leon Parma, a San Diego manufacturer. These are some of the "big" businessmen seen so often with the President on golf links and whose homes he still visits for private dinners. These men think one way: business.

Deep down inside, President Ford's relations with these influence-peddlers bothers the hell out of me. The swiftness of his energy decision bothers the hell out of me.

Thursday, September 25, 1975

PRESIDENT FORD still privately insists that he must and will continue traveling. On that basis, I am writing a draft for use on October 7, 1975, at Kings Mountain, North Carolina, the site of a patriot victory in the Revolutionary War. He will speak of the need for mutual trust and understanding, of his travels and efforts to build such bridges in our society.

What does the President hope to gain by this speech? Who is he trying to reach by that address? What is the aim of accepting a speech such as Kings Mountian?

No one has the answers.

For the past week, there's a new wrinkle in our operation. Bob Hartmann has asked, according to our secretaries, that the names of the speechwriters not be contained on the copy that goes to the President. He's quoted as saying this might influence the way Mr. Ford may feel about a particular speech.

This is an odd request because the writer of each speech usually sees the President personally when a draft is ready for his consideration. The President will see the writer face to face which, according to the logic presented us, would influence the President's feelings about a speech as much if not more than the writer's name on each draft.

It turns out, at least in the examples I have seen, that the writers' names are now being eliminated from all draft copies. No one on the staff is sure of the reason but there is considerable conjecture about it. This includes the fact that Hartmann does no more original speechwriting than any member of the staff. As a matter of fact, many weeks he does less.

Rumors about a shakeup of the speechwriting staff persist. WTOP, a local round-the-clock news operation, reported yesterday morning that White House "sources" say an "overhaul of the speechwriting staff" is in the wind. Hartmann and Rumsfeld deny it, according to the broadcast, but obviously someone is leaking such a story.

Friday, September 26, 1975

BOB CONSIDINE, a friend and colleague of many years, died in a New York hospital yesterday. I wrote today a statement for the President on Bob's passing. It has been botched by the front office with the usual paintbrush approach to writing. I recount it here, the way I wrote it and the way Bob's friends would have written it, because Bob Considine has been a good influence on mine and many others' lives for nearly a quarter century:

"Bob Considine was a great reporter—one of the greatest. He always said that was his greatest accolade: reporter. Bob was also a great man. It can be said without fear of challenge that Bob never made an enemy in the world, and that is saying something because the world was literally his beat. It is likely that no reporter in history traveled as much or was as prolific as Bob. The quality and scope of his writing, his personal courage and his outstanding character all made him a superstar long before the term was ever used. Bob used to say that only three things mattered in life: work, family and faith. He may have forgotten a fourth: friends. No reporter in America had more friends than Bob, in and out of his profession. We will miss him. We will miss his stories, his gentle good humor and, above all, his sterling example of personal integrity. I join Bob's dear wife, Millie, and the Considine children in their prayers, in the words that Bob was so fond of quoting: 'May the angels lead thee into paradise and may the martyrs receive thee at thy coming . . .' "

Some of the old days walk through the mist of the past into the present. . . .

I can see him standing there at the counter of the tiny coffee bar in Castel Gandolfo, just off the main square near the papal summer home. Bob is belting down a double Scotch and orders another. I know we have to write and I take an orange soda pop. Bob is talking:

"Jack, I was moved in there, genuinely moved. Like the centuries were coming together and history was pounding on me saying that this was momentous—really momentous."

Bob was referring to the fact that we had gotten inside the papal villa, up a stairway and into the death room of Pope Pius XII. We were, according to those present, the first lay people to see the Pope dead. Eugenio Pacelli, the Roman nobleman surrounded by six tall candles and clad in the raiment of a dead Pope, was serene in death. I wrote most of a column about his hands, as if chiseled by Michelangelo. Bob and I knelt for a long time looking into the face of the dead pontiff, catching the colors in the room, the hum of priests' prayers for his eternal soul. I felt I could hear our two hearts beating.

Bob wrote under a dateline I suggested: "At the Bedside of the Pope, Castel Gandolfo, Italy." Red Smith, a Catholic and great sportswriter, later kidded Bob and me about that. "How the hell did you get a typewriter to write in there?" Red asked. Of course, we didn't. But what a dateline!

There was the time that Bob and I went to the small, farm town

173

of Sotto Il Monte and spent the entire afternoon interviewing Pope John XXIII's brothers and other relatives. Bob kept egging me to obtain a bottle of their "Dago red" and I did. And his quip: "How the heck does an Irishman like you speak such good Italian?" He drank "the Pope's wine" with buddies at Toots Shor's.

Walking through the streets of Paris in the night rain with Bob, talking about the love of God and, limping from a few drinks too many, wondering where we could go to Mass in the morning. . . . Sitting in a Milan restaurant—it could have been anywhere, spoofing one another about Italy's contribution to America. He would say Enrico Fermi and I would counter with Eddie Arcaro. He would say Enrico Caruso and I would blurt the DiMaggio boys. He'd say Columbus and I'd say Carnera (the fighter). What a crazy, wonderful world that was, far from the home office, far from its politics, thinking that we were the inheritors of Hemingway, Fitzgerald and others who cast part of their lot in Europe, away from the rat race.

That is past.

The President's daily news summary quotes Don Rumsfeld as telling people that Ron Nessen is through. Bill Greener, Nessen's deputy and a former assistant to Rumsfeld at the Cost of Living Council, is quoted as telling reporters that he will take over as press secretary within a month or two. But, as Greener was saying that, Rumsfeld is quoted as telling still others that Greener is not up to the job. He wants someone with "prestige"—like columnist Dave Broder of the *Washington Post*. It's my understanding that Broder turned down the offer before Nessen accepted it.

The news summary quotes an article entitled "The Manipulated President" by Richard Reeves in *New York* magazine which says:

"The tone of the gossip radiating from the White House these days is also more vicious than anything I ever heard around McGovern. It is a day-to-day demonstration that Gerald Ford has never really gained control of his White House. A lot of people there seem to be in business for themselves—ambitions and the pettiest passions are running loose, and underlying the whispers is implied contempt for the man at the top."

This analysis was manifested yesterday afternoon while I was waiting with some of our staff to see the President. Dick Cheney, Rumsfeld's assistant, came out of the President's office. He stopped at Nell Yates' desk in the waiting room to phone Frank Zarb, asking

Zarb to meet him in the White House. Paul Theis made a deliberate effort, going out of his way to walk over where Cheney was standing as he phoned, to speak with Cheney. When Dick hung up, Paul said hello and asked Cheney how he was. Cheney acted as if he had never seen Theis in his life and rushed from the room.

The old Rumsfeld-Hartmann feud was again exemplified. Here were two grown men in vital positions in the White House unable to communicate, engaged in the childish jealousy demonstrated by their staffs.

The atmosphere was quite different in the presence of Mr. Ford. He zipped through the speeches quickly, relaxed and ready with a smile. I felt refreshed seeing him so steady after the latest assassination attempt and amid the unhealthy atmosphere around the White House recently.

It is the wettest September in Washington in forty years. Because of the floods around town, most of our staff did not arrive at the office until about 10:30 A.M. Perhaps it is the weather. Maybe it is one of the valleys amid the peaks at the White House. But I decide to do something I haven't done in a very long time—to go to a bar and lift a glass to better days with old buddies like Bob Considine.

Monday, September 29, 1975

GOSSIP IN THE WHITE HOUSE today is a bare-knuckles political punchout. Hartmann and the Rockefeller team are blamed but no one is sure of the source of the "hatchet job" done on Rumsfeld by Evans and Novak over the weekend. The Washington columnists blistered Rumsfeld, implying he's trying to dump Rockefeller from the Ford 1976 ticket and obtain the nomination for himself.

Some believe Hartmann, already notorious for leaking stories, to be the source of the column because of this quote:

"While the Ford campaign is technically removed from the White House, Rumsfeld actually runs it."

Hartmann, still listed as a top political adviser to the President, is known to be very upset. He believes Rumsfeld connived behind his back to obtain the job as Mr. Ford's liaison with the Republican National Committee, as well as to place Bo Callaway as the director of the Ford Campaign Committee. Rumsfeld's answer is to treat Hartmann's abilities with contempt. This is done privately, of course. Hartmann, a rough-and-tumble two-fisted fighter who is known as a "mean" scrapper, scares Rumsfeld. That is why Rumsfeld is so circumspect in his criticism of the way Hartmann runs the speechwriting staff. He drops slight digs and lets others pick up the line.

Others insist that the Rocky people have begun a counteroffensive against Rumsfeld. They won a major victory by receiving presidential acceptance of Rocky's $100 billion energy program. The second victory came over this weekend when the *New York Times* ran a three-column front-page story with a photo of the Vice President headlined: "Rockefeller Making an Impact on Policy."

Evans and Novak write of a "fascinating manifestation of backstage intrigue with far-reaching implications" at the White House. Dick Cheney, Rumsfeld's thirty-four-year-old assistant, is reported increasingly taking care of White House business. They are right on the button because Cheney is moving more and more into such areas as energy, agriculture and staff work. Rumsfeld sidles more and more into politics. That prompts talk inside the White House and out that Rumsfeld is making a run at Rocky's job.

As Evans and Novak correctly point out, Rockefeller's foray to win substantial southern conservative support is considered mediocre at best and a failure at worst. The Harris poll shows Rockefeller to be a drawback to the Ford campaign.

Republican Senators Brock and Baker of Tennessee and Ambassador Bush are considered possible Veep choices, but none is considered the suave gut-fighter that Rumsfeld is, and none works at the President's elbow.

The Rockefeller staff is particularly upset at reports that Rummy is bad-mouthing their boss to conservative Republican leaders as he speaks to them on party matters. It's suggested that Rocky is getting old.

It's my feeling that Nelson Rockefeller, a real gentleman, will move heaven and hell if it comes to a fight with Rumsfeld. I have seen him at close range as a reporter, and I know Rocky is about as shrewd and tough as they come if angered. Rumsfeld, who many in the White House know prefers quiet battles in private, would not be permitted the luxury of a clandestine battle by Rocky and his men. Rumsfeld might well back away because Rocky could wipe him out politically and professionally forever. He would be far better off biding his time since he's only forty-three.

The *New York Times* story, based on an interview with Rockefeller, is meant as a warning to Rumsfeld and those who oppose the VP on energy. He's saying that he will fight for the program. The story is consistent with indications I get from the Domestic Council staff. This quote in the interview is stressed to me by one of Rocky's aides:

"I understand the people around the President and how these things work, and I was determined that I was not going to let anything get between me and the President, that I would not cause him trouble with his own people or with the cabinet or anybody else, you see.

"Because that's when they cut you off. If you can't see the President, you might as well forget it."

Wow! That's Rocky talking to both the President and Rumsfeld via the *New York Times*. And Rocky talking to all of Washington, saying, according to his colleagues:

"I'm a team player, fellas. I'm open about this. I'm leveling. So I won't accept any stonewalling from anyone."

It's too early to determine Rocky's chances for success, but it's obvious his proposal faces a real fight in the Congress.

At this moment, on the basis of events of the past several weeks, I look back on all the arguing, backstabbing and quibbling another way. Where is the post-Watergate morality in the White House?

The leaks are pouring from the White House almost daily. Bo Callaway's ungentlemanly treatment of Rockefeller is "old politics." Feuds are erupting all over the White House. The exodus continues of good men from the Justice Department, the CIA and other government agencies under fire. Where is the "new direction" for the nation? The truth is: there is no new direction. We are living with the old morality and, inside, it hurts.

Theis calls a staff meeting in the late afternoon. The speechwriters as well as the people in research and the secretaries attend. It is a rather astonishing session—astonishing in its absence of substance although this is the first staff meeting in months.

Theis opens it by thanking all for working long hours. He explains this has been a difficult period with a flood of presidential speeches, but the staff has done well.

The real word around the White House is that some of the speeches are poor and the President should get one or two new speechwriters. This word is coming from Rumsfeld and Nessen. Few know just how chaotic the situation really is; the staff still gets very little direction from anyone and each speech continues to be edited by as many as sixteen different people. Instead of new writers, the President needs to restructure the entire speechmaking process, from the reason for acceptance through the research and writing of the speech to actual delivery.

At the meeting, the researchers zero in on the Library of Congress. They say the White House receives little assistance there since the librarians insist they function for the Congress, not the White House. I suggest that we take the library's "green sheet," which lists new publications, and simply order those which look promising. Friedman says we must be careful not to exert any kind of pressure on the library staff because "many of them are liberals and super-liberals. They may try to get to the *Washington Post* to cause what they hope will be a scandal."

Friedman continues with an attack on our researchers saying in effect that he doesn't need them. I defend the researchers, stressing that they should continue an "issues file" so that when the writers have to produce a speech on short notice they will have sufficient material to work with, particularly interpretive articles.

Theis explains that the White House is now trying to set up a retrieval system to obtain material from the Republican National Committee. What material do they have that we do not? Nothing much, Theis adds, they clip the newspapers and magazines as our researchers do. In short, they might have an article or two that we might not have.

The session drones on for more than an hour. It offers little more hope than the meetings that we held nine months or a year ago. One new thought is offered. Theis announces that Friedman will chair meetings once a week with appropriate White House and other government officials on upcoming speeches. This is a welcome possibility. However, I don't understand how it can be done since we sometimes are covering three or four different topics.

The meeting closes quietly. There is no more agreement among the researchers and speechwriters than there ever was. We have solved nothing. Theis did hold out hope that we might get some direction from appropriate officials. Apparently, we may no longer need to plead for their time or ease around them by talking with their speechwriters or public affairs directors.

After the meeting, Theresa Rosenberger, one of the researchers, confides to me that there's a feud between their staff and Friedman. He will not work with anyone but Agnes Waldron, Theresa says, and collaborates with Agnes only under duress.

Apparently, there's also a feud between Friedman and some secretaries. Theresa and other researchers claim Friedman is rude and Judy Morton supports them, saying she will not work with Friedman outside the office on the road. Judy advises the researchers that she has reported this to Theis.

One might conclude that this is worthless office gossip. However, I am beginning to conclude that such trivia is not unimportant. The reason is simple. We are not pulling together in the President's behalf. Mr. Ford is not being well served.

As I return to my office, Kaye Pullen gives me some more bad news. Theis has advised her that she is being dropped from the staff. He also suggested that a second writer might be dropped. Paul says it's an economy move dictated by Rumsfeld.

At face value, the move is not an intelligent one. The staff is drowning in speech assignments and this does not appear a propitious time to cut it. As a staff, we are barely meeting our deadlines. Even if the President cuts back his schedule, it will still be very heavy. Something is wrong here. There is something missing from this puzzle. One thing is certain. The President will not be better served by fewer speechwriters.

Kaye is crestfallen. She has done her best but concludes:

"I guess I said once too often how screwed up this place is—how we are left to do everything ourselves. I can't help it but that's me. I've got to say what's on my mind. And the truth is the speechwriting staff is without a leader."

Kaye adds that two researchers also will get the axe.

I think back to what Theis said about all of us doing a better job, about working together more, about getting ready for the campaign. That was much of his theme today. We must prepare ourselves for the campaign. We must be ready to go full speed. Yet, the fact is that as many as four people may be cut off from our staff.

It is after 7 P.M. when I leave the office for the walk across the Ellipse. The sun has set. It has been a beautiful, sunny day but somehow the sunshine has disappeared in more ways than just the evening darkness. I am disturbed by our proclamations on directness, openness and candor. Are we really direct, open and candid with one another?

Tuesday, September 30, 1975

"CREDIBILITY" is a critical public problem. There are many questions about it these days in the Ford White House.

Ron Nessen has been double-talking to the White House press corps ever since Sara Jane Moore took a shot at the President in San Francisco. We are being told one thing internally while Nessen spouts another publicly. The scheduling office, Theis, our researchers, all tell me the same thing. Mrs. Ford, the Secret Service, some of his top advisers and congressional friends of the President have told him that he must curtail traveling for his own safety as well as to avert another national tragedy. Mr. Ford has agreed and made the decision to cut his open-air appearances. For example, I was writing a speech the President is to give at Kings Mountain, North Carolina, to commemorate a Revolutionary War battle. Theis told me to drop it, that it had been canceled.

The open-air speech is considered "uncontrollable" by the Secret Service. Consideration of a side trip to South Carolina to curb the protests of Senator Strom Thurmond complicated the presidential appearance. Nessen implies the trip may still be on and the North Carolina sponsors have not been notified that the President's visit is off.

Why is Nessen so sensitive about admitting the President will not be making as many trips as scheduled for security reasons?

The necessity for all this elaborate smoke-blowing is a statement by the President after Sara Jane Moore shot at him. Mr. Ford declared in strong terms that the President would not be held "hostage" or intimidated by the crazies of the country. He would continue his scheduled travels.

180

Therefore Nessen and Rumsfeld do not wish to admit a curtailment of travel because it might make the President look weak and retreating from his public statements. Thus, two postures must be maintained: the strength of the President's word and purpose; and, the appearance of physical bravery.

No one in the White House would quarrel with either public projection. But it's absolute fiction to maintain, as Nessen does, that the changes in the President's schedule are not based on security precautions. At the moment, Nessen is doing two things that create a credibility gap. First, he is pulling a row-back (meaning a pull-back when one is caught out too far on a limb in newspaperman's terms) and second, he is doing a camouflage job. Neither is working but White House newsmen don't press the issue because this is obviously an embarrassing moment for the White House.

This is a typical Nessen sentence at a recent White House briefing:

"Some of the trips that have been rumored or speculated about, or have been reported as being under consideration or tentative, some of these may not actually be on the President's schedule."

On the other hand, a number of White House aides have told reporters that Nessen is all wet. The President's security is definitely one of the reasons for cutting back travel, but they also point to the frenetic pace of the President's past travels. The President might be burning himself out personally and politically; therefore, the presidential travel schedule has been reviewed. In talking with the press in this manner, these aides undermine Nessen's credibility and enhance their own truthfulness.

This is a vicious practice and borders on the unethical. The aides argue, however, that they operate under a different set of rules than Nessen. He speaks for the President publicly while they do so privately. They see no contradiction in taking different public and private postures. This is, of course, an old practice in Washington. You don't want to attribute the truth to a President, a senator or a congressman, but you want the truth made public to prevent you from looking ridiculous maintaining public fictions.

But why not tell the press just that in diplomatic language? No, the decision was made to do it deviously. And, once again, a golden opportunity is missed to level with the press.

181

I am not all that convinced of post-Watergate morality in Washington. One need only look at the Federal Election Commission, which is trying to keep itself from being buried in Washington's political jungle. The Commission was born of the Watergate scandals. It was to set up legal guidelines for campaign expenditures, to avoid the horrendous examples of laundered political contributions as well as political payola and various pressures involved.

The commission, with four of its six names being former members of the House, is beginning to step on a few political toes. One immediate issue is the slush funds maintained by many members of the House and Senate. They use political contributions of one kind or another for trips back home, including payment of various expenses incurred during those visits; luncheons, newsletters mailed to voters, charity contributions of one type or another, and similar payments.

There is no formal public accounting on the sources of this money or how it is spent. Those on the outside, and even some on the inside, consider this an open door to the acceptance of "slush funds" from wealthy contributors and thus manipulation by business organizations, unions and similar contributors.

The Federal Election Commission members recently decided in a unanimous vote that these funds should be charged against the contributions and expenditures legally allowed for the next congressional election campaign. Congressmen and senators, reserving to themselves the power to overturn any commission action, balked at the recommendation. The rule has now been revised and provides as follows: such funds will be considered campaign expenditures *only* in the last two years of a senator's term and the last year of a representative's term.

Decisions like this make men like me look twice at a politician and politics. If these are public duties, then they should be paid for out of public funds. The fact is, and everyone in Washington knows it, there's a lot of hanky-panky going on with these slush funds and Congress doesn't want to face up to the unpleasantness.

The Congress is undercutting the commission at its very outset. "To the winner belong the spoils" is still a truism around this town, although that mentality is supposed to be discredited.

Yet the men and women of the Congress use every conceivable device to increase their salaries and expense accounts. They have increased their staffs and their incomes by hiding the increases in other legislation. While doing this, they vote against salary increases for the career government civil servants to prove their devotion to a balanced budget. They use cross-balloting to show they voted for an increase at one time and voted against it on another. All this is part of the post-Watergate morality on Capitol Hill.

Is it any wonder that thinking individuals, once past the glamour stages of the Capitol Dome and the front door of the White House, begin to question the real values and motivational forces of American politics?

Chapter 13
October, 1975

"Organization in the executive branch provides the means for performing systematically, promptly and accurately the research and related work essential to the orderly presentation to the President of all the pertinent facts and calculations which he must take into account in making a sound decision on any issue. Thereafter, it assures that his decision is communicated to and essential resulting action is coordinated among the appropriate agencies."

DWIGHT D. EISENHOWER

Wednesday, October 1, 1975

THE ROCKEFELLER ENERGY PLAN is still shaking window panes, chandeliers and heads around the White House. Greenspan, Simon and Lynn continue to oppose the $100-billion ten-year program. Rumsfeld claims to be the honest broker between these big three and the Domestic Council which favors it. The claim is too late, however, since Rocky's men insist Rumsfeld tipped his hand against them; therefore, they refuse to trust him.

The Domestic Council argues:

"We don't have any goals. What the administration needs is a ten-point program or some kind of agenda for the future. Nobody in the country knows what we stand for or where we're going."

I add amen. I have been saying this to Theis for months. The President must begin advocating positive ideas instead of promising more and more vetoes. He must stand for *something*.

The big three want government out of the private sector. The Rockefeller energy program would expand government's role.

It's reported around the White House today that Simon has leaked another story, this one to the *Christian Science Monitor*. There's no way of checking it out unless someone tries to finger Simon. The story, quoting a highly placed government source, says the Rocky plan will probably be killed in the Congress where both liberals and conservatives oppose it for different reasons. The liberals say it's a "giveaway" to business. The conservatives stress it will crowd the money markets as well as taking away private initiative. If not cut down in the Congress, the government source reports, the measure will be killed by the President because the Congress will have burdened the plan with unacceptable amendments.

Rocky aides insist the Vice President is sticking to his guns. When advised of Simon's opposition, Rockefeller replied to his staff, "Who is Simon? Just a bond seller."

Rocky's plan to put the government in the energy business for the next ten years with loans to enterprising industrialists is called "meddling in the marketplace" by virtually all of Mr. Ford's economic advisers. Some are willing to permit a little meddling if it doesn't go too far. Why? Burns, Seidman, Morton and Zarb recognize that the President has political problems and they see positive results from Rocky's plan: a possible break in the energy deadlock with Congress; the creation of jobs; and an acceleration in the nation's economic recovery.

That's how Mr. Ford is thought to see the proposal. However, the President has yet to discuss it in public.

Theis is on the phone saying that "the President is sore." He asks me to look into a report appearing in the presidential daily news summary which says that the United States and Poland have agreed in principle on a long-term grain deal. The President wishes to make the agreement part of his speech in Omaha. Theis says, "Didn't we tell those guys over at State and Agriculture that the President wished to make the announcement on any final grain deal with the Soviets or Poland?" I advise Theis that I told Claude Gifford, an aide to Secretary Butz at Agriculture. It is my understanding that General Scowcroft, of the National Security Council staff, was to advise the State Department. Theis asks me to move quickly.

The Agriculture public affairs office denies that it is the source of the story. I call State and speak with several energy men there. They insist that Secretary Butz broke the story himself yesterday.

Gifford calls in a few minutes and admits that words like "agreement in principle" were used in a news release and, perhaps, should not have been. I relate my conversation of several days earlier to him in which I said that the President wished to make such an announcement. Gifford asks for time to speak with Butz. In careful terms, I let him know that the President is not very pleased at this development.

About five minutes later, Butz phones me. He says that the news release is wrong. There is no agreement in principle for this crop year but for next year's and the future. Butz claims that this is old news, that the President is aware of these developments and that the final agreement will be concluded in Warsaw when the Agriculture secretary visits there at the end of November.

In polite, careful terms, I advise Butz that this is not the way the President is reading the story. Butz counters saying that he's coming to the White House on a tobacco meeting today and will speak with the President on the subject at that time. In the meantime, I am left holding the bag.

I simply change the speech to read that the United States is
now negotiating long-term grain purchase agreements with the
Soviet Union and Poland. For several hours, Theis wrestles with
the language and attempts to show there's a new grain development
with Poland. He asks for my advice and I keep saying that we have
to go with Butz.

As a reporter, I learned that a newspaper or television station
has to go with its reporter. If it does otherwise, it not only
demoralizes its staff in not backing the reporter up but, more
importantly, it is usually wrong.

I pass a Rocky aide in the hall going to lunch and ask him
how they're doing. His reply is captivating: "One run (the
President's approval), no hits, no errors."

Monday, October 6, 1975

I AM GIVEN MY FIRST political speechwriting assignment since
coming to the White House one year ago. It's a GOP fund-raiser in
Milwaukee on October 30. I study President Ford's eight previous
fund-raising efforts. After reading them, I feel a little sick.

As a reporter, I went to many of these fund-raisers and the
rosy rhetoric always came out as dishwater. I always regarded it
as a necessary charade that one endures as the price of
democracy.

On reading page after page of the President's ad libs about
what a great person this or that politician is, I am numbed by the
shallowness of it all. This is a world of unreality in which the
raised voice and the raised hope is virtually valueless. It is a brazen
show, a diverting hour if one has nothing better to do, in which
most of the audience is as much actor and actress as the speaker.

Why am I numbed? Because the show cheapens real beliefs
and real values. It is like watching one clown after another strutting
across the sawdust and the lights where the public pays to watch a
ridiculous situation. Real clowns at least do not ridicule their
audience. But in their overflowing, gushy, rich rhetoric, the
politicians do ridicule the intelligence of their audiences. And I
now see it in a man for whom I have great respect. I cannot help
thinking about the price he is paying, even as President of the
United States.

Monday, October 6, 1975

The President did touch on some issues during these fund-raising forays around the country, but his language is so patently phony and out-of-fashion that I do not believe it does him or anyone else any real good, except raise money for the GOP.

Most of the speeches written for the President could have been written in 1970 or 1960 for that matter. They are a litany on the work ethic and individual freedom. A few paragraphs refer to current issues.

No wonder, I say to myself, that *Time* magazine today reports the President's popularity at its lowest ebb ever. Most of what the President says and does is fuzzed by those around him. No wonder the man appears confused at times. No one appears able to agree on anything around here, except what's vague.

The President's national campaign is disorganized from top to bottom. All are criticizing Campaign Committee Chairman Bo Callaway. Grassroots organizing has never caught fire either. In the early primary states of New Hampshire and Florida, there are virtually no specific plans for direct-mail fund-raising. In the words of almost everyone inside the White House, "We are way behind schedule."

Although many in the White House are still unaware, Lee Nunn resigned several days ago as director of organization for the President Ford Committee. Nunn, an experienced grassroots man, quit because he was left powerless at getting local organizing off the ground. Everyone's campaign wires are crossed.

Stuart Spencer, a longtime California political consultant, is taking over the Nunn post, and also overall political directorship of this part of the campaign. Asked what this means concerning Callaway, one of the top staff men says, "Who the hell knows or cares?"

Bo Callaway, inexperienced in the detail work of a big campaign, appears to be standing aside watching the musical chairs as they waltz around him. The feeling in the White House is that one of them may drop on his toes and sideline him for good.

The top White House staff is uptight. Their hope that Ronald Reagan would evaporate as a threat has not materialized. Most concede that Reagan is in the race for good. The Reagan people have begun their direct-mail campaign across the country, a first mailing of more than a million requests for funds. And the Reagan camp is saying:

"The President was not elected. He has no record to speak of. And the public has no investment in him because the American people have never voted for him as President."

This is hard-hitting stuff, the kind of directness that is edited out of Mr. Ford's speeches.

Another area of conflict surrounds Vice President Rockefeller, who is getting rough with Bill Simon and Alan Greenspan. Rocky says the two should either support President Ford's proposal for a new $100 billion government energy corporation or resign. He explains:

"I think that's the way you have a strong, hard-hitting administration. But to go out and poor-mouth what your boss has decided is not serving him well nor is it serving yourself well . . ."

Rocky also emphasizes something I have been feeling for many months. He uses the word "loyalty" but I would use "agreement":

"You can't have an effective administration, where the President is able to really lead this country, unless you have loyalty in the organization."

I ask myself: "Why are you still here?"

And I answer:

"Because I hope that one day these people will get together. The country needs unity in the White House. And we need a few independent neutrals in the White House who will act and speak objectively."

Seeking equilibrium from the fourth estate, I speak with an old friend, George Romilly, a cameraman with ABC News, who says:

"Everybody's waiting for the next shot, man. That's all the reporters and everyone thinks about. It's like a death watch. Remember, you covered the MacArthur and Eisenhower death watches.

"We're doing security stories like crazy. We film the Secret Service as much as the audience or the crowds. It's morbid, really. Nobody's paying attention to what the President is saying. We're thinking gun."

If "nobody" is listening to the President while he travels, perhaps he should stay home where they might listen.

As the day ends, I take a walk across to Lafayette Park in front of the White House. I keep thinking of a speech which pollster Lou Harris gave a few weeks ago. He said:

"The voices from the top today are by and large not the voices from below."

Harris stressed that the American people are sick to death of politicians who will not level with them.

I wish I could speak with Lou Harris now, to show him the speeches, the "straight talk" that has been edited out of so many paragraphs.

Tuesday, October 7, 1975

IT'S A BEAUTIFUL AUTUMN DAY, cool and crisp, and I take an extra long walk on the way to work. Everyone seems in a hurry. Few glance at the clear sky, wondrous in the morning sun.

Yet it's not to be a beautiful day for the speechwriting staff.

One of our secretaries, Judy Morton, whispers that there was a "blowup" yesterday in the West Wing which houses the top staff. She says Hartmann "exploded" in an argument with Rumsfeld over the President's address to the nation on tax and spending cuts. Judy portrayed an angered Hartmann turning to Rumsfeld and shouting, "You write it."

And Rumsfeld did. Rather, he asked Dave Gergen, an aide at Treasury, to do it.

Dick Cheney, Rumsfeld's aide, had his secretary phone Judy and ask how the President desired his addresses spaced on the speech typewriter. Judy, unaware that Cheney or anyone else outside our office had a speech typewriter, pointed out the availability of our two speech typewriters and was told, "We have our own."

To our secretaries' knowledge, this is the first speech given by the President that has not been typed by our personnel. In addition, it was not cleared by Theis. He never saw it. At the moment, there is some question as to whether Hartmann did.

The President's decision to propose a massive $28 billion tax cut stunned Secretary Simon and Federal Reserve Chairman Burns. His announcement far exceeded any of their suggestions.

Simon, playing the role of the "good soldier," endorsed Mr. Ford's proposal as he helped brief newsmen on it. He took the position that the enlarged federal deficit is outweighed by the long-term benefits of a tentative congressional agreement to slash spending. The package proposed by the President's national budget of $395 billion for the fiscal year starting October 1, 1976, is some $28 billion below anticipated federal spending. The tax cuts would be offset by proposed curbs on spending.

"The President made up his mind on the big tax cuts at the last minute," according to OMB economists. "He wanted something big and dramatic."

Greenspan, Simon and Lynn, who briefed the press, claimed the President's action was not political. The assertion is nonsense. The tax cut is an election-year decision. It will mean more federal borrowing in coming months, which Simon and Burns have always warned could push up interest rates and hinder economic recovery. The tax cuts really begin at the start of next year, while spending restraints will not be effective until the last quarter of the calendar year. Thus, the economy will get an extra shove before election time.

I try to see Paul O'Neill, deputy to Jim Lynn, but his office is swamped. Questions pour in from every direction. O'Neill is the straightest talker of the entire group. Whenever I can't visualize an economic development I see him.

The White House family is not a happy one. The struggle for power at the top trickles down to the rest of the staff in bits and pieces, surprising some, confusing others and fostering a feeling of insecurity among the troops. The foot-soldiers plod on because they are called upon to be "good soldiers." But I have a deep feeling that we need more "good soldiers" at the top.

Wednesday, October 8, 1975

IT WAS APPARENTLY to be another exchange of platitudes. Theis brings in two speakers to advise the speechwriting staff on the issues for the 1976 campaign: Steve Stockmeyer, executive director of the Republican Campaign Committee, and Bill Steponkus, an administrative assistant to a Republican congressman from Ohio. Buddy Rich, doing PR at the Republican National Committee, sits in on the meeting.

Stockmeyer and Steponkus are pessimistic. Stockmeyer estimates the Republicans might pick up "a handful" of House seats in 1976. Steponkus speaks of "lethargy" and later "apathy" in describing the Republican grassroots organization around the nation. He says, "They are still devastated by Watergate. They have never recovered."

Theis eases them toward the issues for 1976. What should the speechwriting staff be communicating in the fund-raising addresses that the President is making around the country?

Neither answers the question. They imply that the election will be won or lost on the state of the economy in the fall of 1976. Both are confident it will improve.

Platitudes.

Steponkus talks about broadening the base of the Republican party. I ask him what he means specifically. He suggests developing it as a theme, working on language and concepts.

I ask how the base is to be broadened; specific appeals to women, the young and black? Steponkus doesn't answer.

Kaye Pullen interjects that the President talks too much, that "the glamor is wearing off Air Force One. He ought to park it for a while. His appearances are getting a little like daytime TV—dull."

Jack Calkins, a political aide to Bob Hartmann and the President, agrees. He says the President is "a lousy speaker" and should do much less of it. All agree that Mr. Ford needs to improve as a public speaker.

Steponkus asks about ideas. Where are the long-range programs and thoughts? What do we think the President plans to tell the nation in 1976?

Theis and Friedman say the President has this program: no programs.

I point out there's a difference between programs and goals. Goals are the President's views on how he envisions America, what kind of country do we want, what are our values. The President can't run an "anti" campaign of being against everything, of being a veto President. He must say something positive.

Theis and Friedman take strong exception to this. They see no need for the President to propose "ideas for the sake of ideas." Friedman suggests that the President should keep his options open to move in any direction when he feels it necessary.

I ask:

"But what does he stand for? I'd like to know what Gerald Ford stands for. I don't think the American people know what Gerald Ford stands for.

"There are innumerable social issues in this country, involving all types of values. Nobody has ever told me where Gerald Ford stands. As a matter of fact, one of the greatest difficulties here is learning what Gerald Ford thinks about anything."

The meeting is getting hot. Theis shoots a sharp glance at me.

Pullen, Butler and Longood of our staff start their attack. There is little or no guidance on speeches. The writer is left to his own devices with little or no input from Hartmann or Theis. There never seems to be any objective to a speech. Most of the time, the writers don't even know why a speech is scheduled.

I continue:

"There has been an incredible change in America over the past decade sociologically. As I understand the Republican theorists, Nixon did a masterful job in bringing together a so-called new coalition of working people, Catholics and ethnics. He won sizeable gains in every state with this new coalition. Should the writers talk about this when they're told to discuss broadening the base? Does President Ford believe in bringing large numbers of hardhats, blacks, the young and women into the GOP?"

Calkins knocks down vision. He says the President need not present many views on social issues; he has the big issue, government spending and taxes.

Theis volunteers the President may run against the Congress.

I volunteer:

"I don't think the President can run on the rhetoric of twenty and thirty years ago. The language is old and it's tired. He has to run on new, positive ideas as well as against the Congress, against spending, against inflation."

Friedman agrees:

"The President is speaking in the language of Harding, Coolidge and Hoover."

Friedman adds that the President is coming off as a man without compassion, as an uncaring individual, as a man without feeling for the downtrodden.

I attack the editing:

"You can't produce a speech with sixteen people editing it as happened in the hardware industry speech I wrote for Chicago. All you have left is bits and pieces. What you have is a string of statements, many of which contradict one another, dangling without logic, feeling or direction. This isn't speechwriting. It isn't even a speech and it's a tremendous disservice to President Ford.''

Theis defends the clearance or signoff procedure, saying it's necessary. I reply that the number of those clearing speeches should be cut:

"We are engaged in a kind of madness. Do you think that Eisenhower, Jack Kennedy, Johnson or Nixon let sixteen different people take a speech apart when they had put it together after some consultation?''

Calkins asks:

"But where are the Ted Sorensons and such writers on our staff?''

I reply:

"That's a very fair question. But nobody on our staff talks with the President in any detail about any speech, except perhaps Hartmann. You can't write when you have no guidance. Our meetings with the President are not consultations about the significance and meaning of what is about to be written and precisely where he stands. They are cursory.

"Ted Sorenson sat down with Jack Kennedy and they talked out speeches. And believe me, Kennedy didn't go back through the bureaucracy to have a dozen or more people tell him what he thought. You've got to take some risks.''

Friedman adds: "This place is a hamburger machine.''

We then come to the critical moment of the entire meeting. Theis and Orben insist that what the President needs in his speeches is not so much substance as rhetoric. As Orben puts it, "We don't want programs. We want vivid writing.''

Theis says that when the choice is between substance and rhetoric, he comes down on the side of rhetoric.

I like Paul Theis. He is a real gentleman—considerate, kind, thoughtful, but scared. He just can't say no to Greenspan, Seidman, Lynn, Zarb, Simon and others who want to express their views by editing the President's speeches.

Theis stresses that he represents the President's real feelings. I disagree:

"The President is being underestimated by a lot of people around here. Let's take just one example. I believe he is at his very best when he delivers a speech that is hardhitting. He pounds the podium, raises his voice, communicates the depth of his feeling to the audience. And he enjoys it. I just don't think he gets across when a speech is so safe that it's boring.''

The meeting breaks up quietly after an hour and a half. Our visitors have said little. The speechwriters have said more than they ever have in the past. Butler, Pullen and Longood say to me after the conference that it's about time somebody spoke up.

I do not believe the meeting has done or will do any good. This outfit is not interested in ideas; it is interested in holding the line. It is less interested in action than reaction.

Friday, October 10, 1975

AL CAPONE would smile. A *New York* magazine article about the President is being bootlegged all over the White House complex. The piece is an excerpt from a new book about Mr. Ford by Richard Reeves. The secretaries and clerks are making a Xerox of a Xerox of a Xerox but even the almost unreadable pages are ''hot copy.'' The article describes the President as a neutral individual, just a nice, accidental President.

Reeves goes beyond the Theis evaluation of Mr. Ford. Theis characterized the President as a ''compromiser'' in our last staff meeting. Reeves claims Mr. Ford has never been a compromiser, a politician who could forge an agreement out of divergent views. He asserts the President is an ''accommodator,'' one who accommodates himself to a compromise already worked out. Reeves views Mr. Ford as an individual who is happiest with ''the least objectionable alternative.''

In my opinion, however, the real ''hot copy'' is in Scotty Reston's column in today's *New York Times*. It is almost as if Reston sat in on our last speechwriters' conference.

Reston makes the following telling points about both Republicans and Democrats, but they appear particularly appropriate, from my viewpoint, to the GOP for 1976. No serious effort is being made to have articulate minds bear on the nation's and party's coming problems. There should be meaning to the campaigns. The national debate must not be left only to distracted candidates and exhausted slogans of the past.

The two parties go on with the same old arguments, knowing the world is different, and not knowing what to do about it.

Both articles seem to bear profoundly on Theis' statement at Wednesday's meeting that rhetoric is more important than substance. The obvious question they raise is whether the 1976 Republican presidential effort will be a public relations campaign or a public policy contest.

In midmorning, Theis unexpectedly calls a meeting of the writers. He begins by saying that Bob Rousek, who has been doing all the editing with him for the past few months, will turn over the editing of speeches to Milt Friedman. Theis explains that Friedman knows the thinking of the President better. He also makes the point that each writer will now be more responsible for the final product. Instead of the final changes being made in the front office, the writer will be allowed a voice in the last draft of each speech.

Theis opens up the meeting to discussion and he is hit by Longood, Pullen and Butler on an old subject. None feels sufficiently backgrounded or briefed to write the President's speeches. For about fifteen minutes, they explain in various ways that they do not understand why certain policy decisions are made, what these conclusions really mean and where they are leading the administration. Theis, who has heard this over and over from me and others for a year, says he plans to ask some of the administration's top people to brief us.

Orben confesses that he has had some doubts about certain administration policies and, in the understatement of the meeting, wonders whether any others have had the same feeling.

Friedman suggests that the office find a computer information retrieval expert and have him placed on detail to Theis for a month so that the writers can have sufficient backup material to compose coming speeches.

The message is clear. Theis, Friedman and Orben, who have formed an inner circle clique on our staff, are willing to discuss the cosmetics of change. The fact is that only two minor concessions are being made. Some adjustments in our editing process are being considered; they do not eliminate the madness of a dozen different people clearing the speeches. Second, a commitment is made to take research more seriously.

Hartmann, whom we were advised would attend the conference, never shows. With an atmosphere of intellectual disagreement if not revolt pervading the staff, he declines to appear.

About 2 P.M., I receive a phone call from Agnes Waldron. Agnes has been at home on vacation for the past two weeks. No conversation, since coming to the White House, hits me with greater impact. Agnes is deeply emotional:

"Never in all my years, and I have been around politics for a long time, have I been so disturbed. It's almost despair. We are confused, mixed up and doing all the wrong things. And we're hurting one another."

I tell this good, decent woman that I could not write the speeches assigned me without her research—that if I have accomplished anything in the White House, she shares the achievement.

Obviously, Agnes is deeply discouraged and disappointed at working conditions and morale. The tragedy is that no one apparently offers her a kind or encouraging professional word.

I promise to speak with her when she returns to work. Being the lady that she is, Agnes quietly says her thanks and gently slips her phone receiver into place.

I find it difficult to think for a minute or so after the call. But I cannot help but wonder about others on the White House staff. Is the Ford "team" coming apart at the seams?

Chapter 14
October, 1975

"In politics we have to do a great many things that we ought not to do."

THEODORE ROOSEVELT

Wednesday Evening, October 15, 1975

BOB HARTMANN is telling a war story. The presidential yacht, Sequoia, cruises down the Potomac River. The speechwriting staff, writers, researchers, secretaries, office boys, and Hartmann's political aides, Jack Calkins and Gwen Anderson, sip drinks as the sun slips beneath the horizon in a ball of orange flame. It is a social evening and Hartmann is at his best.

"We were on Bougainville in the Pacific," he tells me. "And they send me H.V. Kaltenborn with a letter from Mrs. Roosevelt saying that we should show him the war for his news broadcasts.

"The Japs infiltrate a little bit at night and we flush them out in the morning. Kaltenborn has never seen a Jap. But he had done a broadcast about the white napkins in our Navy Officers' Mess.

"So I take him out for a ride with this Marine driver one day. All the Japs are asleep because it's morning. And I order the driver to stop so Kaltenborn and I can view the Japanese positions. Of course, I don't know where the hell their positions really are.

"Kaltenborn walks ahead a few paces, and I tell the driver to stay with the jeep. I also tell him that when we cross a small hill, he should put two bullet holes through the windshield of the jeep on Kaltenborn's side. And I tell him that's an order.

"So I walk H.V. for a while, and sure enough, we hear firing. I tell him the shots must be coming from Jap snipers and we better get the hell out of there. We return to the jeep and Kaltenborn sees the holes on his side of the windshield and says: 'Oh, my God, I would have been killed!'

"He begins his next broadcast, with all the emotion in the world, saying he was under fire from Japanese snipers. There were no more stories about white napkins."

Hartmann roars. He loves his own punch lines. He is captain of the ship this evening.

About an hour out of the Washington Navy Yard, the Sequoia's regular berth, Hartmann assembles us inside the deck to read a letter thanking the two staffs for all of their hard work. At the close, he says:

"And it is signed by—guess who?"

A voice calls out: "Donald Rumsfeld!"

200

Some laugh but Hartmann reddens and falters. He quickly recovers:

"Not quite. The signature—and it was not done by one of those machines—is that of a friend of mine who loaned us his boat this evening—Gerald Ford."

The Rumsfeld-Hartmann feud did not escape direct comment by Hartmann:

"Our little voyage was planned long before the Aldo Beckman story in the *Chicago Tribune*. It's been in the works for weeks. However, if anyone wants to make a confession on the Beckman story, I'm going up to the top deck."

The Beckman yarn hit the speechwriting staff like a lightning bolt. Last Monday, which was a Columbus Day holiday, the phone rang at our home. I had taken my wife and our youngest son, Lawrence, for a ride outside the city to see the changing colors of autumn. On return, my mother-in-law said: "Call Paul Theis. It's urgent."

I phoned Paul who wasted no time: "Are you the source of the Aldo Beckman story?"

I asked Paul what he was talking about. He replied:

"It's about the Hartmann-Rumsfeld feud. About the tax spending cut speech of the President. About the fact that our staff didn't write it."

I told Theis that I had not leaked the story, had never met Beckman in my life, and had never communicated with him in any manner, shape or form. Theis, obviously strained, backed off and hung up.

Beckman, the *Tribune* White House correspondent, had written a front-page story highlighting not only the feud but the fact that Hartmann had been passed over by the President on this major address. Rumsfeld, Lynn, Seidman and Greenspan, working with Dave Gergen, a Treasury aide, had written the speech. The article referred to complaints from White House aides on the quality of the President's speeches, including some unhappiness on the part of Mr. Ford. A speechwriter is quoted that the Ford administration is getting the reputation of not having a "social conscience."

For the first time, the discontent on the speechwriting staff is beginning to surface in the media and Theis is determined to discover the leak.

From all accounts, including her own words, Kaye Pullen met and discussed some inside grievances with Beckman. But the Theis call particularly upset Bob Longood, the new writer, who confessed precisely that to me and said he was leaving the staff. Longood, an able and experienced speechwriter, said he was dumbfounded when Theis phoned him asking the same question about leaking the story to Beckman. Longood, a direct individual, was personally and professionally affronted. He said he wanted to leave the staff with his head high and reputation intact.

Power and lust for it are destroying the Ford White House. Power, which Gerald Ford had not sought but came upon by accident, is becoming a curse. And no ride on the Sequoia could put our staff completely back together again.

On the drive home, I have time to think about events of the day. Rod Hills (husband of Carla, who is secretary of HUD), with whom I worked on the hardware industry speech, is leaving the White House. He will become chairman of the Securities and Exchange Commission and confides to associates:

"I don't know if I am being railroaded in or railroaded out" (into SEC or out of the White House).

Hills has come under fire inside the White House. He speaks his mind in the President's presence which annoys some top staffers, including Rumsfeld. And he apparently suggested to newsmen during a background briefing, that the President might establish an independent inspector general for the CIA. The inspector general would be independent of the agency and, in effect, oversee it.

Actually, the President has such a post in mind but not precisely as reported in newspaper headlines. Hartmann and Nessen also wondered about the source of the story. When they learned it came from Hills, word went out that he talks too much.

Hills' departure leaves Phil Buchen, the President's old law buddy from Grand Rapids, as the only White House legal counsel. Mr. Ford doesn't like to hear criticism of Buchen, a white-haired gentleman with no proven track record when it comes to a big crunch. Phil Areeda, a brilliant legal scholar from Harvard, quietly left, and other lawyers are leaving, such as Bill Casselman. The White House is losing good men like Hills and others because of obviously weak links in the President's chain of command.

Thursday, October 16, 1975

More and more, I conclude that the President's view of his office is limited. Kissinger, Schlesinger and Rockefeller are the only proven pros on his staff with vision and the guts to back up their views.

I am not surprised by the challenge which Vice President Rockefeller tosses at the President on the issue of helping New York City out of its financial crisis. It comes as a shock to most White House staffers when Rocky dramatizes his differences with Mr. Ford at a Columbus Day speech in Manhattan. Without consultation or clearance of any kind from the President, Rocky demands congressional action to bail out New York.

Rocky's staff plays the speech down. They say the VP is trying to switch blame to the Congress if New York City goes under and there is a ripple effect, causing further economic strain in the country.

Bill Safire, former Nixon speechwriter and a conservative columnist for the *New York Times,* leads the conservative charge against the VP. In an offkey approach he laments the closing of one of his old saloon hangouts by the Rockefeller interests connected with Rockefeller Center. Safire's attack on Rocky is harsh. Summing up, Safire says Rocky has "left the reservation" of the Ford White House by his New York speech. He writes of "team play"—a term of no endearment to those of us who believe this Nixonian concept carried the United States to the brink of political catastrophe. Safire suggests Rocky is likely to be "dumped" by Ford. The oft-expressed hatred of Rockefeller by conservatives still surprises me, even after these many years of listening to it. I think what Bill Safire needs is not an old saloon but a new song.

This is becoming a very uptight ship and the national election is still more than a full year away.

Thursday, October 16, 1975

PAUL THEIS and I meet for about a half hour this morning. It's very polite but "tough" talk. I tell Paul that the speechwriting staff should go on the offensive. We now have that opportunity.

"We go to California at the close of the month. Reagan will be there. He will hang tough. He'll deliver a great speech with plenty of punch, style and sock-it-to-'em emotion.

"The President may lose that battle. We can't give him just
another ho-hum homily to the party faithful. This speech ought to sing.

"Let's say we lose—the President does not equal Reagan.
Envisage that four-hour ride on the press plane from San Francisco to
Milwaukee—four hours for the press corps to sit down together and
drink and conclude that good old Jerry was upstaged by a great actor,
Reagan.

"But it needn't end on that note. We give 'em a helluva speech for
Milwaukee."

Theis nods in agreement, not that he's sold, only that he's willing
to continue listening. I give Theis a proposed speech in rough draft. I
wrote it in an attempt to provoke discussion within the administration
on the 1976 issues.

*I am here this evening to restate and renew the common
aspirations of the American people. I speak not only of our common
heritage but of our common journey into the future. I address not only
the proud principles of our past but the principles upon which the
United States will build its future.*

*The United States and the Republican party are thoroughly linked,
past and future. No history of this nation can be written without that of
our party, and no historian can chronicle the GOP without returning to
our country's traditional beliefs and values. You here in Wisconsin
know that better than anyone. The Republican party was founded in
Ripon in 1854.*

*But what of the future? Does the Republican party have a role in
the future of America? What is that role? Who are these Republicans?
What do we have to say to the United States? . . .*

*Our answer is a policy of openness. For young and old . . . rich
and poor . . . black and white . . . Independents and deserted
Democrats . . . we must create new vistas in American politics. We are
the party of positive principles, not pessimistic posturing . . . the party
of answers and solutions, not the disseminators of doubt and despair
. . . the party of reason, responsibility and restraint, not those who
promise the American people more rule and less reason . . . more
freedom and less responsibility . . . more spending and a weaker
dollar.*

*In the final analysis, we oppose government without consent—the
increasing encroachment of government in our lives and futures—as
well as irresponsible government action on the local level.*

It is neither responsible nor compassionate to spend a city into *bankruptcy. It is neither responsible nor compassionate to erode the value of peoples' hard-earned money through inflation by piling government program on program on program and financing them through continual budget deficits. This is not compassion. This is irresponsible hypocrisy.* *

I conclude by telling Theis that the party should listen to guys like me who do not believe the GOP has all the answers. He must get off this Republican versus Democrat kick and open up the GOP. Independents like myself will be attracted to it if the GOP will only listen to some people outside the party once in a while instead of paying so much attention to its right-wingers.

Theis promises to read the speech carefully. I infer that he's telling me it may not be butchered because it's different. Perhaps, he will take it to Hartmann.

On return to my office, Agnes Waldron is there. She shows me the latest Harris poll, published today. It says:

"Public confidence in America's leaders has fallen to the lowest point in many years, and the public believes many are simply out of touch with the people they represent and whom they are supposed to be serving."

Harris reports that by an overwhelming seventy to twenty-three majority most Americans believe their leaders treat them as twelve-year-olds. Their number one target is the federal government, Congress and the executive branch. Federal leadership does not comprehend the changing values and aspirations of the average American citizen.

The survey supports my differences of a week ago with Theis. Americans want serious and constructive approaches to inflation, recession, energy and other problems. I applaud one Harris observation. Americans are responsive to the press and radio-TV news because these media are not afraid to take on the establishment with investigative reporting.

Monday, October 20, 1975

I REDISCOVER OVER THE WEEKEND that there's another world out there. Columbus, Ohio, for example. It rains most of the weekend but nothing can dampen Midwest enthusiasm for college football.

For entire text see Appendix, p. 339.

Columbus is mad about its Buckeyes and they run away from Wisconsin, 56 to zip.

I was there to address the local chapter of Sigma Delta Chi, the Society of Professional Journalists, on energy. Their attentiveness and interest startle me. These people are positive, not negative. They are amiable, not assertive. They are polite, not pushy. They are relaxed, not in a hurry. And they laugh easily.

This is the first time that I give a speech under White House auspices and that magic description draws four radio stations, two television channels, the *Columbus Dispatch* newspaper and the Ohio State University *Lantern* newspaper.

I spend a few hours at Ohio State speaking with some professors. Their primary interest is HEW—the rules jungle and the paper-pushing of the Department of Health, Education and Welfare. Their questions come with a grace and warmth that can beguile a visitor. The professors carry the same inner intellectual toughness and discipline of the East, but they grace their actions with a civility that is infrequent in Washington.

There was not one question during the entire weekend on the possible financial collapse of New York City. However, the first thing I hear on return to the White House is should President Ford bail out New York?

Bill Seidman seems to be holding the cards on New York City. Seidman, despite criticism of his abilities by many of the President's other economic advisers, apparently is feeding New York developments to the President.

When Abe Beame, New York's mayor, wants to speak with the President after midnight, Beame is advised that Bill Seidman is keeping Mr. Ford advised. The President is asleep, Beame is told, and Bill Seidman is handling things.

But it is Alan Greenspan in whom the President confides privately for one-half hour when it comes to the crunch. What the President needs is arguments, logic, articulation, and Greenspan offers him that. Mr. Ford long ago made up his mind to fight attempts to bail out New York. It is a natural, self-made political issue.

The President doesn't believe he has the authority to provide any long-term aid to New York City. Even if the President did have that authority, he would not do it because he doesn't believe any "quick fix" of federal government millions will solve the Big

Apple's long-term problems. Mr. Ford believes New York City has had the opportunity and means for a long time to clean up its own financial mess. The problems amount to the 6 per cent spread between what the city is spending and what it's taking in. The city has not closed that 6 per cent spread in the past ten to twelve years.

Behind the scenes, the President has made it clear to everyone that New York will be a big issue in 1976. He doesn't have to shout it. Mr. Ford simply tells everyone:

"It's absolutely against my philosophy (the way New York has been run)!"

Tuesday, October 21, 1975

I HAVE A FRANK TALK this morning with one of the President's key black assistants. He is ecstatic about the President's speech before the National Baptist Convention in St. Louis a month ago, but nevertheless is generally unhappy:

"Morale is low, man, as low as I've ever seen it. Rumsfeld is holding a knife over everyone's head. No one knows who will be cut in these staff reductions.

"One of us blacks is leaving. But Rumsfeld wants to put his own man in the job, someone who will be loyal to him. It's not that the top black in the administration must be a bright, intelligent individual. It's that he must first be loyal to Rumsfeld."

He pauses, reminding me that he has watched Rumsfeld operate for many years, and continues:

"I know of no staff in the White House where people are happy except Personnel. They are doing the chopping and hiring for Rumsfeld and they do nothing without Rumsfeld.

"They're cutting out titles. That's Rumsfeld's way of separating the chiefs from the Indians. He doesn't like titles like 'special assistant to the President' because he wants to emphasize control, man. That's the most important word to describe Rumsfeld—he wants complete control.

"But we need those titles out in the field, out in cities talking with people, trying to let them know that we count with the President, that we're not wasting their time. That we need them and they need us.

"And he cuts the number of people receiving the President's daily news summary in half. That's control, man, He's using a little gimmick to say: 'Tighten up, I'm tightening up. You tighten up. Everybody tighten up.' "

The presidential aide is calm, a cool guy, not a talker. It's obvious he has been thinking this way for a long time. He adds:

"You are the only guys who don't come under his thumb in some way—the speechwriters. Everything I hear indicates he's out to undermine your staff because he doesn't control you. Remember, it's control, man. That's his bag—control.

"So he fights with Hartmann. He drops a comment here and there to the President about the speeches—this one or that one is not too good. Another one could be better. That's the way he operates—quietly through the back door."

He muses that he has considered quitting but he will stay through the 1976 campaign. He says:

"Right now, if the President doesn't straighten this place out, he's going to lose. He's got to unify this place. The President has to run the White House, not Rumsfeld.

"Baroody goes to Marsh. He can avoid Rumsfeld. But Rumsfeld still wants to put his own people in here without considering whether this or that person will work well with our staff. All he cares about is his man or woman inside. That's not serving the President, as he always talks about. That's serving Donald Rumsfeld."

The aide asks me not to discuss our conversation with anyone in the White House. He doesn't want his name used. I tell him that I may write a book some day. He replies:

"That's okay. Just say I'm black. I am getting out of politics—as far away as I can get. I'm sick of it. I want my pride back from guys like Rumsfeld."

Others who have blistered Rumsfeld swore me to silence, to use their quotes but never their names. They are staying in politics. They see Rumsfeld as a possible Republican power one day although he may have reached his zenith in this administration. This is the kind of power that Rumsfeld wields in the White House—the power to intimidate White House staff members; the power, perhaps, to destroy some of them. This is his game. This is what he apparently relishes. Will power corrupt him also as it corrupted so many men in the Nixon administration?

President Ford, suffering from sinus congestion and a temperature of 101 degrees, has an even bigger headache from the press today. Tom Wicker, of the *New York Times,* and Jim Gannon, of the *Wall Street Journal,* deliver one of the strongest one-two wallops to Mr. Ford since he assumed the presidency.

When news commentaries are particularly sensitive and close to the mark, few if any staffers want to discuss them. Such is the case today.

Wicker describes Mr. Ford's "political shrewdness" in pardoning Richard Nixon and closing the subject in the minds of many Americans, even if "unsatisfactorily." Wicker insists that the Democrats should bring the episode back into the public consciousness by raising it as a 1976 campaign issue.

He accuses Mr. Ford of misleading if not untrue statements during his confirmation hearings for the vice presidency. The President implied, according to the Wicker argument, that he would not issue a pardon to the man whose resignation would make him President.

The Democratic issue, according to Wicker, is simply the President's veracity.

Wicker then discusses the Nixon tapes. He suggests the possibility that Mr. Ford might be holding back the September 15, 1972, Nixon-Haldeman-Dean tape in particular. The President and White House have taken the position that the tapes are the property of Nixon and should be placed in his custody at San Clemente.

Wicker suggests Mr. Ford may have helped stop the first congressional investigation into Watergate under orders from Nixon. The September 15 tape might show Nixon ordered Haldeman or Dean to get to Ford to halt the investigation.

In his vice presidential confirmation hearings, Mr. Ford insisted he was not acting on White House instructions when he helped lead a successful drive to deny congressional subpoena power. This effectively killed a planned investigation.

The tapes are in the hands of Phil Buchen, an old friend of the President and White House legal adviser. Indirectly, Wicker suggests, Buchen might be protecting his old friend from embarrassment if not from perjury.

A biting attack like Wicker's, suggesting perjury by a President, would shake up any organization. This includes the White House, particularly a White House with a poisoned past.

Thus, Wicker opens up questions in the minds of those who serve Gerald Ford. His article causes me to stop and think. Jerald terHorst quit as press secretary because he believed he had been misled by Buchen and others, the same Buchen named by Wicker.

What about the crony system in the White House? Is that why Seidman and Buchen, men obviously ill-equipped to handle the full responsibilities of their jobs, are here? Does Ford contemplate possible embarrassments in the future, and therefore, must he have old standbys who will act and take the heat in his behalf?

This self-searching becomes significant, however, when someone is forced to look in the mirror and ask:

"Could the President I work for have been a liar and a perjurer? A liar and perjurer to obtain the presidency itself? Would and could he have lied to me and, therefore, I lied in writing his speeches?

"How much are men being used in this White House? Is it inextricably part of the game? Do men betray their own minds and hearts to stay on, to hang on to power? How far are they willing to go? Who are the weak and strong around me? And what about me? Do I have a price? Would I ever, under any circumstances, betray the trust of my wife, parents, family, friends and country to salvage the presidency of Gerald Ford?"

Jim Gannon, an excellent reporter and a man from my old alma mater of Marquette, poses these questions in another way. His analysis of the President's economic policies in today's *Wall Street Journal* is devastating. I respect Gannon as an extremely able and honest individual and thus his points appear to be particularly telling on a personal basis.

Gannon begins simply. President Ford is often ignoring the counsel of his top economic advisers. White House policy on economic matters is particularly "confused and contentious."

What are some of the confusing elements?

Mr. Ford's sudden decision to propose a bigger tax cut than even liberal Democrats dare, tied to restraining federal spending. The President had said that renewal of the 1975 tax reduction would depend on the state of the economy this fall. In essence, the President would "probably not recommend a continuation of the tax cut" if the economy were coming out of the recession without inflation danger. The economy was doing just that when Mr. Ford dropped his bombshell of a tax cut. The President rejected the no-tax-cut advice of Bill Simon and Arthur Burns, and he went far beyond the advice of economic aides like Alan Greenspan and others.

The President says his plan isn't aimed at affecting the economy at all. The goal is to get a handle on government spending. But this is a real switch from his drawing the line on government spending. The proposal of the big tax cuts increases the national deficit. What happened to Bill Simon's and the President's arguments about "crowding out"—that big deficits and heavy Treasury borrowing would push up interest rates and crowd other borrowers out of the market.

The Rockefeller plan proposed by the President to create a new $100-billion government energy corporation will not reduce federal spending and government interference with the economy. Simon, Greenspan and others battle fiercely inside the White House to kill Rocky's plan but their attempts fail.

A year ago, Mr. Ford wore a WIN button asking Congress to fight inflation by raising taxes. Yet he cut taxes.

Gannon's argument is that President Ford has changed his mind and changed courses so many times on economic matters that he is not particularly credible any longer. The political factor has become the dominant influence in policy formation. It is certain to do so for the next campaign year.

Gannon sums up his thesis with some ironic but convincing rhetoric. The President promised the Congress "a policy of communication, conciliation; compromise and cooperation." He concludes:

"But now the Mr. Nice Guy period is over. The old four C's are replaced by a new set: confusion, contradiction, confrontation and can't do. . .."

Once again, I ask the same questions which seem more pertinent than ever:

"How much are men being used in the White House? Is it inextricably part of the game? Do men betray their own minds and hearts to stay on, to hang on to power? How far are they willing to go?"

Behind the scenes, many of the President's economic advisers continue to be critical of one another. They leak stories to the press that favor themselves and damage the image of others. They vehemently oppose some of Mr. Ford's decisions and yet—yet, they remain.

How do they rationalize and philosophize this? They oppose presidential decisions privately and find arguments to support them publicly.

They produce rapid-fire, almost split-second affirmations in meetings once a presidential decision is announced. It is as if sudden, new reasons to support the President existed all along. Simon is particularly good at this but he is not alone. Greenspan, Lynn, Seidman, Burns—the mighty have a prepared plan for any eventuality. On any project or program, they are ready to accommodate themselves three different ways. This is called "survival" by most honest men. It is called "diplomacy" by Henry Kissinger. And it is called "politics" by Gerald Ford, Bob Hartmann, Paul Theis and others.

One can say with ease from a living room sofa that my discomfort is naiveté at its worst. The White House is not academia or the pulpit. This is America as it is lived in the power circles.

To the uninitiated like myself, whose mind and heart still think and beat as a reporter, this world of contradiction and cronyism is losing much of the luster it manages to project under the umbrella of patriotism and the good of the country.

It is not that I do not believe Gerald Ford. It is the atmosphere and accommodation with which he works and has worked much of his career. It is the "game of politics" which I am coming to question. It is the price which people pay for power.

Where does politics end and ethics begin?

What about me? Can I continue without compromising my own character?

Barry Locke, a longtime Republican political information official, always describes me as "an accident. A guy who accidentally became a speechwriter to an accidental President."

Barry, a hard-nosed Jewish kid with a beguiling smile he learned from his Irish neighbors near Boston, has few political hangups. I sometimes question the nature of politics and politicians and he always says:

''Take it a day at a time. Look at it that way. Politics isn't history. It's today, man. What do we gotta do today?

''Tomorrow. We'll think about that tomorrow. There's an answer. There always is. There always has been. And when you don't have any more answers, then you are a has-been.''

Wednesday, October 22, 1975

''THIS SPEECH IS LUDICROUS. It's laughable.''

His face flushed red, his voice faltering, his hand slashing in the air as if crossing out sentences and paragraphs, this is a Paul Theis that I have never seen before.

''Ludicrous . . . laughable . . . ridiculous . . .'' Theis repeats himself over and over about the Milwaukee political speech.

I say nothing. I listen and, more than ever before, I take an objective look at this man. His pen never leaves his right hand. His desk, piled in disarray that has caused so much confusion over the past year, is submerged in paperwork. I can't help but reflect on the mountains of federal paperwork that we have promised to abolish in our speeches.

Theis runs pen and hand through his hair many times. He shifts in his chair, nervously rolling it back and forth. Surrounding him, in all parts of his vast office, are signed photos of various Republican politicians over the years. That is Theis, the Republican, first, last and always, the loyal staff man of the party. Loyalty, that is a word and description which falls easily on his shoulders, like an overcoat.

Theis has never really been either a reporter or an editor. He has been a ''liaison man'' between his political party and individual congressmen during the prime of his career. He was, in the harsh terms of modern Washington, a ''political hack.''

It's exceedingly difficult to sit here and write this because I have always attempted to characterize Theis in my own mind as a gentleman. And he has been a gentleman to me. But in these past few months, he has been coming apart—shouting, angering his staff, ridiculing people, and communicating less. Theis, in the parlance of his political mentors, is ''running scared.''

After his long and angry harangue, I ask Theis if I might make one comment. He does not seem to want it so I say nothing.

He makes a long defense of the President's political speeches saying, "This is the way the President is."

After this rambling rhetoric, he concedes me a moment and I say:

"Paul, I spoke with you for a half-hour on October 16—a week ago—and told you this speech was different. That it might serve as the basis for discussion within the administration.

"I wrote you a note when I handed the speech in on October 15 saying we had time and opportunity to work on different approaches and ideas. And now, a few hours before I leave for Syracuse University, you tell me the speech is laughable.

"We seem to be in a perpetual crisis around here. I don't want to debate or argue any point. I'm learning that debate or discussion are not what's desired. So let me put it this way: I will toss this one in the wastebasket and write another speech along the same lines as all the old ones."

Theis starts in again—shouting, having lost control of himself, insisting that the President doesn't want a change-of-pace speech. I say nothing. Still flushed red in the face, Theis waves me from the room.

Saturday, October 25, 1975

I LEFT FOR SYRACUSE UNIVERSITY early Thursday morning and addressed 380 Communications frosh on the subject of "energy and the press—as seen from the White House." It's a free-wheeling, exciting one hour and forty-five minutes. My remarks cover thirty minutes and questions rock-and-sock for an hour and fifteen minutes.

It's a hostile but good-natured crowd. I stay on the offensive, insisting that we must solve our energy problems and Congress is copping out. And the media need to stay on the politicians' back—all the politicians' backs—if the nation is to come up with the needed answers in energy. They love it. Here again, I quote the late Bill Lawrence, for many years the *New York Times* and ABC News White House correspondent: "The only way to look at a politician is down."

A roar of laughter and applause.

I'm mobbed after the talk and the refrain is the same:

"I never thought anyone from the White House would talk like that. You really laid it on the line. You did President Ford a lot of good because you didn't try to bullshit us."

Meeting the students at the S. I. Newhouse School of Public Communications at Syracuse is like taking a cold shower. A bit of a shock treatment at first but exhilarating and uplifting. I spend two days talking and being interviewed by the student body. I come away, immensely in their debt.

How different from life in the White House! These students are truly open and candid; it's not an affectation. They are genuinely inspired by thoughts and ideas, not playing it safe. They are in love with what they're doing—writing, articulating, gesticulating, learning, living. They are relaxed, not uptight. Most of all and best of all, they display little or no envy. I leave Syracuse with a deep sense of sadness. The kids have gotten to me. And I say to myself:

"They will solve the energy problems. They don't have all of our easy habits. They will see the necessity and provide the will. Most of all, they have the guts to do it!"

As the plane lifts off over the rolling countryside of upstate New York, I say a little prayer for two men: S. I. Newhouse, the man who gave so many millions of dollars to Syracuse's School of Public Communications, and his representative in Syracuse, WSYR general manager for radio and TV, Curly Vadeboncoeur. These men are true giants. The greats are not in the White House, they are out here in the so-called hinterlands—men and women who have risen above their daily toil to help lift the lives and spirit of their fellow citizens. It is a prayer of thanksgiving.

Tuesday, October 28, 1975

HARTMANN IS PUTTING A BRAVE FACE on the fact that Reagan is definitely running:

"The Boss likes competition. And it will be a good thing for all of us—get us on our toes for the Democrats."

Although the former California governor hasn't officially announced, his top people don't care who knows it, "Ronnie's running."

Despite his bluff that a Reagan race will be good for the President, Hartmann is deeply concerned. He privately warns about the Ford team weaknesses, specifically Bo Callaway, who is in nominal charge of the President's campaign. When Hartmann feels expansive about Callaway, which is not often, he utters a single syllable: "Dumb."

Callaway's name seems to be on everyone's critical list except the President's. If so many have so little confidence in him, I ask myself, why don't they find someone to run the operation and let Callaway remain as a figurehead? I am forced to believe that is an intelligent question, so penetrating that it's too hot to handle except by the President. If there is a tone of irony in those words, it is because such irony creeps into much of the White House talk these days. Over and over, people say:

"Let's get organized. Let's get together. Let's pull together."

I keep thinking back a year to when I joined the White House staff. Those are the precise phrases that I heard then, only the differences and divisions were blamed on "those Nixon people."

Wednesday, October 29, 1975

BOB ROUSEK, OF OUR STAFF, tells me that the President is acting "a little scared" about the California trip which begins today. He relates that Mr. Ford rejected speeches by Friedman and Hartmann saying they were "too dull." Rousek explains that the President wants "tough, positive" speeches for Los Angeles and San Francisco "because that's Reagan country."

I see Agnes Waldron and ask her about the "tough" speeches and she says:

"Yeah, Friedman has a line about being 'fighters, not patsies!' "

I groan and ask: "You're kidding?"

Agnes replies:

"What else is new? There's nothing new in the speeches—just rhetoric."

I search out a copy of the Milwaukee address to see what happened to what I had written. My draft is gutted. It's replaced by the old phrases which Mr. Ford has been using for months.

A few thoughts of what I had written are included in the final version. What remained was:

"It is neither responsible nor compassionate to spend a city or a nation into bankruptcy. It is neither responsible nor compassionate to erode the value of peoples' hard-earned money by piling government program on program without the revenues to pay for them. . . ."

The President goes to the National Press Club at noon to deliver his heralded speech on New York City's financial nightmare. Someone leaked the essence of the speech to the *New York Times* yesterday. Today the *Times'* front page announces that the President will guarantee essential city services, such as police and fire, but will not bail out New York.

Hartmann, who wrote this speech, showed it to only a select few. Yet the President's intended remarks are substantially reported in the *Times* and parts also were made available to the wire services and select newsmen. Just what the President's advisers hope to gain by these leaks remains a complete mystery to me.

Kaye Pullen slips into my office to relate she has just had a three-hour lunch with Senator Bill Brock, a Republican from her home state of Tennessee. Kaye says:

"Bill sums it all up in one word: leadership. He's tired of the same stale language and concepts. He's turned off by statement after statement that says nothing new. He told me this:

" 'I feel like standing up before the entire GOP at the Republican National Convention and saying: Let's abolish the party and start from scratch! Because that's how I feel!' "

Kaye quotes Brock as saying "gloom and doom" is spreading among the Republicans on the Hill. She says:

"They don't think the President has a handle on things. Take the economy. He's inconsistent. They don't know what he's going to say or do next. They don't think he's clicking out there. Something is missing."

Tom De Cair, an assistant in the White House press office, is telling Michigan reporters that inept staff work is hampering the President. Leaving the White House for a new job, De Cair says: "Something is wrong."

217

In the press office itself, relations between Ron Nessen and newsmen are again deteriorating. The correspondents, cooling it for several months after Nessen blasted them for "mindless arrogance," are again on the offensive. They are now heckling Nessen, groaning aloud at some of his explanations, and sniping at the press secretary with personal insults. Nessen's old buddies claim he has "sold out" to Gerald Ford and has become a "propagandist." At the moment, Nessen is trying to maintain an equilibrium in the press office. He hopes that once the New York City "bailout" story is over this new surge of rancor will subside.

———————

"Flash!" Agnes is talking, her voice rising. "Flash! Henry Kissinger has just killed the San Francisco speech!"

I question Agnes slowly and carefully. She reports the President has left on Air Force One but the Secretary of State phoned here making "the strongest representations" against the President's giving the speech. Friedman, writing on the United Nations, had received most of his material from UN Ambassador Pat Moynihan who extolled our, rather his, attack on the "tyranny of the majority at the United Nations." The Friedman version attacked the Third World à la Moynihan and Kissinger blew his stack. Agnes says:

"The speech was all Moynihan and no Kissinger. Friedman never checked out the speech with Kissinger until the last minute and now, Kissinger says, we have no speech. We must do another one."

There's a flurry of activity in Theis' office. He and Friedman are talking with Hartmann on Air Force One. It's a major flap which only the President can settle. Apparently, Mr. Ford has never read the final or fifth draft so it's impossible to predict his reaction. One thing is certain. We now have the beginnings of a Moynihan-Kissinger battle. It's time to call it a day.

Thursday, October 30, 1975

THE WINNAH AND STILL White House heavyweight champ—Henry Kissinger! Our secretaries recount the quick knockout: Milt Friedman and General Brent Scowcroft, who is Kissinger's National Security Council representative inside the White House, get on the phone to Bob Hartmann on Air Force

Thursday, October 30, 1975

One. The Moynihan scenario of "tough talk" to the Third World is toned down to a light left jab in the President's San Francisco speech. Mr. Ford, warning the United Nations about the tyranny of the majority, pledges continued, strong support of the global organization. Henry has done it all through Scowcroft—without lifting a glove!

I cannot help but wonder: Where was the President in all this? Why wasn't he consulted? The answer appears to be that Hartmann didn't want to rock the boat.

Hartmann has been under pressure about some of the President's speeches. Hartmann has rarely worked as hard as he has in the past week, trying to come up with some ideas, pushing to make the speeches punchier. Theis reflects Hartmann's concern, coming directly from presidential criticism. Theis looks grief-stricken but he confides to me he hopes to get away for a while by flying to China as part of the White House advance team.

Chapter 15
November, 1975

"The President is the unifying force in American life. He alone of all our elected officials has the entire people as his constituency, the entire nation as his charge. He must, in a large sense, embody the national will and the national purpose.

"Every man who occupies the office will bring to it the special stamp of his own character. Yet, fundamentally, there are but two approaches to the presidency. To Theodore Roosevelt, the President's duty was 'to do anything that the needs of the Nation demand, unless such action is forbidden by the Constitution or the laws.' William Howard Taft, in sharp contrast, believed the President possessed 'no undefined residuum of power which he can exercise because it seemed to him to be in the public interest.' Where Roosevelt elected leadership, Taft chose stewardship. My own preference is clearly for the President who leads."

NELSON A. ROCKEFELLER

Monday, November 3, 1975

THE WHITE HOUSE is in quiet uproar. That isn't a contradiction. When something really big is up, people walk and talk more softly. But the steps are quicker and the words are sharper.

The nation's newspapers are awash in bold, black ink: "Sunday Massacre." Mr. Ford, cornered in Florida by newsmen, would only say: "I love you all." But the headlines report he has fired Defense Secretary Jim Schlesinger and CIA Director Bill Colby, and removed the title "Chief of the National Security Council" from Henry Kissinger.

It's rumored the President will replace Schlesinger with Don Rumsfeld, and Colby with George Bush, our diplomatic representative in China; and give the Kissinger title to Air Force Lt. Gen. Brent Scowcroft.

In the press office, John Carlson and others blame the furor on Joe Laitin, public affairs chief at the Pentagon. They say Joe leaked Schlesinger's firing to a national magazine and another source. This is causing a wild, frantic day of reporters' questions. I don't believe them—not for a second. I have known Joe Laitin for ten years and there's not a man or woman in the press office capable of carrying his typewriter. Joe is a pro all the way—a class guy with professional principles, not a deliberate leaker.

A second rumor, a trickle that has now become a flood inside the White House, suggests that someone on the staff leaked the firings to the press so that the President could not change his mind.

The President is canceling his appointments for the day. Ron Nessen's regular morning news briefing is called off. The President has called a news conference for this evening.

Mr. Ford is now meeting with staff members, discussing what he will tell the American people tonight. In the midst of this, I learn that China has not cleared the arrival of the American advance team in Peking and the flight is called off. No one knows why Peking is stalling on having the White House team complete arrangements for Mr. Ford's upcoming visit.

Ron Nessen, at a special afternoon news briefing, makes a stunning announcement. He reports that Rockefeller personally handed a letter to Mr. Ford this morning stating he does not wish to be considered for the 1976 GOP ticket. The announcement startles the entire White House staff.

I am surprised but not as much as many. Rocky's Domestic Council assistants have been hinting to me for months that the Vice President is "frustrated" and "can't seem to get any real action out of the White House." They blame Rumsfeld, but Gerald Ford has been taking sharp issue with the Vice President, particularly his public language in the New York anti-bailout speech.

Some staffers ask: Is it really Rumsfeld and not Kissinger, as the reports imply, who is the "architect" of the "massacre"?

Rumsfeld attended the recent meeting of the President's kitchen cabinet in which they told Ford he must project a decisive image.

Rumsfeld thus has had the opportunity to initiate action to project this image.

Rumsfeld, in the estimation of many, gains far more than Henry Kissinger. He gains a cabinet post which allows him to make a "name" in his own right, offering more public exposure. The move also puts him in a position to challenge for the vice presidential nomination and, thus, he would be in a position to make a run for the presidency itself in 1980.

If the President appoints Dick Cheney as his chief of staff, this will be a total Rumsfeld victory because Cheney is his closest confidant. It will also indicate Rumsfeld has pulled many of the strings to launch the sweeping changes.

I learn late in the day that Schlesinger and Colby were fired in "cool" face-to-face meetings with the President on Sunday morning before Mr. Ford emplaned for Florida where he met with Egypt's President Sadat. The scenes are described as "cool" because the President planned to make the announcements next Wednesday with proper staging and considerable planning. Both men were taken aback, although Schlesinger had been hinting he might not agree with the President on proposed budget cuts in the Defense Department. Thus, he was running a serious risk with Mr. Ford and knew it. Colby, however, had no indication of his impending firing.

Agnes Waldron comes to ask my opinion and I speak with her in confidence:

"If Cheney gets Rumsfeld's job, this is Rumsfeld's master stroke. Schlesinger, who's a very honest guy and a fighter, could cause the President real trouble in three months by standing up at some small college and saying in a speech that the President doesn't know what he's doing in foreign policy—that he's a captive of Kissinger. The word 'captive' is a political killer. Finally, it's Rocky's team, the Domestic Council, that can make or break the President's 1976 campaign. They are the idea and issues guys. If they sit on their hands, and their morale is really low now, then Gerald R. Ford is in terrible trouble.''

Other developments are beginning to tie together. Mike Duval, who has been the energy man on the Domestic Council, recently switched to the legal office with these words: "The council is a sinking ship." He confirms the discouragement and disillusionment that I have found there. Thus, these Rocky people must somehow be pulled together by a Vice President who is not running. I believe this to be a critical situation which could cause the defeat of the President next year.

Bob Orben, our gag writer, has been attempting for months to obtain a special position with the President: special assistant on Mr. Ford's speeches. Orben, who cannot write substantively, nevertheless feels he understands the issues and audience reaction as well as elocution sufficiently to become the President's chief adviser on his public appearances. Bob Mead, the President's television aide, and Ron Nessen believe they are more competent in this field. Nevertheless, Orben has managed to have himself manifested on all Air Force One flights as the President's chief adviser on his public appearances.

Orben's few attempts at explaining issues to the other speechwriters (e.g., an attempt to throw together a basic political speech which should serve as a model) were considered totally inept by us. The attempt was so bad that several of us suggested it be destroyed so as not to embarrass anyone.

Orben indirectly criticizes Hartmann and Theis, suggesting he has the answers to Mr. Ford's public speaking problems. He is thus undermining not only his superiors but also the speechwriting staff with other White House staff members. Some writers claim Orben is attempting to disassociate himself from the staff. The real difficulties are, as I have outlined many times in the past, that too many people are editing the President's speeches and the entire speechwriting operation is being mismanaged. Only I have said it to Theis and the entire staff on the record and face to face. Orben operates with a clandestine approach.

Kaye Pullen, Orben's most vocal critic on our staff, tells me she's pulling out. She plans to leave our staff and join Sheila Weidenfeld in working for Mrs. Ford. Blasting Orben in bitter terms, calling him a "snake," Kaye feels she has been undermined by him. It's plain that our staff is now divided and dismayed. The President has another no-win situation on his hands.

Our finest secretary, Judy Morton, is quitting. Upset at long hours and crisis after crisis, Judy plans to move on. This is an unnecessary and tragic loss because Judy is cool under fire. We need her. However, with Theis procrastinating on our speeches and constant last-minute crises resulting, there's little to fault in Judy's decision. Our staff is being seriously weakened and, again, it's a no-win situation.

The seeds of defeat in 1976 are being sown. When the final results are in next November, if the President should lose, I will mark today as important in Mr. Ford's loss of the presidency.

Ambition . . . self-promotion . . . discouragement . . . dismay . . . lack of far-reaching discernment . . . these are sorrowful seeds that promise a bitter harvest.

Monday Evening, November 3, 1975

THE PRESIDENT, ON NATIONAL TELEVISION at 7:30 P.M., confirms the reported changes in his staff. In addition, Mr. Ford announces that Commerce Secretary Morton will step down after the first of the year and be succeeded by our current ambassador to Britain, Elliot Richardson.

The President tells the nation that the shakeup was his own, personal decision and no one else's. Very few knowledgeable people in the White House believe this. I have found no one, thus far, who believes it.

Pure and simple, the action is interpreted by most as an attempt by the President to demonstrate to the American people that he's a decisive leader. The leadership factor, in the face of all the disarray that I see in the White House, has become Mr. Ford's number one liability. His kitchen cabinet is telling him that, and I understand that is also Rumsfeld's line to him. He must show everyone who is boss. This should be a lesson not only for the country and Congress but all government leaders. It should be a warning to the staff that the President will run a tight ship during the campaign.

Rumsfeld's fine hand is everywhere. George Bush, an old friend of his, takes over at CIA. Richardson should be grateful to him because Richardson's ego has been bolstered by this new post, as well as Richardson's acknowledged ambition. Kissinger will no longer play God each day with the President. He will meet with Mr. Ford only a few times each week on the same basis as Rumsfeld. Rocky is out of Rumsfeld's way to the VP post on the 1976 ticket.

It's now known, however, that Rumsfeld has been discussing a staff shakeup with Mr. Ford for some time. Mr. Ford is known to be a man who finds it difficult to fire anyone. This is why so many Nixon loyalists managed to hang on for months before being quietly eased out of the White House and several other critical places. It's reasoned that Rumsfeld coldly laid out the plan.

The President offered both Schlesinger and Colby new posts. Schlesinger was to become head of the Export-Import Bank, and Colby was to become ambassador to NATO, dumping Al Haig, a Nixon loyalist. Each declined the offer.

However, the leak of the firings blew up careful plans by Rumsfeld to orchestrate calm and reasoned announcements on Wednesday. Rumsfeld's reputation as a conniver is so pervasive among White House staffers that some suggest he may have leaked the story himself so Mr. Ford could not possibly change his mind. I find that tale too extraordinary to contemplate, but it's an indication of the controversy which Rumsfeld generates.

All of this must make outsiders wonder about the openness and candor proclaimed by Rumsfeld and the President. In this situation, Schlesinger and Colby apparently conducted themselves with far more candor and openness than either Mr. Ford or Rumsfeld.

It's now known that Schlesinger told the President in a Saturday meeting that he might not support Mr. Ford if he cut the defense budget too greatly.

Colby, in testifying before senators investigating CIA conduct, chose to come clean and tell all—or as much as he possibly could without compromising his agents. This candidness, including Colby's confirmation of assassination plots linked to past Presidents, has never been well accepted inside the White House. He has been second-guessed by Rumsfeld, Phil Buchen and others.

When fired, both men were reported "cool but correct" with the President. Colby, in particular, surprised Mr. Ford with his calmness. The rejection of jobs by both, while not entirely surprising the President, reportedly set him back on his heels because they acted with such firmness. Neither considered such a possibility for an instant although it's known both men are of modest means with large families.

Bush, in contrast to Colby, is well-heeled. He is personable and is known for his loyalty. That means much to Gerald Ford these days.

Rumsfeld, while not rich, doesn't have to be a millionaire because he has a job—unlike those fired.

I have always respected General Scowcroft. He's an intelligent, soft-spoken man with a quiet sense of humor. Dedicated, a man who normally works a thirteen-hour day, Scowcroft is wise without any trappings of arrogance. He has a somewhat poetic touch at times, as I have noted in his reviews of speeches that I have written, but is a hard-core military man. Some claim he may become independent of Kissinger and I hope so. However, Kissinger undoubtedly will attempt to influence most of Scowcroft's work. Intrigue and power are instinctive to Kissinger.

When all is said and done, it comes down to the fact that Mr. Ford, fifteen months after taking office, is still trying to be "presidential." He has been told by his best friends that he leaves many Americans with the feeling that he's floundering in the Oval Office; one result is the Sunday Massacre.

With many men now jockeying for the vice presidency . . . with Rumsfeld gone from his side to Defense . . . with his old anchor, Bob Hartmann, partly cast aside . . . with conservative Republicans joining Ronald Reagan to denounce the firing of Schlesinger . . . with still no satisfactory explanation of the shakeup forthcoming . . . with David Packard and Lee Nunn, two pros, resigning from his campaign committee, saying it was not being run efficiently . . . with great difficulties in raising funds for the 1976 GOP campaign . . . with the Republican left or progressives threatening to put up their own presidential candidate . . . with Elliot Richardson returning from London, pleased at his new appointment as Commerce secretary, but not hiding the fact that his main ambition is an elective office . . . with a continued and rising battle between Press Secretary Nessen and the White House correspondents . . .

with John Connally making contradictory noises about the state of the economy and the nation . . . it is difficult to see how the President can tell the nation: "I am very happy."

And it's almost impossible to accept the word being passed down from the top:

"This is a great moment for the President. He's starting off with a clean slate!"

Tuesday, November 4, 1975

DICK CHENEY WILL REPLACE RUMSFELD. I learn this early in the day. Thus Rumsfeld has won a smashing victory.

I happen to like Cheney. He is modest without seeming to work at it. He is tough without being abrasive. Cheney is loyal without wearing loyalty on his lapel. He is intelligent without displaying the arrogance and studied aloofness of Rumsfeld. Cheney, thirty-four years old and a University of Wyoming graduate, has the ability to be his own man without Rumsfeld, who has been his mentor. It is critical to his success, and that of the President, that he demonstrate his independence from Rumsfeld at this point. Otherwise, it will be said that "Rummy" is still "running the White House" and that would be fatal for Cheney and, perhaps, the President.

Details of the firings of Schlesinger and Colby are beginning to leak out. Speculation inside the White House is rampant. For openers, one White House veteran confides to me in private:

"That seals the door on Hartmann if anyone ever had any doubts. The President is telling him and all of us that Hartmann couldn't cut it as his chief adviser. Hartmann is a lousy administrator. Cheney is an up-and-coming kid with the moxie to do the job.

"That raises a further question—all the rumors about Hartmann not doing a good job with the speechwriting staff. It's not being run right. I fear that Hartmann may escape the axe because he has so many years with the President. So you have to ask: Who's going to get it?"

The story on Rockefeller, pieced together from Rocky's staff, appears to be this. Rocky believes he's being hassled by the President's staff, particularly Rumsfeld. The tale is long and tortuous, beginning with the sniping at his place on the 1976 GOP ticket by Bo

Callaway and ending with Rumsfeld's sitting on some of his staff's position papers while professing friendship.

The VP has a low opinion of Mr. Ford's top staff, regarding most of them as "amateurs" who couldn't make his team. He believes they lack experience in national affairs but have the effrontery to act like experts. Rocky concludes the President has too many self-seekers too close to him.

Rocky's most severe criticism is that the White House staff is disorganized. He believes it's wandering, drifting without goals or principles. Mr. Ford is not exerting vigorous leadership on behalf of the country and, at the same time, is not allowing Rockefeller to demonstrate his abilities as a leader.

It seems ironic to me that Ronald Reagan is basing his candidacy and campaign on Rocky's exact premise.

All reports from New Hampshire and Florida clearly indicate that Reagan's forces are better organized than Mr. Ford's people. I hear from Gwen Anderson and Jack Calkins, political operatives reporting to Hartmann, that there's much work to do but they're "optimistic."

With these two opening primaries only four months away, some attribute the recent White House shakeup to "clearing the decks" for the campaign. This appears to be partly true, but it's obviously only part of the answer. There's entirely too much subterranean politicking for personal gain inside the White House to accept such a simplistic analysis. The real answers must be found in the maze of political and personal conflicts which seem to epitomize this White House. It seems to be each man and each clique operating on the basis of self-interest, not the interests of the President and the country.

Wednesday, November 5, 1975

THIS MORNING'S TALK around the White House is that everyone lost in the Sunday Massacre. President Ford, Schlesinger, Colby, Rockefeller, Rumsfeld, Bush, Richardson—none has gained by the top-level shakeup. My personal observations support this view.

The President's credibility is being severely challenged in the press for the first time. Newspapers across the country indicate Mr.

Ford has been much less than candid in his firing of Schlesinger and Colby. Reporters criticize the President's unwillingness to reveal whether he tried to talk Rocky into staying on his "team." Some flatly refuse to accept the President's assertion that his actions were neither "personal" nor "political." Many ask searching questions on why Mr. Ford apparently will no longer tolerate "intellectual dissent" among his top advisers while still claiming "candor and openness."

The administration has lost because Schlesinger's articulate distrust of the Russians will no longer be voiced in the highest councils of the land.

Colby has lost because he will no longer be in a position to "rehabilitate" the CIA. He hoped to accomplish this by being direct and honest with the Congress. Although he will remain as CIA chief for a while, his bargaining power has been significantly reduced. Colby, accepting himself as the "sacrificial lamb" to preserve much of the strength of the American intelligence system, is a man worthy of respect.

Rockefeller has lost because he appears to be closing the door forever on his presidential hopes despite his aides' denial. Some claim privately that Rocky's "resignation" is a "Declaration of Independence" from Mr. Ford. If the President receives the Republican nomination, they suggest, the Vice President may not campaign with zeal for the 1976 GOP ticket. And if Mr. Ford falters in the first few primaries, Rocky may reassess his chances, resign and run for the presidency himself.

Rumsfeld has lost because his name is headlined across the nation as an intriguer, conniver and political hatchet man. He is called the architect of the Sunday Massacre. His "victory" in becoming the Secretary of Defense may be the biggest defeat of his personal and professional life because, as a result of this penetrating publicity, Don Rumsfeld may never again be trusted by his fellow politicians and the American people.

Bush has lost because he is basically a politician. The American people will find it most difficult to accept "politics" mixing with the CIA. It's a foregone conclusion that the Democrats will not easily accept it and Bush may become a political liability to Mr. Ford.

Richardson, not really part of the shakeup because he succeeds

Rogers Morton who is resigning as Commerce secretary, may lose by association with the Sunday Massacre. He gained fame by refusing to go along with Nixon's Saturday Night Massacre and it's ironic that his name should be associated with another. This may be unfair to Richardson but then the game of politics is unfair.

Why am I so convinced that the President and the White House have lost so heavily? Because the confidence of this President and this White House rises and falls by what the media say and do.

The President and his staff will read of the "clumsy handling" of the firings, the "disarray exposed in the White House" and other comments. Most will privately conclude that they made a mistake. In fact, this is already happening. However, there's some sharp hairsplitting. Most staffers blame the negative reaction on the "leak" and subsequent "handling" of the firings. This is false. This is what the Nixon people believed, that they were "done in" for reasons of public relations. Now, the Ford team is repeating that mistake. The firings have nothing to do with public relations. They have everything to do with substance.

Some of the President's top men are trying to separate their image from the President's. Kissinger is swearing to James Reston, of the *New York Times,* that he had nothing to do with Schlesinger's firing. Rumsfeld also appeals to Reston, insisting he opposed the Schlesinger dismissal. It is incredible to think that either would discuss such a delicate matter with Reston since each is implicitly placing all the blame squarely on the President. It's all the more unbelievable since both intend to continue as leaders in the Ford administration. Most incredible of all, Kissinger and Rumsfeld appear confident they can get away with it—at Mr. Ford's expense!

So the old question, which I've been asking myself for many months, returns again: Who is in charge of the government?

Those closest to the President are passing down the word that the President acted as he did because "he didn't want to hurt good men."

That's nonsense. Good men have been hurt—even humiliated.

I write these words with a sad heart and record these thoughts with deep dismay. Yet there is still time. The President can still seize the hour and the day—and the presidency.

The phone rings and a secretary tells me that Bob Hartmann wants to see me. Hartmann is all business. He wants me to write a major speech on energy in twenty-four hours. He lists several points, including the fact that "the President wants to hit Congress hard on energy." Suddenly, Hartmann fires a broadside question: "What's wrong with the speech department?"

I say nothing for a moment, recognizing an obviously dynamite question. Hartmann puts his hands together on his chin, as if in deep contemplation, and he begins a rambling discourse:

"The President isn't exactly overjoyed at the speeches these days. I am written out—burned out. That's the President's fault although he doesn't recognize it. He's talking too goddamned much. And he wants a brand new bellringer every time."

Hartmann pauses, rubs his hands through his gray hair, and lowers his voice:

"Something is wrong in our department, though. And I've got to get to the bottom of it before someone does it for me. People are taking potshots. The President is unhappy. And I don't want Cheney to start getting involved. I want to be ahead of them. Now, you tell me, what do you think is wrong?"

I tell Hartmann I wish to say nothing·that would reflect on Theis although some of my observations may. Theis is "hard-working, dedicated, loyal and honest."

Hartmann interjects: "What's wrong?"

My mind keeps telling me: If he doesn't know what the hell is really wrong, sitting where he does, then we are in much worse shape than I have ever believed. Does Hartmann genuinely seek information or an "out" for the criticism aimed at him and Friedman recently in their handling of the two California speeches? The President kept rejecting their writing. I privately agreed with Mr. Ford. Both addresses were devastatingly dull and badly written. Is Hartmann looking for scapegoats? Is all this an elaborate ruse to blame the other speechwriters? Is this the bottom line—survival? I decide to navigate slowly:

"There are too many people involved in the editing process, in clearing the speeches. For example, in the Chicago hardware speech I wrote, at least sixteen and I think as many as nineteen people took a crack at that speech. It was a nightmare. This has been going on for the entire year I've been here. Too many people are writing critiques and our speeches are written by committee."

"What's the answer?" Hartmann asks. I reply:

"The answer is that you have to cut down the number of people clearing the speeches, to about five at most. And the editor has to be tough. He can't let too many people bulldoze him on style and theme. He has to stand firm."

Hartmann presses me for hard answers, appearing not to know the obvious so I am forced to continue:

"I hand in all major speeches to Theis ten days ahead of time. That's his rule. But Theis' desk is piled high with letters he's answering and a lot of other junk that he shouldn't be handling. Theis seems to be obsessed with the trivial. So the speech sits there for a week. Three days before the President is to give it, Theis suddenly discovers the speech. We are then in a crisis. This first draft still has to be cleared by everybody and his brother,-to say nothing of the possibility that the subject matter may not be exactly what you or the President want." (This is a broad hint to Hartmann that he and the President are not giving us sufficient guidance and direction on presidential addresses. He pretends not to notice it.)

Hartmann prods further:

"So you think Theis should clear his desk of this other work?"

I answer:

"I would take the other work and give to Bob Rousek. Let him compose letters to high schools and constituents. So what if he blows some letters. That's not like blowing a speech to millions of people. Theis should dump all that stuff in a wastebasket and give it to Rousek."

Hartmann reflects:

"What you really seem to be saying is we should divide our work between the written and spoken word. Isn't that really it? Which job would you give to Theis?"

I reply without hesitation:

"The written word. Theis is a compulsive editor and procrastinator. That puts us in perpetual crisis. He also edits for the eye and not the ear. And he's not tough in holding off all the people who want to edit the speeches. He's editing speeches by committee."

"Who would you get to edit the speeches?" Hartmann asks.

"I don't know. Maybe a guy like Dick Whalen. I don't know Whalen, but I have read his books and he has a lot of good ideas and is an excellent writer."

233

Hartmann remarks that he doesn't know who Whalen is so I offer further information. He voices suspicion, saying that Whalen worked for Nixon. I say, "Just briefly, and then left him because he didn't trust Haldeman and Ehrlichman." Hartmann asks me for other names. I tell him I need time to think about it. Nevertheless, I am surprised that he offers no names since he knows as many if not more newsmen and writers in Washington. Hartmann, in casting suspicion, draws suspicion on his own remarks.

Hartmann suddenly asks me if I would edit the speeches. I tell him that I am perfectly happy in what I'm doing and, as a matter of fact, have no desire to take on the job.

Hartmann then drops his voice:

"I am trying to save Theis—and maybe myself."

Hartmann smiles. I know the smile. It is one of his old habits when he wishes to show he is deadly serious.

"I am going to handle the speeches directly from now on. I'll deal directly with the writers. This second- and third-hand stuff doesn't work."

Hartmann mentions that he will be speaking with the other writers about what is wrong. He may be making some moves to strengthen the staff. The conversation ends almost as abruptly as it begins. I walk back to my office and cannot help but reflect on Hartmann's crucial observation about saving Theis and himself.

These are the words of a desperate man battling for survival. And so I ask myself:

Is Hartmann a man of integrity? Is he looking for honest answers to improve the President's speeches? Or is he looking for cosmetics, a change here and there, to imply that he's acting to improve the speeches? Or is he so desperate that he will sacrifice anyone to survive, and hope that anyone he brings in may do a better job? Is he so desperate to buy that kind of time?

The answers to those questions await us all.

Thursday, November 6, 1975

WE SEEM ON THE VERGE OF CIVIL WAR inside the White House. The Rockefeller people are talking very tough. It's almost like my first days here when the Ford and Nixon teams fought each other.

Rocky's people say he's declaring independence from the President. I ask if it's "secession"? The answer: "It's political freedom." Would he run against Ford? Smiles from the Vice President's aides.

Rocky himself says in a news conference that he would not campaign for the President because that would be "illegal." Ridiculous. No Vice President has been stopped by any such campaign rules or laws in the past.

Rocky's men say all of the President's rationale for utilizing Rockefeller, with all his government and administrative experience, has collapsed. Mr. Ford's words about broadening the party with the Vice President's help ring hollow to Rocky's aides.

My greatest fear for the President's future appears a foregone conclusion; he will not have sufficient support from the Rockefeller-dominated Domestic Council to conduct an issue-oriented, substantive campaign.

In addition to the Rockefeller problem, the word "credibility" is back on the White House scene. The last question at Mr. Ford's recent news conference was:

"Are you saying, and intending to be understood to say, that neither personal nor policy differences between Dr. Kissinger and Dr. Schlesinger contributed to this change [Schlesinger's dismissal]?"

The President replied, "That is correct."

No one in Washington apparently accepts that answer.

The image of a candid President disappeared from the nation's television screens last Monday evening. Mr. Ford disappointed me greatly. I recall sitting in front of the television set for a long time, seeing CBS news commentators discussing the President's performance, but I could not hear them. My mind had frozen on the fact that Mr. Ford had stonewalled it. He talked of "my guys" and refused to give a straight answer to why he fired Schlesinger and Colby. Gerald Ford had humiliated two good men and now, I feared, the sword might be pointing at him.

Friday, November 7, 1975

PAUL THEIS QUESTIONS ME about my meeting with Bob Hartmann. He wants to know "how things went." I am surprised. For one reason or another, even if it's a ruse, Hartmann is deliberately going around Theis to speak directly with some of the writers. If he felt Theis should be at these meetings, presumably he would have asked him.

So the question is unfair. But Theis is uptight these days, seemingly unable to control his concern. I tell Theis three things. I told Hartmann he, Theis, was an honest and hard-working individual. There are entirely too many people editing the speeches and some of the editing is very poor. All of the unimportant matters should be cleared from Theis' desk, given to someone else, and all of our efforts should be concentrated on the President's speeches.

When I finish, Theis says quietly, "You are right."

Theis begins a long and rambling monologue, saying the President has told Hartmann that the speeches must be improved. Theis talks of being "tired and worn out." On and on, Theis wanders over the White House landscape, portraying the general situation as going from bad to worse. He is, in effect, crying out for help. However, I know the only way I can help him is to write better speeches and hope he will not butcher them. Theis has become a creature of Milt Friedman, whose professional judgment is not the best and whose personal ethics are questionable in the minds of some of our staff. Friedman will not save Theis. Friedman will save only himself.

This is the kind of atmosphere that pervades much of the White House under President Ford. He encourages competitive rivalry but doesn't want any blood on the carpets.

The names need not be Schlesinger versus Kissinger. The names could also be: Hartmann versus Rumsfeld; Greenspan versus Seidman; Simon versus Hartmann and Rumsfeld; Nessen versus Kissinger; Friedman versus most of the other speechwriters; Theis versus Bob Goldwin; or, Callaway versus Rockefeller. The list could go on and on.

Mr. Ford extols options, the need for different people to offer him various opinions on decisions. When he sets this rivalry in motion, he seems to expect no conflict.

I have asked myself a dozen times: Why does he expect no conflict?

The only conclusion I have been able to ascertain over the past year is that as a congressman, Mr. Ford became accustomed to cloakroom compromises. He had been conditioned to feel comfortable with accommodation. The difficult decisions reaching the White House involve deep personal and professional principles. Apparently, Mr. Ford doesn't want to face—I do not believe he cannot see—the difference between compromising moral principles and compromising legislative positions. Men and women sometimes cannot and will not compromise their principles. And they should not be expected to do so.

The White House staff is asking itself: Who are "my guys" that the President referred to as necessary for him to run the White House properly? They are, as best as I can determine: Hartmann, Marsh, Buchen and Seidman. This is a mediocre crew. It is quite doubtful that any of them would ever reach the White House on professional ability.

I deeply feel that Mr. Ford's firing of Schlesinger and Colby was uncharacteristically cruel and startlingly revealing. The object was quite egotistical; he proved he had the guts of a national leader. But such an abrupt action with the explanation that he was not at ease with these men boggles the mind. The careers of these men are at least equal to if not greater than that of Gerald Ford before his appointment to the White House.

This prompts another question: What does Mr. Ford seek in a staff? Mediocrity. Why mediocrity? Is Mr. Ford a true believer in Sam Rayburn, the veteran Democratic House leader, who provided young congressmen with this "sage" advice: "To git along, you got to go along."

The atmosphere in the White House after the Schlesinger-Colby firings by the President appears to be consistent with Sam Rayburn's advice: "Keep your head down and your mouth shut." Why? The 1976 campaign is beginning. We're in a new phase. The aim is to win.

More and more, I am coming to the conclusion that Mr. Ford just wants to "hang in there," hoping to come out on top without ruffling many feathers. He's less interested in "leadership" than he is in "survival." This may explain what is happening to the speeches that I and others have been writing. Direct, tough, straight speeches are deliberately compromised into "safe" speeches that won't cause too many waves. Hartmann and Theis appear far less interested in leadership for the nation than in their own personal survival.

My phone rings. It's Bob Rousek. He says Theis wants me to turn in all my material on the North Carolina Central

University speech. Rousek says Theis wants ten minutes of jokes. Bob Orben, our gag writer, will take over.

I ask Rousek what's going on. He says that Red Cavaney, the President's chief advance man, phoned from the university saying the speech should be jokes. I ask why Cavaney is suddenly deciding the content of the President's speeches and Rousek replies:

"It's orders from Theis, Jack. That's all I know."

Theis is busy so I advise Rousek that the President cannot go to this black college on the 50th anniversary of its founding, a solemn and historic occasion, and tell jokes. It would be an unmitigated disaster.

Rousek insists he must follow orders but agrees to speak with Theis.

I call John C. Calhoun, a black aide to Bill Baroody, on the matter. John says:

"Listen, man, we're sick of hearing jokes and getting the soft shoe from Whitey. That's been going on for a hundred years or more. The worst thing the President could do would be to address a formal gathering like this with jokes. Man, that's absolutely unbelievable. I just can't believe it. Has Theis gone nuts?"

I need Calhoun to back up my argument. I phone Rousek and quote Calhoun. Rousek says I had better prepare a serious speech if I feel that strongly; then my address would be available if needed. He says he has spoken with Theis, who would like to see what I come up with. In the meantime, they have alerted Orben.

I have had many disagreeable professional experiences since coming to the White House. This equals any of them.

Monday, November 10, 1975

THEIS, THE ENGAGING LAMB, has become an enraged bull. For weeks, Judy Morton has been indicating this to the staff. The two engage in another hot exchange this morning. Theis insists that Judy forgot to give him the reading copy of the President's address to the Marine Corps. Calling from the waiting room just outside the Oval Office, Theis begins screaming at Judy, who responds that she had earlier asked him four times if he wanted the Marine speech.

Theis also vents his anger at me. He claims that a *New York Times* story disproves a statement I wrote for the President. In essence, the *Times* sees the Marine Corps' first amphibious landing, on March 3, 1776, near British Nassau, as a failure. Pushed by Friedman, Theis leans into me, suggesting that I did sloppy work and he would consult with Agnes Waldron in the research office. Agnes rebuts Theis verbally and in a written memo. I respond via memo since Theis hangs up the phone on me.

Agnes sums up our office morale in these words:

"I was in the 1960 campaign, and that was bad. I was in the 1972 campaign, and that was worse. And I watched Nixon fall, thinking that was the lowest level. But this atmosphere is absolutely hysterical. No question; this is hysteria. And we're not even into the campaign."

Tension is precisely that which the President says he's trying to avoid in the White House. On "Meet the Press" yesterday, Mr. Ford said that "growing tension" caused him to fire Defense Secretary Schlesinger. The President's exact words were:

"I need a feeling of comfort within an organization: no tension, complete cohesion . . . a comfortable feeling . . ."

Bob Hartmann apparently has received this message. For the first time since coming to the White House, he has begun to attend the morning senior staff meetings at eight o'clock. Sitting to the left of Dick Cheney, directing the staff meeting as Rumsfeld once did, Hartmann stuns his colleagues. Some of those present indicate Hartmann ended his boycott because the President is insisting that internal feuds must end. Others say Hartmann will now start directing the speech staff personally. Both interpretations appear correct.

But the most important question remains: Will Hartmann and Cheney work effectively together?

In the late afternoon, Judy Morton advises me that Hartmann and Theis discussed with the President the speech I had written for his appearance at North Carolina Central University. They met at 12:30 P.M. today without me or Pat Butler, who wrote a North Carolina fund-raising speech. In other words, a new policy may be developing in which some of the writers are excluded from meeting with Mr. Ford on the speeches they write for him.

I ask Butler about this and he mentions that he has been excluded from such meetings with the President for several weeks. He says:

"Hartmann and Theis want to control things. They don't want any questions. They want total control."

Butler is bitter. He laments that the speechwriting staff has been divided into cliques—Theis, Friedman and Orben who have formed a self-protection clique, and the rest of the writers who are subject to blame for whatever happens.

I tell Butler that the real responsibility for poor speeches belongs to Hartmann, Theis and Friedman since Mr. Ford has been rejecting their speeches. The "lousy writing" and "lack of direction" starts at the top.

Butler confides that "I cannot serve the President in this manner. I am being blockaded on all sides. They cut up my speeches without rhyme or reason.

"If things don't happen dramatically for the better in the next few weeks, I'm leaving. I just can't go on like this. I'm treated like a second-class citizen and made to feel as if I'm not even wanted."

Butler feels that he may be made the "scapegoat" for failure at the top.

Judy calls me to say briefly:

"Mr. Theis is still editing your North Carolina speech."

And I reply:

"Judy, Paul Theis has been editing my North Carolina speech for longer than it took me to do all the research and writing. I don't go by my watch. I look at the calendar."

Tuesday, November 11, 1975

I JUST FINISHED MY THIRD speech assignment of the week, when Judy Morton, our top secretary, phones at midmorning and asks to see me privately. She comes to my office and, for an hour and a half, pours out her heart about her work.

Judy, a refined and reserved young lady, bitterly criticizes Milt Friedman. She describes Friedman's "tirades" which belittle her as "incompetent and worse." Judy describes him in bitter terms and says:

"He's dividing the staff and Paul is letting him do it. I told Mr. Theis several times that Friedman was destroying his working relationship with the other writers. But Paul always goes along with

Friedman. Paul rarely touches what Friedman writes and always agrees with what he says. He wants to swim with the current.''

Judy spends a long time lamenting Theis's insecurity and dependence on Friedman. She concludes:

"Friedman is always telling us, the secretaries, that he's the only competent writer on the staff. And Paul Theis cannot see that Friedman is destroying the staff's morale. He's really working against the President when you come down to it.''

Judy tells of a dozen or more private talks with Theis, begging him to treat all the speechwriters equally. She talks of shouting matches with Theis, and concludes that her White House dreams have collapsed. She's beginning to hate the White House as well as her job. Her sense of honor and privilege about serving the country and the American people has faded. Judy says: "I worked in the Nixon White House. Nixon was in charge and you knew it. There was a lot of work, a lot of long hours, but you knew what you were doing and why. No one knows what he or she is doing around here any more because the President doesn't seem to be in charge or giving us direction. Everybody is going his own way and bumping into the next person. It's chaotic.''

Judy leaves and Theresa Rosenberger, one of our researchers, is soon on the phone explaining why she could not obtain on schedule for me the material needed for the President's talking points for an upcoming meeting with magazine publishers. Theresa claims there's "no communication" between the White House communications office, a liaison office with the news media outside Washington, and the White House press office. She relates that the two staffs can't seem to agree on functions which overlap. This has caused some sharp feelings between the staffs. Thus the communications office, which is involved with the magazine publishers' meeting with Mr. Ford, did not know the number of formal interviews given by the President. In fact, Theresa relates, this office told her the information was not available. She found the number, fifty-five such interviews, in the press office. And the press office staff told her: "The communications office doesn't know what it's doing.''

The final draft of the West Virginia energy speech, edited by Hartmann and Theis, is before me. This is the first speech that I've written after meeting with Hartmann on how to run our office better. At that time, Hartmann gave me the following instructions on the West Virginia address:

"The purpose of this speech is to get the President out in front of the Congress on energy. And he wants to hit the Congress hard. Therefore, the thing we have to emphasize is this: congressional legislation, as it now stands, stresses the conservation and allocation of energy. Nothing that the Congress proposes will increase the production of energy. The President's proposals of last January do just that in two ways, by offering industry the incentive to produce more domestic oil by gradual decontrol of prices, and by supporting new energy production through the Energy Independence Authority."

I wrote a hard-hitting energy speech following Hartmann's guidelines. I summarized by saying that the current congressional proposals would not "produce one drop of oil in the name of energy independence for this country." And I continued:

"In energy, we are standing still. The Congress has not moved one inch.

"The choice is up to the Congress: to stand still in energy—to retreat from responsibility and reality—to threaten our economic recovery—or to move forward with legislation that will produce energy and economic stability for this nation.

"I believe the American people want, as they always have, responsibility and reality. We in the Republican Party are prepared to provide it."

I ended the speech there.

Here is how Theis and Hartmann ended the address:

"Let's make sure we decide for an America at peace, for a nation renewed, for a people with pride, for a future that summons us to new achievement and glory and greatness. With your help, we can do it! Thank you all very much."

I wrote above it in red letters: Baloney!

The difference between the two speeches is remarkable. Theis and Hartmann had written another marshmallow, after all of Hartmann's emphasis on a "tough" energy speech. They killed most of the "tough" lines in my draft and handed the President of the United States another serving of bland platitudes.

Thursday, November 13, 1975

GEORGE WALKER, A NEW SPEECHWRITER, stops me in a hallway and wants to talk. Walker tells me he's trying to understand a "new system'' introduced by Hartmann and Theis. He asks why two writers are now being assigned to the same speech. Theis requested that both of us write a West Virginia speech for the President.

I paid little attention to the fact at the time because of Hartmann's explanation to me. Hartmann said he considered it ''unfair'' to ask a new man like Walker to tackle such a complicated subject as energy. Yet he wanted to see what Walker could produce under pressure. Since I had been writing most of the energy speeches, Hartmann said he wanted a backup speech.

Walker explains he now has a second such assignment. He and Pat Butler are writing differing versions of a presidential fund-raising speech before North Carolina Republicans. I now understand Walker's earlier expression about a ''new system.'' He believes the assignment of two writers to the same speech is now a regular procedure.

George wants to know how or why such a procedure developed. He has never seen it previously. Nor have I.

George continues:

''Theis called me in and asked me what I thought about this new system. I said I didn't think much of it because it pits writer against writer on the same staff. This is bound to cause personal and professional friction. I told him I would divide the speeches according to knowledge and capabilities of each writer—a feature writer, an energy writer and so on.

''I also told him that this was writing a speech by committee. You just can't blend two different speeches very easily. When you do, both will suffer. On top of that, we are already writing speeches by committee because of all the people who clear the speeches.''

George asks me how many writers have come and gone on the staff. I list them for him: Earl Culp, John Coyne, Fred Bird, Aram Bakshian, Bob Longood, and Kaye Pullen. Walker then says:

''You might as well add another name—mine. I've just been told they won't need me after this temporary period. But they may call me back in the future.''

Seven speechwriters will have come and gone in the fifteen months that President Ford has been in office. That's one about every two months. All voiced the same complaint: ''You can't write a speech by committee.''

Now, as Hartmann and Theis apparently battle for survival, they increase the committee by assigning two writers to a single speech.

243

My phone is ringing as I return to my office. Theis asks me to come to his office immediately to discuss the North Carolina Central University speech. Aaron Spaulding, a relatively new black appointee in the personnel office, is with Theis. Paul tells me that Aaron has some suggestions for this address, which I have completed writing. Theis warns me that I have only forty-five minutes before the speech must be presented cleanly typed to the President. So I ask Spaulding his suggestions and he replies, "A new speech."

"Beautiful," I reply. Theis appears shocked and he moves away saying he is working on another deadline.

Spaulding says he is a graduate of North Carolina Central and what they want and need is a speech on education. I tell Spaulding that I cannot write a major speech on education in forty-five minutes—also that a speech on education means a speech on busing. The President has nothing new to say on busing. Even if he did, I would not advise him to give such an address at a virtually all-black college. The university leaders in their correspondence left the choice of speech subject to the President.

After the meeting with Spaulding, I advise Theis that the speech should remain basically as I wrote it. It was a discourse on competition, opportunity for blacks and other minorities in American society. The address concentrates on the contributions of blacks to American life and the growing interdependence of the world and American society. Competition breeds harmony, not division. Lack of competition breeds division because people then feel they do not have a chance, that society or the world is denying them opportunity. The speech is a call to American black youth to join American competitive life through a good education and to seize educational opportunity because it may never pass their way again.

Theis asks me to accompany him to a meeting with the President on the speech and two others by Friedman and Butler shortly. When I show up to attend the meeting, Theis says I am not needed.

Butler, however, is deeply hurt that he cannot discuss directly with the President the speech he wrote for a North Carolina GOP fund-raising event. Theis rules him out. However, Paul invites Orben and Friedman to the meeting. Butler says he is about to quit because he's being treated so shabbily.

Agnes Waldron, Kaye Pullen and Butler hold a meeting of their own about the speech written by Friedman for a Georgia GOP fund-raising dinner. In it, the President calls for rebel yells, talks about Georgia peach fuzz and exhorts those present to stage a "comeback" of the GOP in Georgia. The Republican party has never been anywhere in Georgia, Agnes points out, and therefore it can't make a "comeback." The trio agrees. It is the worst speech written for Mr. Ford since he assumed the presidency. When asked later, I remind them that such griping solves nothing and that they are powerless. I say that if Mr. Ford cannot perceive a bad speech, then perhaps he should suffer through it.

The three retire in disarray. It has been another day of frustration and disagreement among the White House speechwriting staff.

Tuesday, November 18, 1975

I FIND ON MY DESK TODAY a September 26, 1975, speech by Ronald Reagan to the Executive Club of Chicago. Attached is a note from Hartmann asking everyone on the staff to read the address. He points out this is Reagan's "new" campaign speech. I ask myself why it took nearly two months for Hartmann to send it to us.

Don Rumsfeld is gone as the White House staff coordinator amid strong denials that he was involved in the firing of Defense Secretary Schlesinger. Rumsfeld took pains to stress his innocence. Yet many in the White House still do not believe him. They look to his successor, Dick Cheney, for less controversy.

Cheney is impressing many with his reserve. He doesn't press his opinions on others, and particularly the President, as Rumsfeld did. Cheney makes sure that everyone who should be heard on a question is heard by Mr. Ford.

There is much less tension in the West Wing. Hartmann, for example, is not as uptight with Cheney as he was with Rumsfeld. He's satisfied with his access to the President and his current role. So far, Cheney is not trying to second-guess him.

Others continue to second-guess Hartmann. A good number inside the White House are disturbed by the gap between the president's rhetoric and reality. In a recent conversation, Mike Duval expressed this view strongly as we chatted in his office.

Duval, now working on matters involving American intelligence troubles on Capitol Hill, insists Mr. Ford is a strong conservative on the campaign trail and a weak compromiser in the White House. He advises me that he has expressed the same view to Cheney. On energy and the New York financial crisis in particular, the President has captured many headlines for his toughness but appears to be retreating from his original positions in favor of accommodation.

Thursday, November 20, 1975

THERESA ROSENBERGER, one of our researchers, stops by for a chat. She asks me what I thought of the President's recent Georgia fund-raising address. I decide to mumble my way out of the question, but Theresa provides her own reply:

"It was the worst speech Mr. Ford has given as President. And written by his worst speechwriter, Friedman."

I say little since I'm trying to stay out of front-office politics. But Theresa decides to ramble back to the Ford vice presidency. She recalls: "The Nixon speechwriters were doing his speeches for him. Aram Bakshian and John Coyne wrote virtually all his speeches as Vice President. Remember when Mr. Ford said he was his own man and believed in Nixon. The press kept claiming that the Nixon speechwriters were doing the Ford speeches. And the Ford people maintained it wasn't true. Of course, it was true.

"Then came the famous Atlantic City speech. That was written by Aram Bakshian. And it caused a real uproar in the press. All the reporters said Mr. Ford had gone overboard in his support of Nixon. And then Bob Hartmann leaked the story to them that it was true—this speech was written by a Nixon speechwriter.

"I remember that Dave Gergen, who was running the presidential speechwriting staff, had words with Hartmann about that. He told Hartmann to get his own writers.

"The first person they offered a job to was Bakshian. He declined. So they went to John Coyne and he didn't want the job. So Milt Friedman was a third choice—a third choice."

Theresa and Friedman agree on little if anything, so I let the comment pass. But Theresa continues:

"That's why Theis and Friedman worked together to give Bakshian such poor assignments. Because he was a threat to them.

He was a good writer and they knew it. So he left. He had no choice.''

I go for a walk at lunchtime. It's a magnificent fall day, the most beautiful autumn in Washington within memory. The sun is warm and there is not a cloud in the sky.

Friday, November 21, 1975

IT'S THE MORNING AFTER. Ronald Reagan formally announced his candidacy for the presidency yesterday.

Our Presidents, from Eisenhower to Nixon, are implicated in CIA plots to assassinate foreign leaders. A 347-page Senate Intelligence Committee report charges that our chief executives failed in their duties to prevent such plots.

The nation's Roman Catholic bishops launch an anti-abortion drive with major political implications. Calling for Catholic political effort in every congressional district across the country, the bishops of forty-eight million Catholics are injecting the Church into the 1976 campaign to a degree unparalleled in American history. The grassroots campaign favors a constitutional amendment prohibiting abortion.

Jim Cannon, chief of the Domestic Council, is passing around a position paper on abortion which he recommends that the President sign. Dated November 17, 1975, the recommendation makes two points. The President should take the position that the Supreme Court has spoken and Mr. Ford will follow the law of the land (a 1973 Supreme Court decision struck down states' restrictive abortion laws and allowed abortion within the first six months of pregnancy). The President should, at the same time, indicate abortion decisions should be in the hands of the states.

This shallow thinking is astonishing. The position paper straddles the issue and puts Mr. Ford once again in the position of being unable to make up his mind.

I am further astonished that the position paper offers little substance on the issue, one of the most complicated moral questions in the world today. Instead, it meanders off mentioning Mr. Ford's past stands on abortion and the fact that the Defense Department has reversed itself from the Nixon days and allows abortions in military installations. It notes such abortions are paid for by Medicaid. These well-known facts add nothing new to anyone's insight. No meaningful moral choices are offered the President.

I'm appalled at such cursory staff work and so is Agnes Waldron. Since I'm busy writing a speech, I urge Agnes to write Hartmann and sock it to this weak position paper. She does.

This subject is important not only in itself but also because the President is being pounded almost daily in the press across the country for too much vacillation. Mr. Ford is portrayed as constantly wavering back and forth on New York and energy as well as a number of other issues. One pollster says the President's negative performance rating may be irreversible. Surveys point out a "lack of firmness and sense of vision."

I go to Jim Cavanaugh, deputy director of the Domestic Council, to obtain some direction in the writing of speeches. Cavanaugh, an able and direct individual, tells me:

"I know precisely what you mean. Direction is precisely what we need. We have got to get organized."

I tell Cavanaugh that I have written many speeches for the President with virtually no direction from him or anyone else. I begin listing some of the speeches, including one to the New Hampshire state legislature.

The New Hampshire address, considered by the media a major address on the President's political philosophy, was entirely what I thought Mr. Ford's political views might be. Cavanaugh looks at the ceiling and replies:

"I know what you mean. Believe me, I see it. We've got to get ourselves organized for the campaign."

I explain how difficult it is to write without guidance—how Mr. Ford's speeches have been criticized as lackluster.

Cavanaugh concedes that very little has been done to determine "the eight to twelve issues that will be the thrust of the campaign." He continues:

"We need to form some kind of board. We've got to get up a position paper on every important issue. And then we have to play these as themes in the President's speeches."

I point out that I need to know what the President stands for, not in terms of fiscal programs, but his goals for the country and his vision of America. I explain to Cavanaugh:

"Theis keeps telling me that Hartmann thinks 'vision' is a Kennedy word. He doesn't like it. 'Vision' belongs to the candidate who uses it. The important thing, however, is that we know specifically what the President thinks about the future of this country. I've been asking for these answers for many months without any success."

Cavanaugh suggests that the President must start having meetings with his political advisers on such specific questions and it should be the Domestic Council's job to follow through on Mr. Ford's direction. But, Cavanaugh concedes, he doesn't know how or when such work will begin. He promises to keep me informed.

I hope that Cavanaugh and the Domestic Council can begin making themselves heard to those who will control the President's campaign. The press and others generally agree that Ronald Reagan has a better campaign staff than the President. Dick Cheney, political liaison to the campaign committee, has no experience whatsoever in a political campaign and is a Rumsfeld, not a Rockefeller, man.

If Mr. Ford loses to Reagan, he would become the first Republican President since Chester A. Arthur in 1884 to seek the nomination and be denied it by his party. The argument that Reagan shouldn't test the President because such a battle might divide the party is not an argument the Democrats have bought in recent times. Senator Eugene McCarthy in 1968 challenged the incumbent; however, the Democrats went on to lose the presidential race.

Monday, November 24, 1975

I FIND NO ONE PLANNING the campaign other than in the most general terms. The "gut" issues are not defined nor is the direction or theme of the campaign.

Instead, staffers gossip about the role Mrs. Betty Ford may play in 1976. The First Lady clearly will campaign for her husband but tells interviewers that she may not agree with him on every issue. Wow!

Mrs. Ford quickly adds that she will not talk issues. And just as quickly, she injects the view that she doesn't support the

President's tough stand against aid to New York City. In a word, Mrs. Ford appears to be spelling trouble in 1976.

The White House has enough of that today. Pat Moynihan, our UN ambassador, is seeing the President. Moynihan's aides leak word that Pat came to the brink of resignation last Friday and discreetly conveyed the idea that Secretary Kissinger was at fault. The UN ambassador's aides slipped word that Moynihan is not being sufficiently backed by the State Department and Kissinger, nor does he have enough room to act as he sees fit.

The mercurial Irishman apparently affronted moderate African leaders in his biting criticism of Uganda President Idi Amin. Moynihan further alienated the Third World by his sharp rebuttal of an Arab-sponsored anti-Zionism resolution in the UN.

Kissinger, however, is appealing to the Third World in terms of energy and resources and calls for global cooperation. The so-called inside word at the State Department is the differences boil down simply to style.

Inside the White House, it's felt that a resignation by Moynihan at this time would only highlight the infighting that has been so characteristic of the Ford administration. It would portray the President as not in control and further publicize disorganization.

The President will thus cool down Moynihan, a five-month appointee, and defuse the squabble. It's still a long way to the convention and the 1976 November election.

In midafternoon, I receive an edited version of the President's Pearl Harbor speech. The following remarks, which I had prepared, are butchered by Milt Friedman:

"We are building across the Pacific a new bridge of understanding between the old nations of Asia and the still young country of America. Between the ageless cultural and intellectual civilization of Asia and the young culture and civilization of America. Between the younger institutions of Asia, socially and industrially, and the world's oldest republic and its most industrialized society which is America.

"Asia is old and yet young. America is young and yet old.

"My mission to Asia was to reconcile the old and manifest the new. That aim is one and the same—to find and demonstrate harmony in diversity. That we have more in common than we do in contrast. And that which one continent has in contrast to the other complements both.

"I am here today at this historic hour to rededicate the United States to the cause of lasting peace in the Pacific and all of Asia:

"We seek not hostility but harmony. We seek not confrontation. but cooperation. We seek not bitter rivalry but a balance of power and interests in Asia. We seek to restrict none but expect all to restrain themselves. We seek not the end of old revolutions but the beginning of new evolutions. We seek less our self-interest than others' self-reliance. We seek the territory of none but the eventual trust of all. We seek lasting peace but not at any price."

Friedman has eliminated all of the first paragraph except the first sentence. He, therefore, has left the following paragraph without proper explanation:

"Asia is old and yet young. America is young and yet old."

Friedman has also eliminated most of the last paragraph where each sentence begins with the words "we seek."

The speech has been, in a word, gutted.*

Bob Rousek agrees and says: "Friedman's changes definitely hurt the speech. They don't make sense in the first place. And he kills the most quotable part of the writing. I've given up on trying to understand the editing around here."

Rousek tells me that Jack Marsh, counselor to the President, "wants more of an old-fashioned Pearl Harbor speech. Marsh wants the speech to say more about American casualties. He says the gold star mothers are not going to like it. He wants your version killed and a new speech written."

I ask Rousek what the Chinese and the Japanese will think if the first remarks President Ford makes after his visit to Peking and Asia is a speech on the casualties and the infamy of Pearl Harbor thirty-four years ago. I say to Rousek:

"Marsh is nuts. This is not a campaign speech. It is supposed to be a statesmanlike five or six minutes about our desire for lasting peace in the Pacific and Asia. Marsh apparently would rather insult the Chinese and certainly the Japanese—and right after the Hirohito and China visits."

Rousek says he's astonished at Marsh's request for a rewrite in behalf of the gold star mothers. I add:

"Let Marsh arrange for a gold star mothers' speech somewhere in Virginia at an appropriate time and place. But not

---

See Appendix, page 351.

the President's first speech after the Asian trip. How the hell can he give the President such advice?''

It's the close of a typical day, a day of quiet desperation.

Wednesday, November 26, 1975

IT'S GEORGE WALKER'S LAST DAY. He returns to his wife and kids in Michigan after a month as a presidential speechwriter. George is the most dismayed and, perhaps, the angriest writer to have come and gone from our staff. He puts his intellectual rage this way:

"I wrote the President's remarks for the judiciary dinner. Friedman cut my stuff to ribbons and then filled it with cliches and platitudes. Even if they asked me, I don't know if I could stay here.

"This place is a closed shop. Theis, Friedman and Orben will cut up any writer to save themselves. Friedman can't write. That's why the President is having so much speech trouble. And if you ever write a magazine article or a book on this place, for God's sake quote me. They're killing the President.''

Walker's deep disappointment rings like an old refrain to me now. So many writers have come with such hopes and left with such bitterness that the words don't knife through me with the same sharpness as in the past. I listen to his last words:

"Any new idea, any new thought, any new phrase is cut. It's replaced with pablum. How can President Ford make it? Tell me. How can he possibly win in '76 under these circumstances? He's surrounded with incompetence in Theis and Friedman.''

I say nothing. I shake hands with George, wish him luck and allow myself the private thought that he has not been given a fair chance as a writer.

Kaye Pullen has pulled up a seat in front of my desk and asks: "Did you hear what happened yesterday?'' When I shake my head in the negative, her face beams in anticipation of her story. Kaye reports:

"Friedman asks Judy Morton if she's leaving because of Paul Theis. Judy says she doesn't know what he means. And Friedman says that there are going to be some personnel changes in our office and she doesn't have to leave if it's because of Theis. In other words, he's telling her that Theis is on the way out.''

Friday, November 28, 1975

I ask Kaye: "I thought Friedman was Theis's friend?"

Kaye whispers:

"For all we know, it's Friedman who's putting the knife to Theis. What better time than when Theis is on the advance trip to China? So Friedman is trying to keep Judy by suggesting that Theis is out."

I interject:

"I think Judy is worth keeping. She's held this place together for them."

Kaye says:

"Apparently Hartmann thinks so, too. He called Judy over to his office and wanted a rundown on what's going on. That can't help Theis or Friedman. After Hartmann spoke to Judy, he had her talk to an efficiency expert about the office—how to straighten it out."

I smile at that. The problems are far deeper than shuffling paper.

Friday, November 28, 1975

ANOTHER DAY OF BACKBITING.

It centers on the New York City financial crisis. The President announces that he now favors short-term loans to see the Big Apple through its seasonal cash flow troubles. The loans, up to $2.3 billion, will continue until mid-1978.

Inside the White House, staffers like Mike Duval privately suggest the President has "caved in" and the American people will perceive his decision as weak and indecisive. Others assert Mr. Ford won in terms of principle but lost politically. They claim he has lost crucial New York state for the 1976 election and hasn't gained that much around the nation in political returns.

The President's chief economic advisers, Greenspan, Simon and Seidman, privately blame Hartmann for putting Mr. Ford out on a limb on New York City. They complain that Hartmann's hardline, tough speech, written for the President's National Press Club appearance, was far rougher than necessary. Thus, they argue, Hartmann didn't give Mr. Ford room to maneuver.

Hartmann is firing back by calling them a bunch of unprintable names. He argues that Simon and Greenspan are responsible for pushing Mr. Ford into a hard line against New York and then began having second thoughts. Hartmann accuses Simon as the first to back down and run for cover after being the first and hardest hardliner against New York.

Painters and decorators finally begin work on a small, hideaway office near the speechwriters that Hartmann selected months ago. Perhaps this is an indication of things to come. We may finally begin to receive some consistent counsel and direction.

Chapter 16
December, 1975

". . . To maintain a democracy of effort requires a vast amount of patience in dealing with differing methods, a vast amount of humility. But out of confusion of many voices rises an understanding of dominant public needs. Then political leadership can voice common ideals and aid in their realization."

Franklin Delano Roosevelt

Tuesday, December 2, 1975

THE PRESIDENT IS IN PEKING and all is calm on the China front. The White House is not so calm. Two good reasons: *The New Republic* and the *Washington Post*. Both hit my desk at about the same time.

Writing in the *The New Republic*, John Osborne says, "with some individual exceptions, President Ford is served by the weakest staff in recent White House history."

Osborne, a White House correspondent visiting London, calms his British listeners somewhat by adding that "this President isn't nearly as dumb" as some of them might assume.

Writing in the *Post*, Nicholas von Hoffman disagrees in the most stinging description of Mr. Ford since he assumed the presidency. Von Hoffman characterizes him as a "blunderous leader."

Using examples from a bump on the head after the President dived into a Florida swimming pool to Mr. Ford's falling down, von Hoffman questions whether the President is "catastrophically close to making himself into the national clown?"

As I move about the White House, the question of the hour is whether one has read von Hoffman. The staff is embarrassed and embittered.

It seems to me von Hoffman is missing the real issues. The problems of this administration are reflected in a phone conversation which I had with Jack Veneman yesterday. Veneman, a special assistant to Vice President Rockefeller, is the central idea man for the administration's future policy. I ask Veneman for more input to the President's speeches, more position paper work about how Mr. Ford sees the future of the country. Veneman replies:

"Very little or nothing has been decided. Everything is at a standstill. We've met with the President a few times but he has made no decisions. We can't move ahead unless he gives us some direction."

At the end of July, Veneman had aimed for a September 22 deadline on the position papers. In July, we waited hopefully for substantive material; in December, we still wait. Like our July conversation, this conversation ends with a mutual promise to remain in contact.

Friday, December 5, 1975

KATHY WOOTEN TELLS ME we can have a few hours off for Christmas shopping. I see Judy Morton, sitting at her old desk, but she tells me that she has formally quit. Judy has returned to clear up some final business. As a farewell and thanks for all the work she has done for me, I offer Judy a "goodbye beer" before I start on my shopping rounds. She agrees and we go to a nearby restaurant.

Judy discloses the real reason for her brief return. She has held a second meeting with Doug Smith, the newly appointed administrative assistant to Bob Hartmann. The meeting, at Smith's request, is to answer further questions on the operational management of the speechwriting staff.

Smith, in an earlier conference with Judy, explained the President is "most concerned" about the performance of the speechwriting staff and he must find out what is wrong. Judy says:

"Mr. Smith doesn't understand how we got this far. He's been talking to a lot of people around the White House. He thinks our department is an organizational mess.

"Mr. Theis told me he saw Mr. Smith for a few minutes. But Mr. Smith indicated to me that Mr. Theis saw him for about two hours. And Mr. Theis doesn't want Mr. Smith to talk with the rest of the speechwriting staff. Mr. Theis is really against that. So Mr. Smith said to me that he wouldn't cause any hard feeling by doing that right now. But he's talking to an awful lot of other people."

I ask Judy the crucial question:

"Do you think Bob Hartmann now understands what has been going on in our office for the past year or so?"

She replies:

"No, I really don't think so. Not the extent of the confusion, the chaos. He's beginning to understand. But I don't think Mr. Hartmann feels he should get too involved with the writers."

I reply:

"That's our biggest problem, Judy. Hartmann doesn't speak to us to any extent. For several months now, three of the writers have not seen the President. We don't know what he's thinking. No one tells us what's going on. Instead of acting as a team, helping one another and working together, our leadership is more concerned with petty self-interests."

Judy says: "I said all that to Mr. Smith in a diplomatic way."

Judy continues for about a half hour, calmly and dispassionately spelling out her dismay, and concludes:

"I'm relieved. I'm really happy to be out of the White House. I have no desire to return. It's a good feeling, a feeling of freedom."

We leave our table and part, each wishing the other luck.

It's a sunny, beautiful day with the temperature around fifty degrees and I enjoy the weather as I walk to my car. Fishing in my pocket for the car keys, I find a memo from Jack Marsh, counselor to the President. He calls the speechwriters' attention to the philosophy of the phrase "sovereign voter" and urges that we stress it in Mr. Ford's speeches. As if the GOP is not sufficiently portrayed as elitists, Marsh wants to compound the problem. A "sovereign voter"? Who the hell will understand that one except some of the Republican intellectual right wing? No wonder, I say to myself, that so many Americans have deserted the GOP. What the voters and the President need is a little less sovereignty and a little more humanity. What Marsh needs to explain in plain English is the President's thinking on food stamps and Social Security, not sovereignty. Marsh is out of contact with the country; Hartmann is out of contact with his staff; and the President is in Asia. Beautiful. I drive to a Washington toy store. The place is for real.

Monday, December 8, 1975

THE PRESIDENT IS BACK at his desk in the Oval Office after his Asian trip to China, Indonesia and the Philippines. The rumors, all about Bob Hartmann, begin to fly almost immediately.

Dick Cheney has apparently made his first important move since the departure of Don Rumsfeld. He has, according to a host of sources, offered a job to Dave Gergen. Gergen is the Treasury Department speechwriter who wrote the tax-cut speech for the President several months ago; he enabled Rumsfeld to bypass Hartmann. Cheney thus chose Hartmann's domain to make his personal debut in White House infighting.

Gergen, removed from the White House speechwriting staff by Hartmann when the Ford team took over, may return to replace the two men who displaced him, Hartmann and Paul Theis. Gergen reportedly has asked for time to think about the offer. Cheney would be in a position, with a speechwriter reporting directly to him, to bypass Hartmann and Theis on any significant speech that he chose to control himself. The betting seems to be that Cheney and Hartmann will butt heads, but I disagree.

Contrary to the public impression, Hartmann is more interested in the appearances of power than power itself. This can be seen in the fact that Hartmann has taken part in very few policy meetings within the White House. The formulation of policy for the approval of the President is where power is truly exercised. Hartmann is much more interested in where he sits at the table when members of the senior staff meet with Mr. Ford. He wants to know if his office has equivalent space and furnishings as those of his equals or neighbors. He is deeply interested in his "access time" with the President. Hartmann makes sure he is always in the most appropriate seat on Air Force One.

Because Hartmann is less interested in substance than the appearance of power, Cheney is willing to risk this move. The speechwriting job according to him is one of substance, not appearance. It will mean long hours of hard work. One of the major reasons why the President is dissatisfied with some of his major speeches is that Hartmann and Friedman have been short on the substance discussed in policy meetings. If Hartmann were really interested in substance, he would attend such conferences, which are held literally a few yards from his office.

I have concluded in the past few months that Hartmann is less interested in the President's speeches than any of us has ever realized. He's far more interested in Mr. Ford's "appearances." Otherwise, Hartmann would spend much more time on substance and policy and much more effort in writing. He would cancel some of the two- and three-hour lunches where he attempts to finesse the columnists and reporters.

Hartmann appears primarily concerned about his own survival. Others on the President's staff can patch up his political duties but, until now, no one has been in a position to patch up his speeches. That loophole, as the saying goes in Washington, appears to be closing. Hartmann will fight for his title as the President's "main speechwriter" but he doesn't care to become too involved in either day-to-day writing or administration. He will retain his title if Gergen accepts the post with Cheney but he will lose some of his influence. I conclude Cheney consulted with Hartmann before bringing Gergen aboard.

I'm scheduled to write a farm speech for the President and I speak with Claude Gifford, an assistant to Agriculture Secretary Butz. Gifford says:

"The President is in trouble with farmers everywhere in the country. They're sore because of his moratorium on exports and they're upset because he seems to be more interested in George Meany. I'd say this had better be one helluva speech because the President doesn't have all the time in the world left."

Claude is kind enough to send me a draft on what he thinks the President must say in the upcoming farm speech. It's a good speech. However, it's also a comment on the way the White House is operating when I ask myself: How do I get this fine piece of work past Theis and everyone else without them cutting it to ribbons?

I decide to sleep on that overnight.

Friday, December 12, 1975

IT'S THE MORNING AFTER our office Christmas party. Many of the staff are laid low—not from hangovers but the numbing news on front pages all across the nation. Ronald Reagan picks up an astonishing 31 percentage points and surges ahead of the President in the latest Gallup poll. Surveying Republican and Independent voters, Gallup finds they prefer Reagan over Mr. Ford by the margin of 40 to 32 per cent for the GOP presidential nomination.

No incumbent President has trailed a challenger or potential challenger in his own party, according to the Gallup surveys, since 1967. Robert F. Kennedy then took a brief two-point lead over President Johnson.

Inside the White House, some staffers try to put a brave face on the Gallup results. They express skepticism about Reagan's strength, saying he was helped considerably by the publicity surrounding the announcement of his candidacy. They add that the President was hurt by his cabinet shakeup, particularly the firing of Defense Secretary Schlesinger.

Other staffers express in cautious and indirect terms the need for more "leadership" from the President. In short, he must be President. I agree with this point of view.

The President, from all accounts, is said to be worried by the Reagan surge. The political word is that he's turning a "hard right rudder." I wince. The "right" will not elect him in 1976.

The word coming from the Oval Office is that Mr. Ford will veto the current congressional tax-cut bill because it does not have a comparable spending slash. Greenspan, Simon and Burns are arguing for a veto, even though it will probably be overridden in the Congress. I believe Mr. Ford will sign the tax measure for the simple reason that his history as president has been to compromise, to accommodate.

It's considered certain that Mr. Ford will veto the *common situs* picketing bill, but there are many doubts about whether he will veto the proposed congressional energy bill. This measure would temporarily roll back oil prices and do virtually nothing to advance American energy independence. I regard the energy measure as much more dangerous to the President than the tax-cut bill. His credibility is overwhelmingly on the line on energy. As the individual who has written most of his hard-line energy speeches, I am beginning to feel a deep sense of dismay about his possible acceptance of this "compromise." It's no compromise; it's a reversal of virtually all that Mr. Ford said he stood for in terms of America's energy future.

There is extraordinary pessimism and depression among the White House staff. My wife, Joy, noticed it last evening at our Christmas party. She commented on how little happiness seemed to be generated, even around the bar. She asked me:

"Why are there so many cliques? Why don't people mix? Why is everyone so closed up?"

There is little or no esprit de corps within the White House these days, or the past several months. Work continues from day to day but no one knows who is really running the place or where we are all headed. There's more spirit and manifest desire to win at the high school soccer games that I attend around Washington. Despite his private assurances to friends that he is in the race to the end, I am beginning to be convinced that Gerald Ford will not really make a run for the presidency in 1976. He simply doesn't appear to be serious.

261

Saturday, December 13, 1975

I AM SITTING IN THE FRONT OFFICE, speaking with Kathy
Wooten, when Bob Orben rushes in. He says he has obtained
an advance copy of *The New Republic* magazine and adds:

"If I were Ron Nessen, I would not be going on vacation
now."

Orben drops off a Xerox copy, indicating he has already
delivered the original to the White House West Wing, meaning to
Dick Cheney or the President. Orben's excitement is about an
article by the *The New Republic's* highly respected White House
correspondent John Osborne. Osborne writes:

"It is intolerable that Ron Nessen [whom Osborne has
consistently defended in the past] should be kept by the President
to bait, derogate and sneer at Henry Kissinger."

Osborne implies that Nessen was "permitted if not
encouraged" to attack Kissinger during the recent presidential
journey to Asia. He cites two examples:

A *Newsweek* report that Kissinger personally denied Nessen
access to the Asian trip briefing books and that Dick Cheney
ordered that the books be given to Nessen. Nessen told newsmen in
Peking that the story was true and, according to Osborne, gloated
about it. The press secretary left the impression that he is higher in
Mr. Ford's estimation and "more secure in his service" to the
President than Kissinger.

Kissinger briefed a small "pool" of reporters aboard Air
Force One after the Peking visit. Speaking as a "senior U.S.
official," Kissinger felt he used some possibly indiscreet language.
He therefore asked newsmen to delete that aspect of their report to
protect the President and his policies. The correspondents did this.
Nessen then attacked the newsmen. Osborne writes:

"He [Nessen] then turned on the pool reporters and
denounced them, saying he was amazed they should be so weak
and should grant to Henry Kissinger a favor they would never grant
to Ron Nessen."

Osborne zeroes in on Nessen:

". . . it most certainly was not the function, the place, or the
duty of the President's press secretary to object to deletions and to
denounce reporters for agreeing to make deletions that were in part

intended to protect the President . . . . It amounted to a display of venom that was shocking in itself and evidence that matters are in sad disarray at the top of the Ford White House.''

Osborne continues to attack the White House staff as ''the poorest in a fairly long memory'' in this new article. He describes the President's major address in Honolulu on a ''new Pacific doctrine'' as ''an inferior rewrite and adaptation of a much better and more forceful address that Henry Kissinger had delivered in Detroit on November 24. Some of the President's language and all of the central points appeared in the Kissinger speech, to distinctly better effect than they did after the President's personal staff prettied them up.'' The speech Osborne refers to was written by Hartmann and Friedman after my original draft was junked.*

Orben interprets the article as criticism of Nessen. He misses the real meaning. This is a very strong attack on the President by Kissinger. Osborne clearly suggests Mr. Ford is encouraging and approving Nessen's assaults on Kissinger. At the same time, it is well known—and virtually admitted by Osborne's defense of Kissinger's record in this article—that the writer is close to Kissinger and his point of view.

To top off this rainy Saturday morning, the front page of the *Washington Star* carries a scintillating series of quotes from Vice President Rockefeller. Rocky met privately in Houston with southern Republican state chairmen, who have been critical of him, and told the assemblage:

''You got me out, you sons of bitches. Now get off your asses.''

The Vice President was telling them that now that they have gotten him off the 1976 GOP national ticket, the Dixie GOP chiefs should quit complaining and get out to work for the Republican party.

I smile at this thought: What about a Rockefeller-Moynihan ticket?

Rocky would take on the Republican right and Pat would take on the rest of the world. The country might have a helluva lot of fun. They could run on the old Norman Mailer-Jimmy Breslin campaign slogan when that daring duo combined to run for city hall in New York: ''No more bullshit!''

See Appendix, page 356.

Monday, December 15, 1975

THE *Washington Post* and the *Chicago Tribune* join in a new battle
cry about Ron Nessen. Over the weekend, both newspapers carry
stories attacking the press secretary. I am reminded of a luncheon
with a CBS executive several months ago. With a grin and a
grimace, he told me: "We're going out to get that son-of-a-bitch
some day."

Both the *Post* and *Tribune* cite Nessen's long absences from
the press room in Peking and his offering of inadequate information
when he appeared. The *Tribune* reports that newsmen sought
Nessen's counsel at a late hour and were told he was asleep and
could not be disturbed.

Both alluded to the Nessen-Kissinger feud.

Bill Greener, Nessen's deputy who is respected for his direct
honesty by the press corps, privately tells friends that he's pleased
to leave and work for Don Rumsfeld at the Defense Department.
Greener is upset at Nessen's arrogance and questions his office
procedures. Although other staffers deny they are looking for new
jobs, reports persist that several are searching.

Bob Orben appears to be delighted at events. Kathy Wooten
and I remind ourselves today of his startling comportment on
Saturday.

Orben gleefully handed us the John Osborne article in *The
New Republic* which castigated Nessen. Orben suggested that he,
personally, obtained an advance copy of the article from the
magazine and further indicated that he was distributing copies
around the White House. With Nessen on vacation, according to
Orben's own words, he was not distributing a copy to the press
secretary.

Orben, an individual of ambition and some delusion, may well
consider himself a possible successor to Nessen. As Kaye Pullen
puts it:

"Any Hollywood or New York gag writer who thinks he's an
economic speechwriter is also a gag writer who thinks he's a good
candidate for press secretary."

Toward the close of the day, Kathy Wooten slips me a Xerox
copy of a Sunday article written by Aldo Beckman in the *Chicago
Tribune* which says:

''Some of his (Mr. Ford's) aides are frustrated to the point of threatening to resign. They contend the lack of organization either signals the President's lack of determination or ineptness by his senior aides.''

The story concludes that the President ''has yet to stabilize his White House staff'' and this ''instability'' breeds conflict. It says that Bob Hartmann is looking for some new speechwriters, but fails to mention that Hartmann and Theis have been hiring and firing speechwriters at the rate of one every two months since Mr. Ford entered the White House. The speechwriters' real difficulty is Hartmann's lack of leadership and his personal problems as well as Theis's mismanagement.

Paul Theis phones and asks that I write a two-page New Year's message for the President as soon as possible. I write the message and turn it in to Theis in about a half hour, only to discover that Theis and Hartmann asked each member of the staff to write the same New Year's message. In short, they undercut Pat Butler, who was given the assignment a few weeks ago. This is another example of how the two are destroying the staff. I am forced to wonder how Hartmann would have appreciated other reporters covering each story assigned to him when he was a reporter. Hartmann would have thrown a fit. Yet he plays such games with his staff and, at the same time, expects it to save him from himself.

For the first time since entering White House service, my mind seriously dwells on quitting. Certainly no man is bigger than whatever service he may offer the President of the United States. However, one is still motivated by real leadership—not lack of it—and one is still moved by hope and not humiliation as practiced by Hartmann. The lowly foot soldier may fear defeat, but he fears poor leadership even more. He will fight dishonor and disgrace more than defeat.

Tuesday, December 16, 1975

PAUL THEIS, IN CALM BUT GUARDED TERMS, advises me this morning that he plans to bow out soon as our executive editor. In a private conversation in his office, Theis says he is exhausted from his sixteen months on the job. Leaning back in his chair, clasping his hands with his eyes closed, Paul explains the editing job has drained him physically. He adds that he would find it difficult to go through the "atmosphere" of the 1976 political campaign.

Theis leans forward and suggests that it may be a good time for others to leave. He uses the story of Jack Calkins, a political aide to Bob Hartmann, as an example. Paul indicates that Calkins has been thinking about running for the vacated congressional seat in his home district in upstate New York. So Calkins went to see the President last week about his possible pullout from the White House and Mr. Ford encouraged him to leave.

This startles me because Calkins has been setting up all the Republican party meetings around the nation for the President. In other words, he has been the President's personal contact man in state after state. I ask myself: What's the President's rationale? It doesn't make sense.

Theis returns to the future. He says the President has been encouraging those who are offered good outside opportunities to accept them. Theis suggests that the President would surely write a good recommendation for me wherever I desired to go.

Paul clearly indicates that he plans to move on to something better. However, for the first time since I have known him, Theis appears beaten. Hartmann, Friedman and Orben apparently are making him the single scapegoat for their own inadequacies. Most on our staff agree that Theis deserves blame for the President's bland speeches, but Hartmann, Friedman and Orben equal, if not exceed, his responsibility. All of them should be taking the fall—not just Theis—but all apparently turned on Theis at the end to save their own necks. All proved better at White House infighting.

Pessimism and gloom are ankle-deep within the White House. Slowly but surely, the President appears to be losing some respect among his staff. Some snicker about his stumbling down airplane steps and bumbling his speech lines. The President's penchant for photos, once considered a warm and appealing personal trait, is now being ridiculed, particularly a photo showing Mr. Ford dancing with the wife of President Marcos aboard the Philippine leader's yacht. The tieless Mr. Ford is chugging away with his mouth wide open and his eyes closed.

For weeks and months, I have been telling myself that one of the major reasons why the Ford White House is so disorganized is that it did not join and weld itself together in the heat of a political campaign out of genuine respect and admiration for the candidate. Like Topsy, this staff just grew, in part, although Don Rumsfeld put his cronies in many posts. However, Rumsfeld is now at the Defense Department and some first loyalties are not necessarily to the President.

Perhaps Mr. Ford perceives the pessimism and disarray around him, because he has begun to preside at some of the early morning senior staff meetings. However, he displays little real enthusiasm about the tough campaign year ahead. He speaks of immediate problems, not of the substance that our society should be made of a year or five years from now.

I am convinced that if the President is to be saved, he must save himself. No one on the staff has either the ability, or apparently the will, to accomplish this. Mr. Ford must begin to show personal strength of character and purpose, or history will assign to him the role of merely an accidental President.

Darkness settles early over the nation's capital. The light of Christmas brightens faces in the crowds as I walk down 17th Street. For me, this has been another day of doubt.

Wednesday, December 17, 1975

THE *Washington Post* FIRES THREE big journalistic shells into the White House this morning, shaking this old mansion to its political foundations. Three commentaries on the President, under the four-column headline "THE DECLINE OF A PRESIDENT," hit the entire staff with stunning effect. Some agree with the criticism of Mr. Ford.

Writing under the headline "A Caretaker in the Oval Office," conservative columnist George F. Will concludes that "Mr. Ford not only became President by accident, but has only prospered as President by fortuities, by having had an easy act to follow, and by having had an easy war to win (the Mayaguez incident)."

Will philosophizes that there is something "sadly symbolic" about Mr. Ford's proneness to personal accidents. He writes of a comedian bringing down the house by performing a simple act. The comedian pretends to be the President but does not speak. He just backs up five paces and then strides forward, stumbling into the microphone. (Uproarious laughter).

Will ends on the note that Mr. Ford is now widely regarded as a "caretaker," which is a synonym for a lame duck.

Roland Evans and Robert Novak blister Vice President Rockefeller and Bo Callaway for "bad-tempered" performances at the recent southern Republican conference in Houston. The two so antagonized the conservative southerners—Callaway assailing Ronald Reagan in both personal and political terms while Rocky simply cussed out the southerners—that Reagan fortified his already strong southern support.

Dave Broder, the highly respected political writer of the *Post*, delivers the blockbuster. The President's position has so deteriorated, according to Broder, that Mr. Ford may find himself facing a forced withdrawal as Lyndon Johnson did in 1968. But Broder, who is read and respected by the President, suggests the President can still make a real race out of 1976. He writes Mr. Ford must get tough:

"First, Mr. Ford could acknowledge his own greatest failure, the tolerance of a White House and campaign staff whose mediocrity sabotages his every effort to exert effective leadership. He could clean house of the bumblers he brought from his days in Congress and the vice presidency, and give himself a 'team' that is competent for the political and governmental challenges ahead."

Many in the White House name the "bumblers"—Hartmann, Seidman, Buchen, Friedman and Marsh, among others.

Broder suggests that the President bring in his kitchen cabinet, Mel Laird, Bryce Harlow, John Byrnes, William Scranton, and others to take charge of the White House and campaign staffs. Vice President Rockefeller should be given responsibilities equal to his abilities. The President should work more closely with his top cabinet members. He must demonstrate leadership—that he is a "tough, principled battler with good people at his side . . ." Broder concludes that inaction will doom Mr. Ford's chances in 1976.

Everywhere in the White House, staffers call attention to the three columns, particularly Broder's.

Some of their bitterness is directed at Don Rumsfeld:

"It's the old art of survival. Rumsfeld would never hold the bag for Jerry Ford. Jerry's just another step up the ladder."

268

Wednesday, December 17, 1975

In early afternoon, I receive a phone call from Chris Farrand, an assistant to Secretary Thomas Kleppe at the Department of the Interior. Chris says the secretary is looking for a speechwriter and wonders whether I might be interested. He adds that the post includes being liaison man with the White House and Kleppe is looking for someone who knows the White House.

I agree to meet with him, figuring that a flat turndown would be neither pleasant nor diplomatic, but I ask for time so that I might consult with Paul Theis and obtain his permission. Farrand says he will await my call.

Theis is alone in his office. I briefly outline the phone call and ask his advice. Theis, as depressed as I have seen him in the past several weeks, is more bitter than I have ever heard him.

Our executive editor begins by saying he doesn't know how long he will be around the White House. He complains of not knowing all that is going on.

Theis says over and over again that he's tired. Paul repeats he will not be able to take the strain of the upcoming political campaign. He speaks of his long, midnight hours—of what these hours have done to his health and family life.

Midway through this monologue, Theis' face becomes red and his emotions begin rising to the surface. He indicates that his own position is in jeopardy. He mentions that the staff is being reorganized at the top and concludes:

"I would get out, Jack. Take the job. Kleppe is a reasonable man. You will like him. It would be better than this, better than eighty hours a week and better than all the bickering around here. And who knows what may happen here tomorrow or the next day? Nothing here is sure. Everything is mixed up. You've got a family to think of. Nobody knows what any next move may be. And this may not only be a move out but a move up. You may have a lot more responsibility without all the uncertainty around here."

Theis rises from his chair and shakes my hand. He looks me in the eyes and says:

"Take the job, Jack. Nobody knows what the future may be around here."

I meet with Farrand later that afternoon and he offers me the speechwriting post. I hedge, asking for time to clear the move with Bob Hartmann. I return to my office and report to Theis. I mention a Hartmann meeting and he agrees.

As I leave for the day, I stop by Kaye Pullen's office. She's leaving us soon to write speeches for Betty Ford. Kaye offers an insight into the character of Don Rumsfeld.

Aram Bakshian, a former member of our staff who is now on a fellowship at Harvard, has been offered a speechwriter's job at the Defense Department by Rumsfeld. Bakshian told Kaye these were Rumsfeld's words:

"They're not going to shape up that place over there (meaning the White House, where Bakshian has been offered his old job as a speechwriter for the President). They're just not going to do it. So come on over with me."

First, Rumsfeld is attempting to take away a speechwriter who could help the President. Second, his expressed lack of faith in the President and his former assistant, Dick Cheney, is remarkable for its callousness.

I believe Pullen and Bakshian. Both are truthful people. The cold expediency of Rumsfeld's words and actions inspire very little trust and confidence.

Thursday, December 18, 1975

I SEE HARTMANN FOR FORTY MINUTES in his office this afternoon. His secretary, Neta Messersmith, cautions me that she has given him some bicarbonate. Hartmann's first words to me are that he has had too much Mexican food for lunch.

I quickly give him the facts. Hartmann seems genuinely surprised. He questions me about salary and what my responsibilities would be. Then he launches into a long monologue.

Hartmann reveals that he is taking "personal charge" of the speechwriting staff. He says there will be changes at the top and he'll "have to be the son-of-a-bitch tomorrow at a staff meeting." Hartmann indicates he will remove most of Theis' responsibilities. The words hit me hard, but it has been clear for some time that Theis would be made a scapegoat for whatever Hartmann perceived to be wrong.

Hartmann discloses that he and Friedman will write all of the President's future speeches. He describes Friedman's writing as a "pale imitation" of his own, but stresses that he cannot do all the speechwriting alone. Hartmann contradicts what he told me only a

few weeks ago. Then, he said that he was tired and "written out."
He now speaks of "taking charge and writing most of the stuff."

Hartmann begins wandering off, saying he really doesn't feel
up to taking over so much writing. He says:

"I feel more like stepping out but that would be rattish. I've
got to help The Man. I'm really the only one who can write for
him. Nobody else can."

Hartmann says the other writers will do little more than gather
facts in the future. None will write a speech per se. He asks my
opinion, after indicating the decision is already a fait accompli. I
reply, "I wouldn't be interested in being a researcher."

Hartmann appreciates the point and chuckles, adding:

"The job over at Interior sounds a lot more challenging and
interesting than what the writing shop here will be doing. I'd take
it. It'll be a lot better to write about the open spaces than the
political campaign. And it'll be a lot saner."

I tell Hartmann that I have been thinking about teaching
journalism. Theis suggested the President might write a
recommendation for me. Hartmann says that would be a good idea.
He adds that he would also be pleased to write such a letter.

Hartmann cites the difference between his and my writing. He
says that I strive for eloquence. The President's character does not
call for eloquence, Hartmann explains, it calls for old-fashioned,
plain speaking. He concludes:

"You are a damn fine writer. Some of the stuff you've done
has been really great. But it's not the President's style. You tend to
be lofty in a big speech. The President is down to earth. I'm the
only one who knows his down to earth style.

"I know you don't want to be a researcher. I'm going to have
to do just about every speech. It's going to be a bitch. But that's
the way it is and I'm going to have to live with it or get out
myself."

As I begin to leave, Hartmann reminds me that he and the
President will write letters of recommendation for me. I thank him
and return to speak briefly with Theis. I advise Theis of the
conversation and he seems resigned about Hartmann's calling a
meeting on staff changes tomorrow. He stares vacantly ahead.

I say to myself that here is a man who has devoted most of his
professional life to the Republican party. Now the party is purging
him from his most precious post and I am a witness to it. Pain and

perhaps agony are written across the face of Paul Theis this evening. I feel desperate looking at Theis' crestfallen face so I decide to offer an unusual invitation: "How about a beer, Paul?"

Theis smiles. He replies quickly: "Thanks but I've got more work to do."

I walk across the Ellipse to my car. The President is lighting the national Christmas tree here and he speaks the words that I have written for him:

"America is a national family. We have different dreams but are united at this time of year."

Friday, December 19, 1975

KAYE PULLEN IS CLEANING OUT HER DESK, preparing for her move to the East Wing of the White House as a speechwriter for Betty Ford. I tell her about my meetings with Theis and Hartmann. She reports seeing Hartmann at a recent staff party and blisters:

"Hartmann says to me that he hears I'm jumping ship, moving over to Betty Ford. If it were possible, he would have kicked me out of here long ago. But I just smiled and told him how great it was. That's what Alan Greenspan told me to do, smile at Hartmann and not give him a chance to fire me. I just smiled, Jack, and you just smile your way right out of this crazy place and thank God you're getting out. Smile, baby, smile."

Agnes Waldron returns from the meeting in Hartmann's office and shows me a reorganization chart. Hartmann is combining his political and speechwriting staffs. Jack Calkins, his political deputy, becomes Hartmann's overall deputy. Doug Smith, the new efficiency expert, becomes the number three man.

Virtually all of Theis' duties have been stripped from him—even Friedman is placed in a separate box from Theis. All presidential correspondence, messages and similar duties are removed from Theis' jurisdiction. He is listed as merely in charge of three writers and three secretaries in a new office classified as "speech communications." Our research office is also taken from Theis and placed under Gwen Anderson, a political assistant to Calkins. This change makes no sense since the writers and researchers must by definition work closely together.

There's no indication that Calkins may be leaving the White House. Perhaps he has changed his mind. From the one-time direction of several hundred employees, Theis' authority now extends to only six persons. Four of those six individuals plan to leave, two secretaries, Kathy Wooten and Cheryl Ford, and two writers, Pat Butler and myself. Bob Rousek, an editor on detail from another government agency, tells me he hopes to get a job as a public information officer with the CIA. Thus, only gag writer Bob Orben and secretary Jan Davis plan to stay. The demoralization of the staff is now out in the open. None hides the fact that he or she is actively looking for another job.

I phone Chris Farrand at Interior to confirm my acceptance of the post there. He puts a letter in the mail to my home formally confirming our agreement.

Saturday, December 20, 1975

I RETURN HOME FROM CHRISTMAS SHOPPING and my wife, Joy, says to phone Bob Hartmann at the White House. His secretary has called describing the Hartmann request as an "emergency." I phone Hartmann who asks me if I have made a commitment to the Interior Department. I reply in the affirmative. He presses me for details and I report that Interior mailed me a letter of confirmation yesterday.

Hartmann, in a rare display of indecision, begins fumbling for words. He suggests that I may want to remain at the White House for awhile. I reply firmly that I have given my word, that I am due to report to the new post in a month.

We go on a merry-go-round for several moments, solving nothing. I remain firm in acceptance of the new job, but Hartmann suggests he may need me beyond the State of the Union address.

He offers some violin music and flowers, saying that he also has written a general letter of recommendation for me. Hartmann reads the letter, which states that he has known me from the early 1960's and that we covered such stories as the Vatican Council, the Baghdad revolution and the outbreak of civil war on Cyprus. He concludes the letter with these words:

"He knows the news business at home and abroad, and is an excellent writer and newscaster of creative ideas and has a genuine sense of history. I can unhesitatingly recommend him for your consideration.''

Hartmann's voice trails off. I tell him that I am on vacation for the next two weeks and would like some quiet time to think. I hang up and tell my wife what has occurred— that Hartmann appears to be waffling. She prefers that I leave because the entire White House appears to be in confusion. Neither of us really understands Hartmann's ''emergency.'' However, I promise my wife that I will do my utmost to leave the White House, because the place has become an organizational and emotional seesaw.

I look at my wife. She usually has tears in her eyes at moments like this. There are none, however. Her eyes are blue steel and she says: ''Leave there, Jack. I beg you.''

Tuesday, December 23, 1975

THERE ARE TIMES WHEN WORDS are no longer adequate. This is one of those days. It's a day of vacation but unforgettable in my White House experience. Newspaper headlines proclaim that the President has signed the compromise energy bill. Mr. Ford retreats from virtually every promise and statement on energy over the past year. The decision amounts to a repudiation of all the energy speeches that I have written for him in the past fourteen months. In one of the greatest understatements of his presidency, Mr. Ford concedes:

''It (this legislation) does not provide all the essential measures that the nation needs to achieve energy independence as quickly as I would like.''

The new energy bill, rather than reducing energy consumption, encouraging domestic production or decreasing our dependence on foreign oil, retreats from all three.

One could argue about the possibility of increased inflation if oil prices were gradually raised under the President's original proposal. But Mr. Ford and everyone else on his staff agreed that risk would not be a serious one—that the American people must free themselves from the dangers of dependence on foreign oil.

I agree with the President's original energy program and still do. Most of all, I committed myself to the program. And now it disappears like vapor in the air.

It is argued that Gerald Ford is a political pragmatist, a man of accommodation and compromise, an individual whose goal is chiefly survival. I believe the American people would understand and agree with the President on his energy program if he held firm—if he carried the fight across the nation with conviction. I believe that Mr. Ford dumped the program that is best for this nation.

It's late for me to believe in heroes. And Gerald Ford has ceased to be a hero. But I continue to believe in principle—and the principle at issue is meaning what you say.

Chapter 17
January, 1976

''Under the Constitution the President of the United States is alone responsible for the 'faithful execution of the laws.' Our government is fixed on the basis that the President is the only person in the executive branch who has the final authority. . . . The important fact to remember is that the President is the only person in the executive branch who has the final authority, and if he does not exercise it, we may be in trouble. If he exercises his authority wisely, that is good for the country. If he does not exercise it wisely, that is too bad, but it is better than not exercising it at all.''

HARRY S TRUMAN

Monday, January 5, 1976

THIS IS THE FIRST DAY BACK AT WORK after a two-week vacation. With about two weeks before the State of the Union address, the speechwriters are discreetly asked by staffers and newsmen about what the President may say.

Theis claims he knows little on the subject. Friedman broods alone. No one on the staff seems knowledgeable on the speech, unlike last year, when most of us were involved.

The President and Ron Nessen are saying publicly that the address will be "philosophical." Mr. Ford's views on where America should go in the years ahead will constitute the major portion of the speech. Both say there will be some program substance, possibly about health and welfare, but the speech will accent Mr. Ford's general outlook.

Two aspects of all this seem worth considering. The President and his top advisers have ignored "philosophy" and "vision" ever since Mr. Ford took office. They are ill prepared to discuss it, since all have done so little work on it. For more than six months, I have requested such guidance and have always met a stone wall.

Secondly, in all the meetings which I have attended with the President, he has been a "practical" man, not a philosophical individual. His tendency is to face and try to solve immediate problems, not to rationalize about a hypothetical future. In conversations with any and all of Mr. Ford's advisers in the past year, none has ever suggested to me that the President had any ideas about goals for America. Hartmann, in particular, has always knocked that one out of the park. To suggest that the President suddenly has a vision of the American future seems to be nothing more than a reaction to the criticism that Mr. Ford doesn't know where he's going.

Among his New Year's resolutions, the President speaks of "a dedication to the strengthening of spiritual and moral values." He talks of improving economic well-being at home and abroad as well as world peace. Mr. Ford concludes that he is the only "qualified candidate" to lead the nation for the next presidential term. The President predicts, as he has in the past, that Hubert Humphrey will be his Democratic opponent. Whatever one might say of Hubert, it isn't judicious to suggest that he's unqualified for the presidency.

Tuesday, January 6, 1976

The subject of qualifications is a touchy one around the White House these days. Bo Callaway is still under fire as the number one man on the President Ford Committee. Dick Cheney has neither the time nor the experience to guide the President's campaign. Bob Hartmann was written off by everyone long ago as Mr. Ford's chief political adviser. And now at least two experienced political pros have rejected White House requests that they run the President's campaign. Rogers Morton, longtime friend of Mr. Ford and veteran GOP operative, pleads health reasons for his turndown. Former GOP state chairman Ody Fish of Wisconsin flatly declines the job.

It's unnerving to the White House staff as they learn that one after another Republican pro turns down this traditional plum, a job of considerable power and influence if the President is elected next year. All see the same handwriting on the wall. Mr. Ford is in real trouble and his possible defeat by Reagan would be interpreted as a debacle. None wishes to lend his name to a possible debacle.

Former Governor Bill Scranton of Pennsylvania may take the job, according to several rumors, but he's not jumping at it. Scranton, considered a liberal by the Republican right wing, may not wish to take on Barry Goldwater's forces a second time. He challenged Goldwater briefly in 1964. I covered that campaign as a reporter. Scranton, a very decent and kind man, simply had no organization going for him.

Bo Callaway's lieutenants at the President Ford Committee, who are stung by criticism of their leader and miffed by White House inaction, are telling their friends that the White House political operation is "inefficient." Said one:

"You just can't get an answer out of Cheney or Hartmann or anyone else. They aren't organized at all."

Some of the GOP's cynics conclude: "What the White House needs is a new Bob Haldeman."

Tuesday, January 6, 1976

A GENERAL WALKOUT IS UNDER WAY on our staff. I hand in my resignation today. Jerry Popeo carries the letter to Jim Connor's office. I tell the President it has been a privilege to serve him. Kaye Pullen has written Hartmann a note on her switch to writing speeches for Mrs. Ford. Pat Butler and Bob Rousek tell me they plan to leave. Rousek says he'll return to the General Services Administration. Two of our three secretaries are considering leaving. Kathy Wooten reads the "help wanted" ads daily. Cheryl Ford will move to Michigan. In mid-morning, Theis calls me to his office. He quietly advises me that he's resigning to accept a post with one of the government departments. It's rumored he's going to work for Secretary Butz at Agriculture.

Three people will remain: Friedman, Orben, and their secretary, Jan Davis. I now learn that even Jan is looking for another job.

Theis quotes Friedman as saying he would leave if he had a good offer. Orben has not been heard from because he's on vacation. There's even a rumor, which I dismiss, that Hartmann may be leaving. He would be named ambassador to Italy. The Washington press corps would roar at that one.

Theis confides that Hartmann's reorganization is not working well. Gwen Anderson, to whom our research and presidential messages and correspondence sections now report, apparently has antagonized both Agnes Waldron and Eliska Hasek, who head these sections. Anderson, regarded by many of us as a tough-talking political hack, has no experience whatsoever in research or presidential messages and correspondence. Yet she's bearing down on both Agnes and Eliska, two real pros. All of Agnes' research and checking of our speeches must now go back and forth through Anderson. This means just one more bottleneck in the endless chain of people involved in producing a speech. Rousek advises me that Anderson has been writing "nasty" notes about her "staff" to Hartmann. We seem to plummet from dismay to despair. Morale is at rock bottom.

Butler, Rousek and I meet for a drink after work. The depth of their antagonism toward Friedman and Orben surprises me. Friedman is summed up as a poor writer. Orben is described as an even worse writer. Yet Friedman and Orben will form the nucleus of any new staff. Kaye Pullen, the strongest critic on our staff of Friedman and Orben, is not present. However, she has written them off as "a couple of real losers."

Butler and Rousek agree. Unless the President stops taking advice from Hartmann, Friedman and Orben with respect to his future speeches, they may be instrumental in his losing the presidential election.

Tuesday, January 6, 1976

Friedman is the single cause of one of the President's most serious complaints. Milt is ready with his speeches only at the last minute; then there is not adequate time to make necessary changes. He rarely gets a speech in before deadline. Friedman, who spends much of his time offering critiques of his fellow staff members' work, may well be the poorest writer in the speechwriting department. Virtually all of us agree on this. Hartmann insists, however, that the President's speeches be "plain and simple" and Friedman represents the epitome of uninspired communication. Hartmann himself is an individual of very limited literary interest or ability.

These are our conclusions except for the most important. Unless Dave Gergen, now on Cheney's staff, is given a real voice in the President's future speeches, they will get worse, not better.

Bob Hartmann distributes the following memo today:

THE WHITE HOUSE
Washington
January 6, 1976

MEMORANDUM TO: PAUL THEIS
GWEN ANDERSON
ROLAND ELLIOTT

FROM: ROBERT T. HARTMANN

Due to Mr. Calkins' temporary absence this week the final plans for the reorganization of my area of responsibility in the White House staff structure have been temporarily deferred. Mr. Smith is filling in as acting deputy until Mr. Calkins returns.
At the proper time consideration will be given to reassignment of office spaces, titles, and precise personnel quotas. In the meantime, no such changes will be undertaken without my specific approval and any that may already have been planned will be cancelled. Until the new organizational structure which I outlined to you in general before Christmas is officially announced to the rest of the White House staff, any disclosure of contemplated changes may not only be inaccurate but will result in the peremptory dismissal of persons responsible. Please advise all those under your supervision of the necessity of refraining from speculation or discussion with persons outside our department until the consolidation is both factual and final. Any inquiries should be referred to me or, in my absence, to Mr. Smith.

*The cooperation of all members of the staff is essential to the
paramount objective of assisting in the preparation of the
President's State of the Union message and other important
upcoming communications. I appreciate and expect your support
and of those in your area of responsibility.*

cc: Mr. Calkins
      Mr. Smith

Hartmann, one of the biggest leakers in the White House, is
now attempting to plug leaks on his own staff. He's angry for two
reasons. A new rumor is circulating that he and his staff are in
trouble and may be cleaned out of the White House. He's also
having second thoughts about the weaknesses of his reorganization,
particularly since he faces the walkout of most of his staff.
Hartmann genuinely fears media publicity that his staff walked out
on him. He wishes to control the staff reorganization so that it will
appear as a clean, responsible reshaping under his considered
direction.

Agnes Waldron sums up the state of affairs in the White
House:
"This place is in panic. That's the only word for it—panic.
We're not only going to lose this election but if something isn't
done soon, we're going to get killed. It's a shambles. Nobody's in
charge. The animals have taken over the zoo. Somebody's got to
take charge of this place."

Monday, January 12, 1976

KATHY WOOTEN IS SPEAKING with Kaye Pullen. She's back from
Williamsburg, Virginia, where part of the President's staff has been
working on his State of the Union message. Kathy was originally
left behind. However, a Pentagon helicopter flew her alone to
Williamsburg. Kathy describes the Williamsburg braintrusting in
one word, "fiasco."

The following staffers made the trip by helicopter last
Thursday: Jim Lynn, Alan Greenspan, Bill Seidman, Jim Cannon,
Bill Baroody, Bob Hartmann, Milt Friedman, two pollsters and a
few others.

Kathy reports that the White House entourage was met by a bus at the airport near Williamsburg; however, the bus driver didn't know where to take them. The confusion caused what seemed an interminable delay.

Lynn, Greenspan and Seidman remained only a day, returning to Washington for a meeting at Friday noon. The others, apparently stymied by this decision, did little. One diversion was a cocktail party. Kathy tells Kaye:

"Hartmann and Friedman spent most of their time eating and drinking. They didn't write anything until returning to the White House on Saturday."

She reports that a "very rough" draft of thirty-five pages was written, adding:

"But it's really rough, nothing like a speech. With a week to go, it's far apart. Hartmann spoke with the President about it this morning but I don't know what happened."

Agnes Waldron comments to me:

"You're lucky you're leaving. You won't get mixed up in this fiasco."

Everywhere in the White House, one hears the refrain:

"If the State of the Union message isn't great, forget it. It's all over!"

Theis continues gloomy. He knows little of what's going on but is visiting the staff one by one in their offices to say he's leaving the White House. Friedman isn't writing today, apparently waiting until closer to the zero hour. The "vision" which the President is calling for inside the White House is grim and gray.

Thursday, January 15, 1976

KATHY WOOTEN DOZES AT HER DESK. She and Cheryl Ford, our other front-office secretary, have just completed their first midnight to 8 A.M. shift, another Hartmann innovation. This will continue for five nights until the President has concluded his 1976 State of the Union address.

The coffee is hot and I pour a cup. I ask Kathy about the speech and she replies: "It's not the best, nor the worst."

I inquire about the President's "vision" of the future in the address and Kathy smiles:

"If you mean that Kennedy word you always use, there is none."

In the *Wall Street Journal* today, Irving Kristol needles the Republican party for its lack of "vision" in the twentieth century. He actually uses the expression, called a Kennedy word by Hartmann these many months, saying the Republicans have sadly lacked this quality. For a year, I have attempted to get Hartmann and Theis to offer the country some "vision," as well as some idea of what the President stands for, but they have resisted the thought. Milt Friedman has been as vocal as Hartmann; both insist that Mr. Ford "must keep his options open," presumably for such compromises as the one which the President made on energy.

In preparing for the present State of the Union message, Hartmann never once consulted his speechwriting staff. He discussed the subject with Friedman and Orben, but ignored the rest of us. To my recollection, Hartmann has never asked me for a single idea since my joining the staff. As a matter of fact, Hartmann has accepted counsel only when it has been forced on him, such as consultation with Greenspan, Lynn and others in connection with the State of the Union address.

I return to my office, where Pat Butler reports that Bob Orben will replace Paul Theis as executive editor of the speechwriting staff. Kaye Pullen joins us to learn the news.

Kaye retorts: "I told you Hartmann and these guys are nuts."

Kaye, a good friend of Alan Greenspan, predicts the announcement will send Greenspan, the staid economist, up the wall. She quotes Greenspan as characterizing Orben as a "jerk."

Orben is an intellectual featherweight. His background for such a responsible position borders on the ridiculous. He has little comprehension of the problems facing the country or the substantive issues that may face the President in the upcoming political campaign. Orben is, in the final analysis, a peddler of the cosmetic. Orben, the editor, may well make Gerald R. Ford the laughing stock of the nation.

Aldo Beckman, of the *Chicago Tribune,* to whom Hartmann leaked the Orben appointment, is incredulous. Hartmann, apparently faced with the fact that Beckman planned to write a story saying that most of Hartmann's speechwriting staff was walking out on him, attempted to tone down Beckman's article by philosophizing about the Orben appointment. Beckman reportedly described Hartmann to both Kaye Pullen and Agnes Waldron as a "maniac."

Rogers Morton, former Secretary of Commerce, enters the White House through the front door as Jack Calkins prepares to leave by the back. Morton will become the President's top political operative here and Calkins, an assistant to Hartmann in political matters, will run for the vacated seat of an upstate New York congressman.

As the day ends, I receive a hand-delivered letter from the President accepting my resignation. It is a beautiful letter, as all of these are, with Mr. Ford's "warmest good wishes for the future."*

My White House career will end in somewhat less than ten days. There is a sadness about it all for I will leave something of myself here within these walls. Yet there will be joy at my departure, too, because I have rarely felt at home in the White House.

Friday, January 16, 1976

KATHY WOOTEN GREETS ME: "Bob Orben tells me that he's the new Paul Theis."

I pick up my morning newspapers and say:

"That may be the biggest mistake Gerald Ford ever made. It could become a national joke."

Kathy laughs. She says:

"I hear some of the speechwriting staff said goodbye to Bob Rousek last night."

"Yes," I reply, "Rousek's last day is today. He goes back to his old job at GSA."

I return to my office. Indeed, four of us, Rousek, Pullen, Butler and I, hoisted several rounds of liquid cheer last evening. Pullen was a smash hit. She kept saying:

"The bastards. The stupid bastards. How the hell could they ever dream up making Orben the head of the speechwriting staff? The guy barely made it through high school.

"Do you guys remember the Windex joke? Orben wanted the President to squirt Windex on a pane of glass at a speech in New

---

*See page 296.

Jersey. He talked about government under glass—about cleaning
the glass and getting government out in the open. Real shit! The
President didn't understand it, but Orben kept telling him it was a
great joke. And Hartmann finally killed it by saying it was
un-presidential for the President to be spraying Windex around in a
speech.''

I asked why Orben, who must have some idea of his
intellectual limitations, would want to jump into a job so far over
his head. Pullen and Butler loudly echoed Rousek, who almost
leaped out of his chair:

"Ego! The guy is an egomaniac. And he believes show biz
sells. He's going to make Gerald Ford the next President of the
United States!''

Butler hammered at me:

"Geez, Jack, Orben believes he's the most important man in
the White House besides the President. He knows the American
audience—what turns 'em on and what turns 'em off. Nobody in
this place understands show biz, man, what makes an audience
react. This is Orben's biggest audience, 215 million Americans.
And he's going to show 'em that Jerry is a homespun hero.''

Kaye is even tougher:

"He's been flattering Jerry Ford every second he can. I mean,
can't you see it? He's always saying how right the President is,
how great a job he does, what a beautiful event. He tells Jerry Ford
three times a day, if he can, that Jerry is Julius Caesar. This has
been planned, baby. This guy is on one of the great ego trips of all
time. He's going to make Bob Orben a star. In the process, he's
going to make Jerry Ford the next President and screw anybody
who doesn't believe it. It's ego, kids, not money, not the country,
not the unemployed, not the elderly, not the blacks or the Indians
or the welfare mothers. It's Bob Orben, from Hollywood and from
Broadway, who's going to package Jerry in a soap opera.
Remember sports fans, Jerry Ford is putting him in the job.
Remember that. Jerry Ford and Hartmann think that they and the
country need Bob Orben.''

I spot the Scotty Reston column in the *New York Times* which
notes that many of Gerald Ford's ''own people are quietly shipping
out.'' Reston says that next Monday's State of the Union address
will be critical:

"It may be his last chance, for the feeling here, even within his own administration, is that things are breaking up, and that people are giving up and moving out."

As the day ends, I call Agnes Waldron in research. She has a copy of the latest draft of the State of the Union message. I ask her what she thinks of the address and Agnes sums everything up in one word: "Workmanlike."

I ask her to try again and she replies: "It doesn't soar."

I urge a third and final try and she responds: "Par for the course."

Agnes, the most dedicated Republican that I've ever met, speaks with resignation. I close my office door and say to myself:

"If Gerald Ford loses Agnes, the Republican party will need a pallbearer. And I've got the candidate: Bob Orben."

Monday, January 19, 1976

KATHY WOOTEN, WHO HAS BEEN TYPING most of the State of the Union drafts, greets me as I arrive for work:

"Hear the latest?"

I plead ignorance. She spills out the grim state of affairs:

"You already know that Hartmann didn't produce a workable draft until last Friday. His first draft with Friedman, the one given the President last Monday, wasn't even a speech.

"Did you know that Cheney blew his stack when he read Hartmann's Friday draft? He had Dave Gergen (his new speechwriter aide from the Treasury Department) try to fix it up.

"They met with the President on Saturday—Cheney, Hartmann, Greenspan, Lynn and others. Cheney and Hartmann started fighting about Hartmann's draft. Lynn and Greenspan took Cheney's side.

"The President got angry, really angry. He started pounding the table. You know he never does that. But he was pounding the table. He told them he thought they had done all their fighting at Williamsburg when they went there. Why were they coming to him less than three days before the speech, fighting about the major points of the speech when they should be discussing the fine points?

"I talked with Gail Raiman (one of Hartmann's secretaries) and she calls the speech a 'disaster.' Nobody is satisfied with it.

287

Most people in the West Wing who have seen it don't like it.

"They've been changing it over the weekend. They're still changing it. And the speech is tonight. It's crazy, crazy."

I return to my office and Kaye Pullen arrives to ask whether I have seen the presidential daily news summary. She says that Aldo Beckman, White House correspondent for the *Chicago Tribune,* wrote a Sunday article about our staff and it's in the news summary. Hartmann, the source of the article, told Beckman that Bob Orben was to be our staff's new leader.

Kaye relates that she discussed part of the *Tribune* story with Alan Greenspan by phone last Friday evening. Greenspan, according to Kaye, characterized Orben's appointment as a "disaster." Kaye concludes:

"Alan is very low—low on the President because Ford waffles so much and low at just about everything around him. He thinks much of the staff is incompetent and sees only more trouble ahead. He's not leaving but he's definitely not happy."

I read the *Tribune* story. It reports the President's "growing dissatisfaction" with his speeches. The article says Mr. Ford tends to reject speeches unless they are written by Hartmann, Friedman or Orben.

The story, sensitive to the fact that Orben is strictly a gag writer, tries to make the case that Orben has written speeches for the President. On two or three occasions since I have come here, Orben has been pressed into service to paste together minor remarks for the President. One was an economic luncheon talk in Sacramento. However, when Greenspan learned of this, he strongly criticized the move. Orben also pasted up what he hoped would be accepted as a standard political speech for Mr. Ford. It was so awful that I threw my copy in the wastebasket. This came at a time, however, when Paul Theis was trying to hang onto his job and he hoped for Orben's support. Instead, he received a shove, with Orben taking over his job.

The *Tribune* story, with Hartmann continuing as its source, reports that Hartmann removed the writers' names from speeches to see if the President would accept them. Hartmann has consistently given out this fable. The fact is that some of Hartmann's work was so criticized by the dozen persons clearing the President's speeches, including rejections by the President of speeches written by him and Friedman, that the procedure became embarrassing to him and Friedman.

Monday, January 19, 1976

To my knowledge in recent months, the President has rejected a half-dozen speeches written by Hartmann and another half-dozen written by Friedman. However, the trio, which does not trust one another but knows that each has the President's ear and could hurt another, long ago decided to make private peace in order to survive. Thus, Hartmann, Friedman and Orben have a tacit pact that their survival comes first and the President's speeches second.

The story given by Hartmann to the *Tribune* appears to be the act of a desperate individual since Hartmann knows well he has done little to lead the speechwriting staff.

Since coming to the White House, Hartmann has offered me information about a speech on only one or two occasions. He has held only two meetings with our staff. I have written presidential speeches at the White House with, for all practical purposes, no guidance or assistance from Hartmann, for my entire fifteen months here.

The article outlines a Hartmann plan to hire new writers as "super researchers" for him, Friedman and Orben. One of the unkindest cuts of all is saved for Agnes Waldron and her research staff. The *Tribune* story concludes:

"There was concern, sources said, that several White House aides, whom Hartmann inherited from Richard Nixon, did not have adequate supervision from Ford appointees. So Mrs. Anderson was given responsibility to oversee their duties."

Agnes Waldron, a brilliant intellect, mature, serious, charming, witty, is thus berated by Hartmann. Agnes Waldron is a lady whose professional ability and grace are a genuine credit to an increasingly weak White House. This gentle woman, an individual of class, will never truly be supervised by Hartmann or his cronies in this White House because her abilities are so far above them.

Pat Butler comes by. He's furious at the *Tribune* article. Pat believes it could compromise his future professional life. He's particularly upset with Orben:

"He just called me into his office and said the article was mostly lies. He kept knocking Aldo and the whole story. But he's the one that's lying because he gave Aldo part of the story. Aldo told me that himself. So I got him dead to right in a lie.

"Orben kept telling me that he's going to have difficulty in recruiting—that writers don't want to be researchers. He wants me to stay, saying I would be a writer, not a researcher. Bullshit!

289

"I'm going to type out my resignation today. I'll have it ready for the time I get a job. The minute I confirm a new job, I'm quitting. These stupid people think they can lie to you day in and day out and that you're just like they are. Well, I got news for them. The decent people are getting out of this damn mess if they can."

I had promised to say goodbye to Eliska Hasek and saunter across the hall to her office. Eliska, an extremely refined and gentle individual, is dejected. She says:

"In my twelve years in the White House, I've never been so depressed. I went over to see Mr. Smith, the new assistant to Hartmann, and protested the fact that Gwen Anderson doesn't know what she's doing on presidential correspondence, proclamations and our other work. She's making some really bad mistakes in letters and other judgments. I told Smith that I could not be held responsible for her errors."

Eliska clasps and unclasps her hands. I tell her softly that I am quitting and I want to say goodbye and good luck. She appears nervous and upset and insists on talking about office problems.

"Just about every presidential message to any group is a political pitch. This is unpresidential. I told Mrs. Anderson and Mr. Smith that. And they are sending presidential messages to every Tom, Dick and Harry in the country. No President has ever done that in my time—not even the Kennedys, and they were really political.

"Why is President Ford lowering the presidency to the level of Ronald Reagan? Why can't he just be President and do a good job and have the staff forget about getting every one of these little political advantages?"

I try to change the subject but Eliska continues:

"No one trusts one another in this White House. The infighting is vicious. I'm afraid—I mean it—I'm afraid to call people about my work. I don't know what they'll say or think. This isn't just bad management, it's outrageous that personal esteem is so low in the White House."

We talk a while longer. Eliska, who speaks several languages, is running out of words in English. I get the impression she thinks she could tell me so much more in French, German or Czech. It's a sad parting. I shake her hand and wish her luck. She says softly:

"It's really bad, Jack. Not even in the most desperate days of the Nixon administration—not even when he resigned—was morale so low. I feel like crying . . . "

I close her door quietly and slip back to my office. I close the door, put my head in my hands and say:

"My God, it's really not happening. I wish I could say it's not happening. But it is. And it's happening now, today—the day of the State of the Union message."

At 3 P.M., the secretaries are still madly typing the President's speaking copy of the State of the Union address. Ron Nessen, who had promised it to newsmen by that hour, is making various excuses.

I read the final version.

There is no promised vision in the speech. No promised philosophy. No clear picture of the America which Gerald Ford would have us, as a people, inherit.

The close, calling to mind our motto of "In God We Trust," comes across as an almost crude, callous invocation of God's name. The expressions have little spiritual dignity or particular insight. The address, wordy and devoid of any real character, mercifully ends on a note of bland togetherness.

For me, it all ends with this address. The hopes, the dreams, the thought that Gerald Ford might uplift all of us by giving mightily of himself to the nation, they wither now before my eyes on this cold wintry day. The leadership, the inspiration, the intellectual integrity, the courage of conviction, the trust and belief of men—all of these qualities necessary for the highest office in our land appear wanting in Gerald Ford.

I feel like crying. I see Eliska's fearful face before me. I hear Pat Butler's discouraged voice. I feel Kaye Pullen's deep sense of dismay. I sense the frustration of Kathy Wooten and her desire to find a new job. I close my eyes in discouragement but am quickly called to account. Two men arrive to take away the office radio and TV set assigned me when I came to the White House. They say I am no longer responsible for them.

Tuesday, January 20, 1976

I QUICKLY LEAF THROUGH THE *New York Times* to their editorial page. The President and Hartmann are doing the same thing this morning, hoping against hope for an historic evaluation of the State of the Union address. They read in vain as the *Times* sums up the message:

"It was a standard pedestrian speech of the kind that Mr. Ford often delivered in his days as House minority leader . . . . It was difficult to find a new or inspiring thought in the President's message."

A few other editorials and TV commentaries are not much better. Most people with whom I come in contact during the day avoid the subject. However, our research office staff is outspoken and unanimous—the worst State of the Union message in memory. That old Kennedy word haunts Hartmann: vision. Everyone asks: Where was the vision?

Maureen Brown, a bright and charming young black woman on our research staff, slips into my office in late morning to say:

"I'm sorry you're leaving but you're lucky. You found something. I wish I could find something. I'd leave in a minute."

I ask Maureen why. She replies:

"I'm sure you heard it from others. I'm no different. I've been here nine years and morale has never been lower. I was here with Nixon. Now I feel like an outsider."

I ask Maureen about the Nixon speechwriters and she says:

"When a writer was assigned to write a speech for the President, he was called over to see Nixon. Nixon told him precisely what he wanted written. And Nixon would later call the same writer with changes when he saw the first draft. They really worked together.

"But you writers don't really work that way with Mr. Ford. He doesn't outline any speeches. He doesn't meet you alone. Hartmann is always there and Hartmann really doesn't want you there. And Hartmann doesn't give any guidance."

We promise to stay in contact. Maureen says she'll do research for me if I call her. She anticipates the new front office will not make much use of her talents. I say little except to tell her how good she has been to me, how grateful I am for her work.

Wednesday, January 21, 1976

MORE DETAILS ON THE STATE OF THE UNION infighting flow from the West Wing. The big argument over the speech was not substance but style. My mind returned almost immediately to our last speechwriting staff meeting when Theis and Orben argued: It's not substance that will be important, it's rhetoric.

Yet, as written, the speech was not rhetoric. It was substantive. However, it offered little philosophical basis for belief in it. The fact is that neither Hartmann nor the President is a deep philosophical thinker, not even in the realm of politics.

The speech, as accepted by the President, was a victory for Hartmann over his colleagues. Greenspan and the others argued long against the Hartmann draft. Mr. Ford came down hard on Hartmann's side.

Apart from the arguments over the address, a good number of White House staffers wonder why the President is so prone to listen to Hartmann, so determined at times to defend him. For some time, rumors have circulated in the White House that members of Mr. Ford's kitchen cabinet strongly suggested to the President that he find a different job for Hartmann. They reportedly wanted him out because of his tippling and abrasive personality. Yet the President, sometimes peeved because of Hartmann's poor writing and his inability to direct the writing staff, has apparently never considered firing his old crony.

Friday, January 23, 1976

MY LAST DAY IN THE WHITE HOUSE. I talk with Hartmann in his office for about a half-hour. He talks about leaks to the press. I wince because he is one of the biggest leakers in the White House. Hartmann believes Ronald Reagan may have infiltrated the White House. He's trying to trace a phone call of a staff member. He talks about the positive reaction to the State of the Union message that he has written. I do not quote the line from Bill Safire, former Nixon speechwriter, in the *New York Times*: ". . . in all, a respectable State of the Union for a tie salesman."

Safire used a line that I have echoed over the past fifteen months: ". . . in Ford speech style, you take no chances, you make no mistakes."

I say goodbye to the President in the Oval Office shortly before 11 A.M. He is kind and gentle as usual. Mr. Ford mentions he's sorry about the "remarks in the press" indicating that some of the writers are being shifted out of the White House. He knows that to be incorrect, particularly in my case. Mr. Ford wrote a letter in my behalf in mid-December clearly indicating that I was

293

leaving the White House at my request. He wrote a second letter later.

However, Bob Orben has been busy telling newsmen that four of us who are departing the speechwriting staff do so because we cannot write in the Jerry Ford "style."

Dave Kennerly is snapping pictures. I tell the President it has been a privilege to work for him. He hands me a copy of a speech I had written for his appearance at the Old North Church in Boston to commemorate the ride of Paul Revere. Mr. Ford has autographed the copy to me saying it was "one of the very best speeches" he had given as President.*

I tell the President how much I admire his wife for her courage. He laughs and says: "She's ahead of me in the polls."

We shake hands for the final time and I am deeply torn between my heart and mind. My heart tells me that this is a decent and good man. But my mind tells me this man does not have the firmness to run the White House or the leadership to be President.

On return to my office I find a copy of the *Washington Star* on my desk. It carries a story quoting our new chief, Orben, that indeed the departing writers were not attuned to Jerry Ford's style.

Thus Orben appears to be telling Washington that his close "friend" Paul Theis failed in his job. Presumably, he includes Rousek, Pullen and Casserly—all of whom are literally walking out of the place because the speechwriting operation is in such chaos. And Butler says he plans to leave as soon as he finds another job.

One paragraph in the *Star* story causes a real uproar among the departing writers:

"Since he joined the White House, however, Orben said that he had devoted himself to writing serious speeches. Though some newspaper stories have stressed his background as a gag writer, he said he has never been the 'joke writer to the President.' "

The four of us consider this the biggest joke of our White House experience. Pullen, Butler, Rousek and I know better—and so does Agnes Waldron, whom I consult for the exact record. Says Agnes:

"My records show that Orben has written one serious speech since coming to the White House. That was a Sacramento

See Appendix, page 309.

luncheon speech on the economy—not really a speech, some remarks. And he took virtually the whole thing from your speech written for the hardware industry in Chicago. So if we are really factual, Orben has never written a serious speech for the President.''

Orben comes into my office as I prepare to carry my files out to my car. He carefully looks over the files, obviously wondering whether he should bring up the subject. I simply say goodbye and shake hands. Orben presses me on any assistance he might offer in the future and I respond:

''No thanks. From the newspapers, I think you've already offered enough.''

He begins to talk about my contribution to the staff but I am tired of his conduct and simply ask him to say nothing about me. Flustered because he begins to recognize that I and others may have seen through his charade, particularly his treatment of Theis, he stands speechless as I leave the office.

Before departing the White House, each employee must turn in a checkout form to the personnel office. Officials of fourteen different White House functions must sign a two-page document stating that, among other things, one has paid his mess bills, turned in his parking permit and has no advance funds outstanding. I turn in this statement.

Jerry Popeo, of our research office, shakes hands in the south courtyard. He is the last person I see. As I drive out of the enclave and motor south on 17th Street, I take one glance back. I see the flag flying above the White House and I say to myself: ''It never happened. I was never there. Never.''

I had looked for a new America and Gerald Ford had offered only survival. In the end, it all came down to the concept of vision.

January 15, 1976

Dear John:

Thank you for your thoughtful letter. I will, of course,
accept your resignation effective January 23, 1976, as
you requested.

You do not need to be told that the post of a Presidential
speechwriter is one of the most difficult in the White
House, but I did want you to know that I recognize the
extraordinary demands it makes on an individual, both
professionally and personally. You have met those
demands fully and in doing so have earned the respect
and admiration of your colleagues in the White House
and throughout Government.

You will be missed at the White House, but I am pleased
that we will continue to have the benefit of your talents
as you assume your new duties as an assistant to the
Secretary of the Interior. I am confident the dedication
and outstanding skills you brought to the White House will
serve Tom Kleppe equally well at the Department of the
Interior. You may be sure you take with you my warmest
good wishes for the future.

Sincerely,

Mr. John J. Casserly
The White House
Washington, D. C. 20500

Afterword

DURING MY FIFTEEN MONTHS at the White House, I came gradually
and reluctantly to the conclusion that Gerald Ford and his staff were
unprepared and unable to assume the full power of the presidency.
There were many reasons.

From the beginning, the President and his principal advisors
failed to exercise the political power available to them because the
Ford White House "team" lacked unity and internal discipline.
Unlike the staffs of elected presidents, Mr. Ford's staff had not been
forged in the heat of a lengthy political campaign, where team
strengths are solidified and weaker members winnowed out. The Ford
staff was primarily, and remained, a "team" of individual players.
Only a relatively modest number of White House and other federal
executive personnel owed their jobs and, consequently, their loyalty
to Gerald Ford. The overwhelming majority had been appointed to

their positions throughout the far-flung federal government during the Nixon administration.

Worse, President Ford delegated his power of appointment to Donald Rumsfeld, his staff coordinator. As a result, many White House officials and other important government executives felt a greater allegiance to Rumsfeld than they did to the President. This is not to say that any appointee withheld allegiance from the President, but it was a divided loyalty.

Rumsfeld also used his position as a wedge between the President and Vice President Rockefeller. This further eroded White House staff unity and diminished the potential of both leaders. If this had not occurred, each man would have helped the other much more—the President providing much needed candor and openness and Rockefeller contributing stronger leadership, as well as vision for the country with the help of his highly competent personal staff. But Rumsfeld stepped between them and prevented this collaboration. In doing so, he also reduced Ford's effectiveness as President.

Furthermore, if capable and experienced Republican politicians—members of his "kitchen cabinet," for example—had accepted responsible positions within his administration, Mr. Ford's staff would have been materially strengthened. The refusal of these individuals to fill leadership posts seems to me one of the great tragedies of the Ford presidency.

And finally, Mr. Ford was unable to assume the full power of the presidency because he and his staff were extremely sensitive to the fact—and inhibited by it—that he was not an elected president, and had no direct mandate from the American people.

Initial disunity is not uncommon in newly-formed organizations, but why did this disunity and lack of discipline persist in the Ford White House for more than two years? Why were not unity and direction created out of desperation, if nothing else? Particularly during those challenging months immediately preceding the campaign for the Republican nomination? Who was responsible for this? The answer to these questions was always one individual: Gerald R. Ford. The President had no clearly conceived goals for the country, no vision of what the nation's future should be. Lacking this, disunity among his staff increased.

This shortcoming cost President Ford the election. His lack of far-sighted aims was a human but monumental error. For the

American people perceived they were being offered only a future of continued compromise and accommodation. The Ford White House reached up and out for formal acceptance by the American electorate by embracing the negative: to make as few mistakes and as few enemies as possible; to claim the cup of victory by declaring: no contest.

To a nation with our past and promise, this was unpardonable, and a sitting president was unseated.

Yet, in spite of the so-called fumbles and bumbles of the Ford administration, our government functioned reasonably well. The American people accepted Gerald Ford as the 38th president of the United States. He became a symbol of the continuity of our democratic system, the historical proof that our Constitution works. The Bill of Rights and the amendments of these 200 years are still alive and thriving as America moves into its third century.

What have we learned from this unusual experience in the transfer of presidential power? We've learned, among other things, that the 25th Amendment is no guarantee of better government. The Congress would do well to strengthen this amendment by issuing a "sense of congressional membership" resolution urging an unelected president—because of his unique tenure—to make special efforts to choose the most capable and experienced leaders to serve the country. Individuals of this calibre would replace their predecessors in the previous administration and, presumably, rise above the power politics and petty rivalries that plagued the Ford White House. A policy of bipartisanship should be the price for the betrayal of presidential trust.

The lesson of this diary is simple: the American system of government has survived for two centuries because it has sufficient flexibility to accommodate a wide range of human weaknesses—even to the extreme of presidential betrayal of the public. Our system of government is not above the lowest corruption nor below the highest vanity; its strength, unrecognized in large measure, is its viability beyond extremes, whether vice or virtue.

The American people have always believed in tomorrow. They still do. But this faith in the future, if it is to survive, must be sustained by a substantive and practical political testament, a sense of purpose, a vision of the future. The vision may vary from one political party to another, or from one year to the next; but whatever vision the American people follow, it will be a vision of their own choice.

This is our greatest liberty, our finest freedom: the people's freedom to choose their destiny.

Appendix

NEW HAMPSHIRE SPEECH (as delivered)

This New Hampshire speech is an example of lack of policy input. Neither President Ford nor Bob Hartmann contributed substantially to the address although most White House staffers—and the media—considered it a kickoff speech for the 1976 political campaign. In assigning the address, Paul Theis merely advised the author to sum up the President's basic beliefs. The President read the speech virtually as the author had written it and most of the media interpreted the address as Mr. Ford's political philosophy. The New York Times *and other newspapers offered considerable comment on what they regarded as the President's basic stance for the 1976 campaign.—JJC*

EMBARGOED FOR RELEASE
UNTIL 6:00 A.M., EDT   APRIL 17, 1975
Office of the White House Press Secretary

THE WHITE HOUSE

TEXT OF AN ADDRESS BY THE PRESIDENT
TO BE DELIVERED TO A JOINT SESSION OF THE
NEW HAMPSHIRE STATE LEGISLATURE

STATE CAPITOL

It is a great honor to appear here before the distinguished legislature of the great State of New Hampshire—a deliberative body that is known far and wide as one of the most highly representative, one of the most highly regarded, one of the most highly effective—and one of the most highly paid—in the respect and admiration of all its constituents. . . . Your selflessness and dedication is both to be commended and applauded.

I come here today to say a few words about the past, to offer some thoughts about the present and to talk about the future. The people of New Hampshire are rich in historical heritage.

It was at nearby Newcastle that four hundred of your ancestors stormed the British Fort William and Mary and captured its military stores—four months before the battles of Lexington and Concord. The captured ammunition was used by New Hampshire men who fought at Bunker Hill.

It was New Hampshire that drafted in January, 1776, the first Constitution proclaimed in the colonies, and passed a Declaration of Independence three weeks before such action by the Continental Congress. It was at Bennington that General John Stark led New Hampshire troops against the British with these famous words:

"There are your enemies—the Redcoats and Tories. We must beat them or tonight Molly Stark sleeps a widow." Molly Stark never became a widow. Bennington was an early colonial victory. But John Stark would have fought to the last man, the last rifle, the last round of ammunition—if necessary.

Let us remember the lesson of General Stark and the men of New Hampshire who fought for us then—and make sure this nation's defenses are never permitted to deteriorate to the point where an American must ever be called upon to fight without the best weapons and without ample ammunition—and without the full determination of our government and our people to achieve final victory once committed.

I like your nickname, the "Granite State." It shows the strength of character, firmness of principle and restraint that have long characterized New Hampshire.

Much of the rhetoric in America today tends toward exaggeration, toward over-statement. Such language tends to divide more than unite. It excites more than enriches. It promises more than it can produce.

This is not the time for extremes or excess in language or in conduct. It is not the moment for exaggeration in any direction. It is a time to think and act with reason and restraint.

You and I share a common interest in a subject where we must avoid extremes and excess. That is the general subject of how we manage our affairs—as reflected in your State budget and in the Federal budget.

Amid the climbing costs of Federal and State budgets—particularly in the past decade—New Hampshire has truly balanced its budget. You grapple with your problems without a general income or sales tax. I admire your spirit of self-discipline and self-reliance. You have gone about your business quietly—with restraint—without the exaggerated rhetoric which divides people and without excessive promises that create so much false hope.

In Federal programs and Federal spending, the opposite has been true. In the last quarter-century, Federal payments for individuals climbed from $31 billion to about $160 billion in constant dollars. In other words, from less than one-fourth of the Federal budget to nearly one-half.

America is now spending—if we include comparable figures for State and local governments—about $250 billion annually for various payments to individuals. That is approximately 15 percent of today's national income compared to some four percent 25 years ago.

Most of this spending is centered in a few programs. More than one-third of the funds are spent in Social Security payments, Medicare and Medicaid.

Many benefit programs are highly desirable. For example, a generation ago America devised one of the finest Social Security systems in the world and followed it with Medicare and Medicaid—and recently a Supplemental Income Plan. The American people supported these programs.

We have done many things over the past generation for the aged, the blind and the disabled—those who cannot help themselves. But it is also true that there has been an astonishing explosion in the number of other Federal programs—and in the number of people administering them. Since the early 1960's, the number of Federal Domestic Assistance programs has grown from about 200 of these social welfare programs in the early 1960's to more than 1,000 today. And there has been a massive increase in the country's bureaucracy—on the Federal, State and local level—from about six million employees in 1950 to 14 million today.

If we continue these trends at anywhere near their present rate of growth—more than twice that of the Gross National Product—the result will be this: In two decades, governments would need to collect in taxes more than half our GNP to meet their commitments.

Almost three-fourths of all Federal spending is currently in a category called "uncontrollable." I categorically reject the view that Federal spending is "uncontrollable" and that we must add each year to the national debt. Federal spending is controllable. There are two levers of such control:

The first is with the American people. They can say "no" to those still spreading the notion that it is possible to get something for nothing. Or they can say "yes" to those of us who are trying to curb the increasing burden of taxation and who want to restore fiscal responsibility.

The second lever is the exercise of leadership by the President and the Congress in the control of Federal spending. As President, I have drawn the line on spending. But the Congress is threatening to go far beyond the line. For example: The House of Representatives passed just two days ago its first regular appropriation bill for fiscal 1976. It amounted to one billion dollars more than my request of $6.2 billion for the major Federally-aided education programs. Apparently, the American people must educate the Congress.

The Nation now faces new Congressional multi-billion dollar initiatives. How much are the American people willing to tax themselves to pay for these new proposals? And for how long?

It took this Nation more than 180 years to reach a Federal budget of $100 billion annually. It took only nine more years for that budget to hit $200 billion a year—and only four years beyond that for the annual total to climb to $300 billion.

The Federal Government expects to spend about $322 billion this fiscal year. With the cooperation of the Congress, I plan to hold the budget for fiscal 1976 to approximately $356 billion. I am seriously concerned about the borrowing we must do to support these levels of spending.

In these troubled economic times, however, I believe it is necessary to help the unemployed and to stimulate the economy by a limited tax reduction.

In perspective, Federal receipts for fiscal 1976 would be more than $40 billion higher if the economy were operating normally. This accounts for the most of the deficit in fiscal 1976. If the economy were operating at the rate of only one year ago, the Nation would have balanced budgets both this year and next.

Some believe that this country can continue government spending—Federal, State and local—on most if not all present programs and at least at the current rate of outlays. Others take the position that America is not spending enough to meet social and other needs.

Most of these requests come from increasingly discredited rhetoric—one promise after another. And this is the heart of our financial dilemma today. It is the endless stream of promises made to the American people—in the last generation and continuing today—that the government can and will satisfy most of their needs—and even their wants. It is a language that has now become one of extremes and excess. It is that the government will make your dreams come true—all you have to do is file an application. The

American people cannot live on promises. We must live on production. All of this raises a question—a question of utmost simplicity and yet of profound significance to the American people: How long can the United States afford to run continuous budget deficits?

All levels of government have contributed much to progress during the past generation. But many new programs have failed—leading not only to waste but disillusionment and despair. We have come to a time—in my judgment—where the American people will and must take a closer look at where their money is going. The reason is simple. The built-in momentum of the Federal budget and unanticipated other demands have produced excessive expenditure growth rates. These growth rates are not only rising faster than current revenues but are absorbing our anticipated future growth. This is no time for fiction or false promises. The American people want to know where they stand.

I believe it is time to reassess our domestic policies. I am convinced that the people of the United States do not know where their money is going—and just as important, WHY. This is the 1974 Catalog of Federal Domestic Assistance—some 800 pages of programs—much of it in fine type. It weighs almost four pounds and is a complex maze of programs. Let us look at these programs. Are we getting our money's worth? If not, why not?

It is time to re-examine not only the American budget but the American Conscience and the basic American virtues. We must get our house in order. Instead of more promises, the American people must ask who will pay for these promises.

The United States is now spending—among Federal, State and local governments—hundreds of billions of dollars for social programs. Many are uncoordinated and ineffective. They must be reassessed. We must take a close look at these and any other programs that may be questionable. The American people understand that they pay for all this spending either through their taxes or inflation—or both. This country is not great because of what the Federal Government has done, but what American individuals have accomplished.

We must take the American people back into our confidence and tell them the truth. And the truth is this: The Federal Government can no longer increase spending at the rate it has done in the past. I sound this warning to the American people—here in this Legislature because you are a remarkable example of the early principles and policies that made this country great. You have lived and worked within your means. New Hampshire is more than a State. It is a state of mind. It is the true new frontier of America—because ideas and principles and virtues have no boundaries. You have offered us the horizons—of free men and women—not those burying this Nation and our people in debt. Voltaire once said:

"Common sense is not so common."

Neither are Granite principles and Granite beliefs. Thank you for your invitation to meet with you here today.

OLD NORTH CHURCH REMARKS (as delivered)

This Old North Church address was written by the author with virtually no contribution by the President or Bob Hartmann. More significantly, it was one of the few speeches that escaped staff infighting during the clearance process. This process, whereby as many as sixteen individuals were known to change, eliminate or add to a speech, damaged many of the President's addresses.—JJC

FOR IMMEDIATE RELEASE   APRIL 18, 1975

OFFICE OF THE WHITE HOUSE PRESS SECRETARY
(Boston, Massachusetts)

THE WHITE HOUSE

REMARKS OF THE PRESIDENT
AT THE
OLD NORTH CHURCH

To Jack Casserly, in appreciation on this speech, one of the very best, and your fine help in a tough job. With best wishes. Jerry Ford

8:25 P.M. EDT

Bishop, Vicar, dear friends:

Two hundred years ago tonight two lanterns hung in the belfry of this Old North Church. Those lanterns signaled patriots on the other side of the Charles River British troops were moving by water.

As Longfellow said in his poem: "One if by land and two if by sea."

Paul Revere, William Dawes and Samuel Prescott rode into the night, alerting the colonists the British were coming. When day

309

broke, according to the diaries of the time, the sky was clear and blue. British troops had crossed the Charles River.

They marched all night, and after a skirmish at Lexington, the Redcoats arrived at Concord. There a volley was fired by our Minutemen, what Emerson called "The shot heard 'round the world." The American war for independence had begun.

Tonight, we stand in tribute to those who stood for liberty and for us two centuries ago. Tonight, we bow our heads in memory of those who gave their lives, their lands, their property for us during that historic struggle because tonight we begin as a Nation and as a people the celebration of our Bicentennial.

Alexis de Tocqueville, the French historian, wrote of our beginnings: "In that land, the great experiment was to be made, by civilized men, of the attempt to construct society on a new basis."

Over the decades, there were challenges to that experiment. Could a nation half slave and half free survive? Could a society with such a mixture of peoples and races and religions succeed? Would the new nation be swallowed up in the materialism of its own well being?

The answers are found in the history of our land and our people. It is said that a national character is shaped by the interplay of inheritance, environment and historical experience.

Our inheritance is basically that of Western Europe. From the English we received the tradition of liberty, laws, language and customs.

The American inheritance has been constantly enriched by people from Western and Eastern Europe, from Asia, and Africa, as well as Latin America and many other parts of this great globe.

Over 200 years some 50 million emigrants have been absorbed in our society. Though our national origins are not forgotten, all of us are proud to be simply called Americans.

Our environment includes every variety of climate, soil and resources. The American historical experience has been brief compared to many, many other nations. We are the new world, but we are the world's oldest republic.

The most distinguished characteristic of our American way is our individualism. It is reflected in our frontier spirit, our private enterprise and our ability to organize and to produce.

Our ability to adopt new ideas and to adapt them to practical purposes is also strikingly American. But now we ask ourselves, how did we come to be where we are tonight? The answer is found in the history of the American experience. It teaches us that the American experience has been more of reason than of revolution, more of principles than passions and more of hope than hostilities or despair.

But our history is also one of paradox. It has shown us that reason is not without its moments of rebellion, that principles are not without passion and hope is not without its hours of discouragement and dismay.

It is well to recall this evening that America was born of both promise and protest: The promise of religious and civil liberties and protest for representation and against repression.

Some of our dreams have at times turned to disappointment and disillusionment, but adversity has also driven Americans to greater heights.

George Washington marched from the anguish of Valley Forge to the acclaim of final victory. Reason and hope were the twin lanterns of Washington's life. They enabled him to prevail over the day-to-day doubts and defeats. They have been the lamps that have lighted the road of America toward its ultimate goals—dignity and yes, self-fulfillment—and pride in country.

Abraham Lincoln was a man of reason and a man of hope. He acknowledged the grave flaw of our first 87 years—slavery.

Over 110 years ago, the American Civil War ended with our Republic battered and divided. Many people talked more of survival than of union. One-half of the Nation was on its knees in ruin. Nearly 2 million had been killed and wounded. The war had uprooted the lives and the fortunes of millions more.

Its end was marked by more tears than cheers. But it was also the birth of a new Nation freeing itself from human slavery. Just before the war ended on March 4, 1865, President Abraham Lincoln stood on the East Portico of the Capitol in Washington and delivered his second inaugural address.

He extended the hand of friendship and unity when he said, "With malice toward none, with charity for all, with firmness in the right, as God gives us to see the right, let us strive on to finish the work we are in, to bind up the Nation's wounds."

President Lincoln had relit the lamps of reason and the lamps of hope. He had rekindled pride in America.

Over 100 years ago, as the Nation celebrated its centennial, America looked to the future. Our Nation had emerged from an agricultural frontier society into an industrial age. Our towns were beginning to evolve into the cities of the 20th century. Rail transportation and the telegraph were tying this vast continent together.

When we celebrated our 100th birthday, one of the themes was: "While proud of what we have done, we regret that we have not done more."

There was certainly more to do and more people to do the job. Immigrants were pouring into America. They were welcomed by these words inscribed on the Statue of Liberty: "I lift my lamp beside the golden door."

The great increase in the number of Americans, may I say, made us a formidable force in the world. That force was soon needed. World War I saw American troops fight and die in Europe for the first time.

Many Americans were disappointed and disillusioned by the aftermath of the war. They found the causes for which they fought unachieved.

The American people rejected foreign entanglements and withdrew into a separate existence. They wanted to be left alone.

In 1941, the United States was attacked and once more we went to war. This time across the Pacific as well as the Atlantic. We were proud of this country and what it was achieving for liberty around the world.

Yet, still another time, following victory over our enemies, the American public was jarred and disillusioned by the postwar years. They discovered there would be no real peace. Europe was divided in two on V-E Day.

In the words of Churchill, "An iron curtain has descended across the continent." America had become the stronghold of liberty.

President Truman instituted a bipartisan foreign policy of containment, cooperation and reconstruction. The Marshall Plan moved to reconstruct a free world. The United Nations was born but the cold war had already begun. Soon—all too soon—America was again at war under the banner of the United Nations in Korea.

Little did we know then that American troops would only a decade later be fighting in still another war in Asia, culminating in a broken peace agreement in Vietnam.

In the two hundred years of our existence, it is not war and disillusionment which have triumphed. No. It is the American concept and fulfillment of liberty that have truly revolutionized the world. America has not sought the conquest of territory but instead the mutual support of all men and women who cherish freedom.

The Declaration of Independence has won the minds, it has won the hearts of this world beyond the dreams of any revolutionary who has ever lived. The two lanterns of the Old North Church have fired a torch of freedom that has been carried to the ends of the world.

As we launch this Bicentennial celebration, we Americans must remind ourselves of the eternal truths by which we live. We must be re-inspired by the great ideals that created our country. We must renew ourselves as a people and rededicate this nation to the principles of two centuries ago.

We must revitalize the pride in America that has carried us from some of our darkest hours to our brightest days.

We must once again become masters of our own destiny. This calls for patience, for understanding, for tolerance and work toward unity—unity of purpose, a unity based on reason, a unity based on hope.

This call is not new. It is as old as the Continental Congress of two hundred years ago, as legendary as Lincoln's legacy of more than one hundred years ago, and as relevant as today's call to Americans to join in the celebration of the Bicentennial.

Perhaps national unity is an impossible dream. Like permanent peace, perhaps it will prove to be a never-ending search. But today we celebrate the most impossible dream of our history, the survival of the Government and the permanence of the principles of our founding fathers.

America and its principles have not only survived, but flourished far beyond anyone's dreams. No nation in history has undertaken the enormous enterprises of the American people. No country, despite our imperfections, has done more to bring economic and social justice to its people and to the world.

Yet, we have suffered great internal turmoil and torment in recent years. Nevertheless, in all the explosive changes of this and past generations, the American people have demonstrated a rich reserve of reason and hope.

There are few times in our history when the American people have spoken with more eloquent reason and hope than during the tribulations and tests that our Government and our economic system have endured during the past year. Yet, the American people have stood firm.

The Nation has not been torn with irresponsible reaction. Rather, we are blessed with patience, common sense and a willingness to work things out. The American dream is not dead. It simply has yet to be fulfilled.

In the economy and energy and the environment, in housing, transportation, in education and communication, in social problems and social planning, America has yet to realize its greatest contribution to civilization.

To do this, America needs new ideas and new efforts from our people. Each of us, of every color, of every creed, is part of our country, and must be willing to build not only a new and better Nation, but new and greater understanding and unity among our people.

Let us not only be a Nation of peace, but let us foster peace among all nations. Let us not only believe in equality, but live it each day in our lives. Let us not only feed and clothe a healthy America, but let us lend a hand to others struggling for self-fulfillment.

Let us seek even greater knowledge and offer the enlightenment of our endeavors to the educational and scientific community throughout the world. Let us seek the spiritual enrichment of our people more than material gains.

Let us be true to ourselves, to our heritage and to our homelands, and we will never then be false to any people or to any nation.

Finally, let us pray here in the Old North Church tonight that those who follow 100 years or 200 years from now may look back at us and say:

We were a society which combined reason with liberty and hope with freedom.

May it be said above all: We kept the faith. Freedom flourished. Liberty lived.

These are the abiding principles of our past and the greatest promise of our future.

Good evening, and may God bless you all.

END   (AT 8:45 P.M. EDT)

HARDWARE INDUSTRY CONFERENCE ADDRESS
(first draft and as delivered)

These are two versions of a presidential address to the Hardware Industry Conference at Chicago in 1975. At least sixteen—the author counted nineteen—individuals took a crack at changing the speech as he wrote it. This process diluted and compromised many presidential addresses, leaving them dull and vacuous.—JJC

August 5, 1975
First Draft

PRESIDENTIAL ADDRESS TO THE HARDWARE INDUSTRY CONFERENCE
CHICAGO, MONDAY, AUGUST 25, 1975

America has always symbolized ideas. No nation or society in history has done more to encourage invention, innovation, and initiative. We pride ourselves on being a people of Yankee ingenuity.

The explosion of American ideas began 200 years ago with our Declaration of Independence. That original document has been multiplied across the earth ever since. New Nations use it as a model today to declare their own rights and freedoms.

A century ago, our continent and our society were swept up in wave after wave of industrial invention and technical innovation. Ideas rotated like crops from the Atlantic to the Pacific.

Charles Goodnight blazed new trails in the cattle industry and made the cowboy an American folk hero. Samuel Colt's six-shooter helped to open the plains to new settlers. Elias Howe and Isaac Singer revolutionized the clothing industry with their new sewing machines. Factory-made clothes became a major democratic force in society.

Railroads tied the entire Nation together. Thomas Edison lighted the country. Henry Ford put it on wheels with his assembly-line prices. The telegraph, telephone, radio, movies, television—all united this vast Nation.

Europe's Old World privilege became the New World of the commonplace. This was a boundless America of limitless horizons and unparalleled hopes.

In our generation, America has split the miniscule of the atom

315

while conquering the vastness of space. No challenge has been too small or too great. From a Nation of Originality and Opportunity, we became a Nation of Optimism.

This has been the spirit of America for the past two centuries—a spirit of ideas, innovation, ingenuity. And I might add independence. It was a spirit of private enterprise—churning ahead in a free, competitive system.

We need to be reminded today of these basic facts about America . . . about ourselves as a people . . . and about our way of life. No nation and no people on earth have invested more than we in these past two centuries in human and scientific progress. No one has taken greater risks or experimented more in behalf of mankind's progress than the United States. And none has been more generous in sharing its discoveries with the world.

Today, as we prepare to begin our third century, America is again called to invest, to risk, to experiment in the name of progress. New ideas are to be born . . . new inventions to lift mankind's burdens . . . new innovation and new ingenuity await the touch of new genius.

As our Founding Fathers learned, we need tools to build and rebuild America. We have the principles and we have the people. Now we need the capital. Our economic progress has always depended on capital investment. Our society has increased its standard of living primarily by increasing capital input relative to labor input.

In recent years, there have been at least a half dozen major studies on the country's capital needs. Every single study reports an increased need for capital. It is estimated that about $4 trillion will be needed for the private sector in the next decade. This total contrasts with less than $2 trillion in the dozen years from 1962 to 1973.

Various estimates indicate the Nation may fall short of its capital needs by anywhere from one-half trillion to three-quarters of a trillion dollars. It is sometimes called a "capital gap"—*not* a *confidence* gap in what we can accomplish but a gap in available investment dollars.

I believe that capital investment is a clear, unequivocal vote of confidence in America and in the American economy. And it is a further vote of confidence in the national traits that have always characterized America—its spirit of competition and discovery.

While we listen to this call for capital investment—for new

commitment to the American future—our Government grows faster than the economy which supports it. Not a year goes by but that Government grows larger and shatters previous spending records. We pride ourselves in being a people governed by consent but Government is becoming a state within a state which keeps enlarging itself—not by common consent and the knowledge of our people—but by growing Government's momentum.

If we do not reverse the direction of the Government growing faster than the economy supporting it, the United States and the American people will begin drifting backwards—in terms of production, jobs, and our entire economic, social and political future. We will no longer be leaders of innovation and ingenuity. The great American Experiment—which lifted multi-millions out of poverty to all the avenues of progress—will founder in a sea of stagnation.

I do not believe the American people want to drift into mediocrity. I do not believe that Americans aim at the short-term security of what their Government may give them. I do not believe that the great American Experiment of Democracy has now or ever will choose what Government may do for you instead of what you can do for yourself.

I believe the American people will face the fundamental problem of capital formation in this country. They will do it for many practical reasons:

—The decline in American productivity improvements threatens to perpetuate stifling inflation. It is curtailing needed growth in jobs and income. And it further undermines our ability to compete internationally.

We must have Government tax policies that will direct more of the country's resources into the modernization and expansion of productive capacity. We must not run out of industrial capacity before we conquer the unemployment rate. We must not permit that inflationary shortages show up when the economy begins to speed up again. We cannot and must not be defeated by our own success.

—All of our basic industries report that they are in a capital crunch. These capital needs are growing and yet the capacity of industry to generate necessary funds is declining. Inflation has seriously eroded balance sheets.

—We need capital to expand agriculture to help pay for imported fuels and raw materials. Additional capital will develop

317

marginal domestic resources of energy and raw materials and reduce our foreign dependence. Other capital is necessary to preserve and improve the environment.

The answer for America is this: instead of trying to place increasing demands on a shrinking tax base—we are now witnessing sad and sorry examples of this—we can begin by instituting energizing tax reforms.

This Administration has made such a proposal to the Congress—to stimulate greater capital formation through tax incentives. The proposal—to permit industry the funds needed for expansion—offers corporations and stockholders an estimated $13 billion in tax relief. This would be very carefully phased in over a six-year period, starting a year and a half from now, in 1977. This would be done through lightening the so-called "double taxation" of dividends. Companies would be permitted to deduct up to 50 percent of their dividend payments from their taxable income. For individual investors, the proposal would in effect eliminate taxes on dividends in a 50 percent or lower tax bracket.

This is causing wail and woe among some members of Congress. They oppose the proposal. But, like my energy measure, the Congress has nothing to propose in its place.

The point was then and the point is now: we must start somewhere. We must do something about capital formation as we must still do something about energy. So I say to the Congress today as I said to the Congress last January: Come up with your own plan. I am willing to consider any reasonable proposal in the interest of generating the much needed capital to move the country forward—to generate jobs, income and full recovery. All I am asking is a clear commitment to the Nation's future. I believe the American people want that and I believe the American people have every right to expect it.

America *can* have a sufficient number of jobs for the increasing number of workers now entering the labor market. We *can* meet the great obligations to Social Security and other social commitments. America *can* preserve its clean air and water. Our standard of living *can* enrich the lives of more Americans. But the American people must be given the *opportunity* to demonstrate—as we have throughout our history—that we will experiment, innovate, use our ingenuity, and take the necessary risks to improve our lives. That experiment, that risk involves the formation and investment of capital in the American future.

Americans are over-taxed. Year after year, the Government takes more of their money. Capital pouring into Government cannot be invested. Americans *will* invest in their own land and lives—and their own future—if given the chance. I am asking the Congress to give them that chance—to open the door to new experiment and new genius. This is the stuff that made America. It is the stuff of America's third century.

There is another way to revitalize the American economy and our free market. That is increased competition. Effective competition is a key to a strong and viable free marketplace. To guarantee that, I am now seeking fundamental reform of economic regulation in the United States. To this end, I have spoken at some length. Today I want to mention an essential companion to regulatory reform: antitrust enforcement.

Such enforcement will divest business of unreasonable government protections that they have enjoyed in the past. Specifically, that means such currently exempt activities as cartel ratemaking and market-sharing agreements. These cases will come under antitrust prosecution. We will thus encourage and expand market competition.

If we are to enact these reforms, there must be bipartisan consumer/business agreement for the common good of all. We must think in terms of broad-based understanding to regenerate and renew the American marketplace with a new competitive spirit.

The evils of monopoly are well known: higher prices, slower innovation, less responsive services, and discriminatory practices. However, to an increasing extent, the problem of monopoly is a result of government intervention to create and perpetuate *shared* monopoly. We see many examples in regulated industries—trucking, railroads and the airlines. Government dispensations originated in other industries—through the imposition of agricultural tariffs, enforcement of licensure, control of prices, and legal restrictions on entry.

Not all government dispensations are bad. Patents, for example, are created for a limited duration to encourage technological innovation. More often than not, however, such dispensations represent special benefit programs.

This is not an Administration of special interests. This is an Administration of the public interest. Therefore, we do not intend to permit the continuation of monopoly privilege. It is my job—and your job—to open up the American marketplace to all comers. It is the marketplace which will allocate resources, lay the groundwork for organizing production, and provide economic progress—not the politics of government.

Over the past several decades, the government has intervened more and more to control our economic life. Today, various industries and associations operate in a congenial cost-plus environment because government has decided that the groups or firms they represent need not or cannot compete.

My message today on monopoly is simply this: we must look at the whole range of monopoly—from a small monopoly franchise to a government-sanctioned cartel. We must recognize that the government does as much to create monopoly as to control it. Our concern is with the *cost* of monopoly, however it may be imposed.

It is estimated that each American family pays an average of $2,000 a year for the combined cost of government regulation and restrictive practices in the private sector. That is more than the Federal government collects in most income tax returns. We must reduce these costs. Our economic system must efficiently deliver what we need and want at the lowest cost.

Antitrust underlines our commitment to a competitive market. And competitive markets promote the investment of capital. The investment of capital will launch new discovery.

We must *act* to create a new, dynamic economy. Regulatory reform and antitrust action go hand-in-hand to spark new capital investment and new competition. This is the dynamism, this is the spirit needed to renew America.

Congress is beginning to act on regulatory reform and in antitrust. Both the Administration and the Congress have legislation pending. More is being considered. But the enactment of such legislation will not be easy in the face of powerful opposition.

We face critical choices in the months ahead: Will we work together for a freer economy for the betterment of all? Or will we be stymied by self-interest battling self-interest? Or eventually will we accept some self-sacrifice in the national interest? America must regain its economic freedoms.

I do not expect universal agreement on all that is proposed. Nor will all our decisions come easily. Yet, we must make a start. In today's world, to stand still is to retreat.

So I ask you today to renew your spirit in the *real* America—the America of competition and discovery. As old as our Nation, these are the launching pads to America's third century. These are real promises. These are practical promises. These are the promises that built our Nation and uplifted our people—and they will do so again. Thank you.

END

THE WHITE HOUSE

REMARKS OF THE PRESIDENT
TO THE
AMERICAN HARDWARE
MANUFACTURER'S ASSOCIATION

McCORMICK PLACE

9:37 A.M. CDT

as delivered

Cardinal Cody, Mr. Spencer, distinguished guests, ladies and gentlemen:

It is a very special pleasure and privilege for me to be here this morning and to pay tribute to the American hardware industry and to kick off Hardware Week in the City of Chicago.

Yours is an industry that has taken American ingenuity and coupled it with some of the most effective merchandising techniques known to mortal man.

That may seem like some exaggeration, but a hardware store is the only business I know of where you can go to buy a 10 cent carriage bolt and come out with a can of paint, a new, improved screwdriver, 50 pounds of charcoal briquets, a bicycle repair kit, ten minutes of free advice, 12 picture hooks, six fuses and a lawnmower, and then have to go back because you forgot the 10 cent carriage bolt you went to buy there in the first place. (Laughter)

I have been a typical homeowner most of my life, and my wife Betty knows it. She says that sending me to a hardware store is the nearest thing she knows to playing chicken with our life savings. (Laughter)

Nevertheless, on behalf of all of us "do-it-yourselfers," let me thank all of you here for making possible the wonder of wonders —the neighborhood hardware emporium, more affectionately known as the world's only candy store for grown-ups. (Laughter)

In your business, you constantly seek out those new ideas that are so important to a great country, and so do we in this country. In fact, no nation or society in history has done more to encourage invention, innovation and initiative.

The explosion of American ideas began 200 years ago with our Declaration of Independence. A century ago a tide of industrial progress started to sweep over America. Sewing machines revolutionized the clothing industry, electricity made life brighter and more prosperous, automobile assembly lines put us on wheels. The telegraph and telephone—later movies, radio and television—linked the people of this vast Nation closer and closer together.

In our generation, America has split the atom and conquered space. Americans never shirked from challenge. Courage, originality, opportunity and optimism are national traits.

This has been the spirit of America for the past two centuries—a spirit of ideas and individuality. It was and is the spirit of private enterprise—churning ahead in a free, competitive system fueled by private savings and investment. We need to recall these basic facts about America, about ourselves as a people and about our way of life.

No nation has invested more than we have in humanity and science. No nation has taken greater risks or experimented as much for progress. As a result, no nation has earned such rewards as the United States.

Today America is again called upon to invest, to risk, to experiment in the name of progress. But unfortunately, we have reached a watershed. A decision must be made. The question, put simply, is precisely this: how do we finance both the investment needed for economic growth and essential programs needed to solve our human problems?

Today we are faced with a problem of creating new jobs in numbers greater than ever before in America. Although unemployment is far too high, neverthless we should not forget that 85 millions in this great country are at work and that is about 1.2 million more than just last March.

By 1980, we must create another 14 million jobs to meet the needs of our expanding population. This is our objective, and it will require substantial economic progress.

As always, economic progress depends on our ability as a Nation to foster capital investment and increase the productivity of our workers. The share of our gross national product committed to the private sector investment must increase significantly over the next few years if we are to reach our economic potential. Some, for example, estimate that total investment requirements could reach as high as $4 trillion.

However, as our need for capital grows, the abilities of industry to generate necessary funds is declining. This is essentially because inflation has eroded corporate balance sheets and because our national tax laws fail to stimulate such investment.

In short, our financial ability to increase production is declining. This decline is curtailing needed growth in jobs and income and undermining our ability to compete internationally.

I am very confident once this becomes clear to the American people they will understand America's need for tax policies that will help to channel sufficient resources into the expansion of productive capacity.

At today's level of economic activity, no shortage of industrial facilities exist, but our Nation's economic machine is not now running at top speed. In the future, we have every reason to expect it will, but we must now not permit bottlenecks and shortages to reappear as the economy gains momentum.

We must not condemn our fellow citizens to unemployment because the modern tools needed to compete in world markets are lacking.

Capital, as all of you know, is vital to all segments of our economy to expand agricultural production, to develop domestic resources of energy and raw material, reducing our dependence on oil imports and to preserve and to improve our economy.

This Administration has proposed reforms to the Congress to stimulate through what some call capital formation through tax incentives, but I prefer to use the term ''job creation'' because that is what the proposals would do as a practical matter.

If adopted, they would provide the funds to expand America's industry capability to create jobs, for one thing, by reducing the double taxation on dividends.

As expected, these proposals have raised an outcry from some Members of Congress who oppose them and, as a person who was in the Congress for a number of years, I understand these voices.

The Congress, in this case, as in others, has come up with no alternatives. We have got to push them to action here, as well as elsewhere. America cannot put its faith in wishing wells. We must do something about expanding our sources of capital to create jobs, and we must do it right now.

I ask the Congress to join with me in this commitment to our Nation's future, to increase jobs, income and full economic recovery.

Let us expand the size of our economic pie rather than simply redistributing the pieces of a much smaller piece of pie.

By itself, however, additional capital cannot revitalize the American economy and our free market system. We must also take steps to help restore the vitality of the marketplace and effective competition is the way to do it.

Too often in the past our Government has stifled that competition in the name of economic regulation to the detriment of the consumer. For that reason, my Administration—with strong support of the Congress in this instance—is seeking fundamental reform of economic regulation in the United States.

The problem is simply this: In many industries, transportation, energy, communication, as well as others, Federal regulatory commissions have actually thwarted competition. The bureaucratic monopolies have tackled business and conflicting policies and red tape far, far too long.

The record is clear. They have burdened the consumer with the cost of misdirected regulation.

Although I am greatly encouraged by widespread backing for regulatory reform, I also recognize we still have a long, long way to go to achieve it. With the continued support, which is very evident, with the support of you, as well as your industry, we will reverse the trend of the last few decades.

We will establish as national policy this basic fact of economic life, that Government regulation is not an effective substitute for vigorous American competition in the marketplace.

Having said this, let me add that some—and let me qualify it by saying some—regulations are necessary and appropriate; for instance, involving health, safety and the environment.

But the reforms that we seek would eliminate the impractical, the unnecessary and the obsolete. As part of this effort to insure that we have a strong economic system, we must maintain an antitrust policy which validates our commitment to competitive markets.

If we reduce Government regulation of business, we must make certain and positive that our antitrust laws are vigorously enforced.

Competition, when freed of Government regulation and supported by antitrust laws, is the driving force of our economy. It will drive costs down to their minimum and assure prices based on these legitimate costs.

Yet, such steps cover only a part of the overall problem. It is much more difficult to deal with areas that antitrust laws do not touch, these other regulated and legal monopolies and the Government sanctioned cartels.

For instance, various industry rate bureaus and self-regulatory agencies—transportation rate bureaus, shipping conferences, stock exchanges and professional associations—now seem to operate in a congenial cost-plus environment.

This is simply because Government once decided they need not, or cannot, compete.

They are allowed to fix prices and divide markets under the regulatory cloak, free from antitrust enforcement.

An essential element of regulatory reform legislation I have already sent or will send to Congress will eliminate most of these anticompetitive practices. The remainder of these practices, now immunized from antitrust laws, are undergoing intense review in the Executive Branch of the Government.

In short, this Administration will look at the whole range of Government sanctioned monopoly—from the small franchises protected by Federal regulations, which rule out competition, all the way to Government-endorsed cartels involving entire industries.

We must recognize this: Over the years Government has done as much to create and perpetuate monopoly as it has done to control or eliminate it. As a result, this Nation has become accustomed to certain forms of monopoly. Some are regarded as beneficial, some not.

If an industry combines to raise prices, it violates our antitrust laws, but no laws are violated if an industry can get the Federal Government to build trade barriers, to increase support prices for the goods or services that it produces, or to police against potential competitors or pricecutters.

It is sad but true—too often the Government walks with the industry along the road to monopoly.

The end result of such special treatment provides special benefits for a few, but powerful, groups in the economy at the expense of the taxpayer and the consumer.

Let me emphasize this is not—and never will be—an Administration of special interests. This is an Administration of public interest, and always will be just that.

Therefore, we will not permit the continuation of monopoly privilege, which is not in the public interest. It is my job and your job to open the American marketplace to all comers.

Ultimately, the vital reforms will be viewed—as they should be—as a pocketbook issue. Government regulation and restrictions now cost consumers billions and billions of dollars each year. We must be concerned about the cost of monopoly however it is imposed and for what reasons.

We must be sure that regulatory reform and antitrust actions go hand in hand with incentives to spark capital investment to create new jobs and new competition. This is what I firmly believe is needed to revive the American economic dream.

Before I close, let me share one thought with you. It concerns a subject that affects the lives and the pocketbooks of every American—the runaway growth of the Federal Government itself.

One of the goals I have set for myself as President is to cut big Government down to size—and we can do it this way—to make it more manageable, more responsive, more efficient and less costly. I want to put an end to the mountain of paperwork and the quicksand of regulation which big Government makes every businessman cope with.

Do you have any idea how many different Federal forms Washington sends out and asks you to fill out? Would you believe it is over 5,000—5,000 Federal forms to keep Washington at work and businessmen from their work.

Believe me—and obviously you agree—this is not the way this great Nation was built over a 200-year span. I can vividly recall how my father started a small family factory back in, of all years, 1929. In those dire economic circumstances, everybody pitched in.

My speciality—and it didn't require much skill—was mixing the paint and labeling cans. But, my father was always out there selling the merchandise and doing what makes sense for the business, not what makes sense for the bureaucrats.

The Ford Paint and Varnish Company survived the depression. And I have wondered if it would have if my father had had to fill out all of today's forms and applications and those thousands and thousands of questionnaires, and at the same time, cope with a patchwork of rules and regulations which face today's businessmen.

My objective is to get the Federal Government as far out of your business, out of your lives, out of your pocketbooks and out of your hair as I possibly can.

To this end, within three weeks after I came into the Office of the Presidency last August, I directed the heads of all Federal Government departments and agencies to reduce the personnel for whom they had requested funds for the remainder of the fiscal year by 40,000.

Actually, I can report to you today that their performance exceeded my directive. We ended fiscal year 1975 on June 30 of this year with a reduction or a cutback of 52,000 Federal employees under the planned levels of a year ago.

As far as those 5,000 Government forms, I can tell you this: several months ago I directed Jim Lynn, the Director of the Office of Management and Budget, to examine, to analyze, to evaluate and then throw out as many of these timewasters as he possibly can. And I am going to personally monitor it.

To put it very simply, I want to see the American businessman pushing merchandise, not pencils.

You don't need a lot of bureaucrats looking over your shoulder and telling you how to run your life or how to run your business. We are a people who declared our independence 200 years ago, and we are not about to lose it now to paper shufflers and computers.

Let's take the shackles off American businessmen. That is the only kind of hardware I don't approve of.

Thank you very much.

END

(AT 10:02 A.M. CDT)

MECKLENBURG AND KINGS MOUNTAIN, N.C. REMARKS

These North Carolina speeches were not given by the President for various reasons, primarily because he was being criticized for too much stumping. They illustrate, however, one of the most crucial conflicts in writing for Mr. Ford. He had been consistently criticized for giving plain speeches with a mediocre delivery. In meeting after meeting with Paul Theis, and whenever possible with Bob Hartmann, I maintained we were underwriting for the President—selling him short—that he could deliver a good speech if we gave him better, more sophisticated writing.

These speeches represent two attempts by me to show Mr. Ford in a better light—less emphasis on tired, plain phrases and a richer development of language and thought. Hartmann bitterly attacked both speeches, particularly the Mecklenburg draft, writing me: "We need plain, simple speeches for the President and forget about trying to write another Gettysburg address." Privately and in polite terms I told Theis that Hartmann was "dead wrong" and his "hack" approach only continued the stumbler-bumbler image of the president.

Perusal of these two drafts may allow the reader to make the following judgment: would the Ford presidency and the outcome of the 1976 political campaign have been any different if Mr. Ford's speech image had changed? There were not a few in the Ford White House who believed Hartmann's unwillingness to project a more intelligent, sophisticated President cost Mr. Ford the election. The sharpest criticism was that Bob was a political and writing hack. I simply concluded that Hartmann, in his graying years, had lost sight of Tomorrow—that he had no vision. The point is, I believe very few individuals, if any, more affected the presidency of Gerald R. Ford than did Bob Hartmann; he may have much to answer for in history. Again, let the reader be the judge.—JJC

May 5, 1975
First Draft

PRESIDENT'S REMARKS AT CHARLOTTE-MECKLENBURG, N.C.
BICENTENNIAL COMMITTEE PICNIC LUNCHEON, MAY 20, 1975

It is good to be here amid the fresh air and fertile fields of North Carolina. And it is an honor to be in Charlotte at the traditional celebration of the Mecklenburg Declaration of Independence by southern patriots 200 years ago today.

Spring is always an invigorating time of year perhaps best expressed in the Song of Solomon: ''For lo the winter is past, the rain is over and gone. The flowers appear on the earth; the time of the singing of birds is come and the voice of the turtle is heard in our land.''

I come in the midst of this North Carolina spring today as a seed-sower—to plant some thoughts and ideas here in the South in the hope they may grow to enrich you and the spirit of the American people.

Ideas—like seeds—are small and fragile but they are the precious beginning of new life and growth. We in America are now in a new spring—indeed we are starting a new era in our two-hundred-year history—and it is time to plant the seeds and ideas of that future.

I do not say that we are to disregard our past—that we should, in order to start afresh, ignore many of the darker hours of the past generation. I say rather that our country must think even more profoundly and return to the very roots of this Republic—to our founding principles of individual liberty and individual responsibility.

I believe that we should evaluate our country—our convictions and our character, our dreams and our doubts, our achievements and our losses—in the light of the entire American Experience. We flatter current history to believe or assume that America will somehow rise or fall because of recent events that are only a very limited part of our history.

The American people must avoid extremes and excess in our thinking and in our expression. We must especially not embrace the extremes of either recrimination or self-righteousness. We must develop greater patience to weigh and suspend judgments. We must plant more seeds of patience and reflection in America today.

We seem to be in the midst of relentless inquisition in our country. The motives, intentions and the character of individuals involved in United States policies over the past generation are being questioned to the core. No one denies that there are legitimate areas of inquiry. It is also legitimate to insist, however, that this means should not become our end. We must be assured that the persistent raising of all manner of doubt does not become our objective. Our objective is solutions to our problems. I believe it is time to recognize that we need more solutions than questions—that we need more definitions than doubts. We must plant the seeds of solution in America today.

No one in America asks that we speak with one voice. But neither can we argue endlessly in what is wrong about America. There are some in our country who appear less interested in dialogue than their expression of difference . . . less concerned about the national good than self-attention . . . more interested in personal argument than answers to our public problems . . . and more interested in reviving the past than making reasoned judgments about our future. We must sow more seeds of reason in America today.

What we seek in our nation today is enlightenment. Blind acrimony and argument do not illuminate the problems we face. We must plant seeds of greater enlightenment in America today.

We must use words more honestly and more precisely. In our efforts to express our views, we have an obligation to speak with moderation and civility and seek more answers than doubts if we are to act as reasonable people. Strong words and harsh criticism lose legitimate force with their intensity because no American has a monopoly on right or reason. We must have a reverence for the accuracy of words and expressions. We must plant more seeds of moderation in America today.

I believe in the ideals of America. We must remember, however, that our search for values is not a reach for absolutes. Absolutes are perfection. No reasonable person expects perfection in the world because this would mean we would grow no longer. We seek to grow. We must sow more seeds of attainable growth and basic values in America today.

It was internal conflict that destroyed Greece. It may well be internal conflict—not danger from the outside—that could become the greatest threat to the American future. We cannot control the destiny of the world. Events take place around the world that are beyond the observational range—much less the comprehension—of any single nation or people. But we can to a very large extent control our own destiny. And that is precisely what this country must set out to accomplish—with reason and restraint. We must plant more seeds of restraint in America today.

The strength of every nation's existence is within itself—living and planning as a people. We need the courage to be and act what we are—a conservative people, not a nation of extremes—and follow a reasonable and steady course of action. No nation's course is charted by reaction. We must have the wisdom and self-confidence to choose what is good for our country and people—to stand with free and friendly nations—but reject the notion that we can be all things to all men.

We must assimilate the lessons of the past generation and apply them to America's future. This must be done objectively—fairly—in terms of our trials but also with a true perspective of the many noble sacrifices performed by the American people—without rewards in many instances or even thanks in others.

We are a wiser, more mature Nation today. We deserve to reap from our experiences new wisdom—not the bitter harvest of hate and hostility.

As a people, we are acutely aware of the need for honesty and candor in our land. Excessive hopes and promises—excessive secrecy and silence—excessive rhetoric and excessive reaction to that rhetoric—all of this marks a time of extreme and excess in our national conduct. We must plant the seeds of greater honesty and modesty in America today.

The fate of responsible people everywhere rests in their own hands. We must seek no excuses in the past—no excuses in the present—and offer no excuses about our future. We must plant not excuses in America but replant the principles of our early pioneers—the seeds of individual responsibility and individual liberty.

Democracy and the common good are not theoretical principles about a formless and faceless crowd of people. A democracy—our Republic—is characterized by groups and face-to-face relationships—family, church, school, workplace. Democracy was not and is not inherited by the American people. It is based on the free choice of a free people who wish to live in a free society.

Open and intelligent discussion are indispensible to the functioning of a true democracy. A mature people considers soberly and decides impartially. It seeks solutions through reason. Democracy—like liberty and freedom—requires a fragile balance to exist.

As we balance nature—and nature balances itself—there must also be balance in government. That is why we have a built-in system of checks and balances in our government. These maintain the stability of our government and lead to reasoned, gradual change—not to unreasonable and unrestrained change. We must plant more seeds of stability in America today.

We must remember that all peoples are only pilgrims on this earth. Much of our work is to keep nature and governments in balance for those who follow us.

It is said that life itself is a gift of nature. A good life is a gift of wisdom.

For the wise, the world is always being born again. And that is why a prudent man or woman will continue to replant in America the proud principles of our Declaration of Independence.

Truth has its roots in the long-ago past. It will outlast all the expedient philosophies of the present. We must be a people of truth and trust.

Two centuries ago, we the people of the United States made our essential choices. We called them inalienable rights. Life, liberty and the pursuit of happiness—their essential truth and dignity—represent the American philosophy. Americans have chosen to be governed by the consent of the people.

I say today that we must and will be governed by consent—not dissent. The American people seek reason and restraint . . . truth and justice . . . but, above all, the American people seek answers about our future—not an agony of blame and suspicion.

Our solutions will not be swift and simple. But our wisdom will show us what is right and our will will make it right.

Our horizons will become limitless because there are no boundaries for a people who live and act responsibly. America has come of age in this past decade. We are a much more mature people.

One hundred and ten years ago, our Nation ended a tragic civil war that embittered our people and left half our country in ruins. President Lincoln, in his Second Inaugural address, offered his countrymen words of restraint and wisdom:

"With malice toward none, with charity toward all, with firmness in the right as God gives us to see the right, let us strive on to finish the work we are in . . ."

Lincoln's prophetic vision was not seen by many and, unfortunately, the effects of that divisive conflict persisted for decades. The world will not permit us the luxury of such division today. We have no other course but to get on with the business of America so that we may—in the enduring expression of President Lincoln—"achieve a just and lasting peace among ourselves and with all nations."

END

333

PRESIDENTIAL REMARKS AT BICENTENNIAL COMMEMORATION OF THE BATTLE OF KINGS MOUNTAIN, KINGS MOUNTAIN, NORTH CAROLINA, TUESDAY, OCTOBER 7, 1975

We commemorate today—as part of our Nation's Bicentennial observance—the 195th anniversary of the Battle of Kings Mountain. This battle—a favorable turning point in our Revolutionary War—has been shared historically by North and South Carolina because it was fought on the borders of these sister states. It was waged by combined militiamen from several southern states—including the Carolinas, Tennessee, Virginia and Georgia.

The colonists' victory at Kings Mountain—combined with a later triumph at the battle of Cowpens, South Carolina some 25 miles away—drove the British northward. As we know, the British were finally defeated a few months later at Yorktown in Virginia.

The site and particulars of the Battle of Kings Mountain are a matter for historians, but the fact that all of us have come here today in remembrance of that struggle—to pay tribute to those who fought and fell 195 years ago—is also an historic occasion. It is a tribute to our unquenching thirst for liberty and our unending dedication to individual freedom.

I come here today to restate and renew the common aspirations of the American people—to speak of liberty, freedom and equality and to identify these with today as well as the founding of our Nation. I speak not only of our common heritage but of our common journey into the future. I speak not only of the proud principles of our past but the principles upon which the United States will build the new America.

We Americans believe that past is prologue. The past and present come together here today at this crossroads of the Carolinas to point the way to new pride for our people and new national purpose for our Nation.

This new pride and purpose in America must begin with mutual trust and understanding. These uplifting qualities have not always flowed freely throughout our society in these years.

We speak of generation gaps, education and other gaps, but

perhaps the greatest gaps of all have been the gaps of mutual trust and understanding. Between people and those who have presided over our public affairs . . . between public and private interests . . . company and customer . . . old and young . . . rich and poor . . . we have sometimes failed to build the human bridges necessary to understand the tumult and the shouting at each end of a span of misunderstanding and even mistrust.

Our society is large, complex and diverse. Our decision-making process is equally difficult, complex and diverse. Yet, it is incumbent on all of us to make this free society work. Mutual trust and understanding are the cement of our society. They are pillars in accomplishing the public's business.

Some six weeks ago, I began a program of person-to-person consultation with the American citizen. During that time, I have traveled _____ miles, visiting _____ cities and meeting with people from all walks of life. I had long ago concluded it was absolutely essential that I travel throughout the United States to persuade the American people face-to-face that our best hope for the future is in greater mutual understanding and trust. I believed it essential—for a better interchange of understanding in our society—to throw off the cloak of isolation that has cast a shadow across American leadership for the past decade and attempt to accomplish two goals:

—to demonstrate clearly my willingness to place my trust in the ultimate judgments of our people, particularly to persuade more and more to take an active part in the critical decisions that face our Nation;

—and to show beyond any doubt that this is a two-way consulting process whereby I would listen to the people and not isolate myself from the mood, the "vibrations" of our citizens across the country.

I believe it is necessary for our Government to openly offer more trust to our people.

Two hundred years ago, the American people rejected authoritarian rule. Our young patriots proved that by dying here at Kings Mountain and in similar battles. The earliest leadership of the United States had placed its trust in the *people*. Today, as we begin celebration of our Bicentennial, I believe history has come full circle: rarely has it been so necessary for American leaders—in Congress, on the state and local levels—to demonstrate their own integrity by candidly going to the American people with the problems facing us—to discuss them directly.

I believe American leadership—on national, state and local levels—is in the process of rewinning the trust and confidence of our people, but that cherished hope is yet to be fulfilled. We still need greater confidence of our citizens in government and more trust and understanding among the various elements of our society.

I believe it is the duty of the President of the United States to stress our common heritage and our common goals. I believe it is the responsibility of the President of the United States—irrespective of the differences that separate us—to renew and rededicate our society to one of national unity and national purpose. This can be done in many ways. I happen to believe the best way is face-to-face, person-to-person communication between the people and America's leadership. That is why I am here today at Kings Mountain, North Carolina, and why I will travel from here to Tennessee and later this month to other states.

If mutual trust and understanding are the cement of our society, then *common* decisions in behalf of our *common* destiny are the most constructive force for our national unity.

Many of these critical common decisions are not being made in our country today. I am told by some that our people are divided and cannot reach common consent. That some have lost confidence while others feel powerless and still others are uncertain and even uncaring and, therefore, unwilling to face the decisions before us.

This portrayal of the citizen is not new. It is as old as the human race and represents mankind's lost horizons—those who have lost faith not only in their society but in themselves. Although there have been persuasive arguments in its behalf, pessimism has never been part of the American character. Nor does it typify the American Experience.

Perhaps common consent and national purpose are impossible dreams. Like permanent peace, perhaps they will prove to be a never-ending search. But today—and throughout the celebration of our Bicentennial—we celebrate the most impossible dream of our history: the survival of the Government and the permanence of the principles of our Founding Fathers.

I have said before and I will say again: The American Dream is not dead. It has yet to be fulfilled.

We are a Nation ruled by the consent of the governed. I believe that consent—that common trust and understanding—is as necessary to our country today as it was when Thomas Jefferson wrote it into our Declaration of Independence. Two centuries ago, Jefferson wrote that governments derive their just powers from the consent of the governed.

That consent is the lifeblood of this republic. It does not exist in the rhetoric of men and women—or in the wrongs or rights of laws but it lives and thrives in the *acceptance* of the American people.

I call upon the American people to *accept* the many difficult decisions before us. I urge all Americans to *accept* the critical choices that face us. I appeal to our citizens, wherever they may be and in whatever station of life, to *accept* these challenges of our times and *NOT* accept the counsels of discouragement and dismay.

Ours is not a society of doubt because Americans have always been a people of decision. Ours is not a society of discouragement because we have always been a people of enormous enterprise. Ours is not a society of dismay because Americans have always represented mankind's greatest *hope* of liberty.

That is why I say to you today: adversity has always driven Americans to greater accomplishments. These are days of decisions. Americans have never shirked decisions. So let us be true to ourselves and to our heritage. Let us reach out, my fellow Americans, for common consent, for common understanding, for the common good of all our people. Let us act to solve the problems before us. Let us cast aside the indecision that characterizes so much of our public life. Let us offer one another trust and, in so doing, renew our support for one another as in those final words of our Declaration of Independence: ''we mutually pledge to each other our lives, our fortunes and our sacred honor.''

This is the foundationstone of America—then, now and always—our common beliefs and principles and our common destiny based on our common consent.

END

MILWAUKEE FUND-RAISER ADDRESS
(author's draft and as delivered)

The two drafts given here of the Milwaukee address are a study in contrast between the author's effort to develop new ideas and rhetoric for the GOP, and the old and safe way of addressing Republican gatherings. Hartmann threw out the author's draft as untypical and ordered another speechwriter to write the speech as delivered, which he considered the way to address the GOP.—JJC

October 15, 1975
Author's Draft

PRESIDENTIAL FUND-RAISER ADDRESS IN MILWAUKEE, THURSDAY, OCTOBER 30, 1975

(The President's preliminary remarks)

It is great to be here in Wisconsin—a state with a remarkable history of open, honest government. I commend everyone in the Republican Party—particularly the Republican state legislators—for the battle you have fought this year with the Democrats on openness of government. The Democratic majority has arrogantly—and perhaps illegally—conducted the state's business in secret. The only Open Party in Wisconsin is obviously the Republican Party. That will be much of my theme here this evening—Open Government and an Open Party.

First, I want to take a moment to salute some great Republicans of Wisconsin. Mel Laird who still brings his counsel and friendship to my office. Mel is in the private sector now, lowering his golf handicap. I will have to bring him in for more consultation.

Ody Fish whose handicap will go up next year. Ody will give six full months to make the Republican National Convention a success in Kansas City.

Your fine congressmen—Bob Kasten and Bill Steiger—who are not only outstanding Republican leaders but outstanding men. We need more of them from Wisconsin in Washington.

Bob Froehlke who, we are glad, is returning to Washington to represent the private insurance companies in the National Health Care dialogue. We learned to respect his abilities as Secretary of the Army from 1971 to 1973—doing a magnificent job for the volunteer army.

And George Parker. I cannot say enough this evening about the job George is doing as the party's state chairman. The GOP is beginning a great comeback in Wisconsin and I believe we have entrusted our future to one of the most hard-working and responsible men in the country today.

(Start of author's draft)

I am here this evening to restate and renew the common aspirations of the American people. I speak not only of our common heritage but of our common journey into the future. I address not only the proud principles of our past but the principles upon which the United States will build its future.

The United States and the Republican Party are thoroughly linked—past and future. No history of this Nation can be written without that of our party, and no historian can chronicle the GOP without returning to our country's traditional beliefs and values. You know that better than anyone here in Wisconsin. The Republican Party was founded in Ripon in 1854.

But what of the future? Does the Republican Party have a role in the future of America? What is that role? Who are these Republicans? What do we have to say to the United States?

There is increasing expression in America today that our beliefs and values are rapidly diminishing. Some say this Nation is no longer what it was in many ways. It is suggested that America has begun its decline and, perhaps, fall. Yet, millions of Americans believe in liberty, freedom, equality and justice. They believe in America and in its future. They believe in themselves. This evening, I have a message for them:

The Republican Party is the party of liberty in this country. No party is so committed to individual liberty. No party supports a stronger national defense.

The Republican Party is the party of freedom in this country. No party has fought harder for the independence of citizens and their enterprises from the ever-increasing control of Government. No party will oppose such Government control more in the future.

The Republican Party is the party of equality in this country. It is the party which offers each man, woman and child in America the creative philosophy of developing to their full potential—not advocacy of a number or a quota that will tell each of us our potential in percentage points.

The Republican Party is the party of justice in this country. No party supports more the principle that every right has its responsibility. If some Republicans have failed in the past, it is not because Republican principles have failed *them* but *they* have failed Republican principles. There can be no justice in society if there is no responsibility. The Republican of 1975 and 1976 is a Republican of, first and foremost, responsibility.

We will not run from the cancerous pessimism that pervades part of our society. The Republican platform of 1976 will not be written to profit from the Nation's trials by promising the American people the moon while sinking them deeper and deeper in a sea of debt and self-doubt. The Republican Party will face the issues squarely. We will face the pessimists directly and we will defeat them because the American people will not be deluded by those who preach the new political religion of the beginning of the American end.

The battlelines are drawn for 1976. And it may surprise you when I say that the fight will not be between the traditional Republican and Democrat. It will not be between the traditional conservative and liberal. No, ladies and gentlemen, the election campaign will not be fought between these sides. The 1976 campaign will be fought between the positive and negative forces of this country:

—The counter cultures versus those of us who believe we need to say more about what is right in America instead of carping about what is wrong.

—A battle between those who pose to question the future of democracy in this country and those who believe—and work and struggle for its future every day.

—A fight against those who exploit the lessening of respect for parents and teachers and many other traditional values—including patriotism—and those willing to renew and rededicate themselves to the social, economic and moral principles and responsibilities of this republic.

—A struggle against those who challenge the fundamental authority of our political, social, economic and other basic institutions by those of us who believe less in protest than positive, constructive action to further our Nation's progress.

These negative forces are not new to America. They are as old as the human race and they have paraded through the centuries in the uniforms and clothes of new ideas. I welcome new ideas in America.

But I will not parade them in the diatribe of discouragement, dismay, and despair. That is not a policy or a platform for a national victory. That is a policy and a platform of a Nation's defeat.

Those who would rally Americans in the spirit of dismay and discouragement represent mankind's lost horizons. They have not only lost faith in their society but in themselves.

Yes, we will conduct the 1976 campaign against the pessimists. Although there have been persuasive arguments in its behalf, pessimism has never typified the American character. Nor does it typify the American Experience. Nor will it typify 1976—the Bicentennial of our country!

The Republican Party must rebuild its spirit and the spirit of the American people. Who are these Republicans and where are these Republicans?

You are these Republicans. Your neighbors are these Republicans. These Republicans are here in Milwaukee. They are spread across the state of Wisconsin. They stretch from ocean to ocean—a thin but *continuous* line of them.

They see themselves as the political underdogs of 1976—not as pessimists but as positive people who want to know what to do and how to win. It is our job—yours and mine and many, many others—to see the 1976 election campaign for what it is: we are in the fight of our lives!

That is why I put this question to you at the beginning of my talk: Does the Republican Party have a role in the future of America?

You must answer that question. The American electorate must answer it. I must answer it. My answer is this:

The Republican Party offers the American citizen a choice. The Republican Party offers the American people an alternative. There can be no two-party system without the Republican Party.

Let us put the question another way:

What is the future of our country without the choice of a Republican Party? What is the American alternative without the Republican Party? What is freedom but choice? And what is choice but freedom? Can we have a viable American democracy without a viable Republican Party?

These are real questions at a time when the Republican Party is being really tested. What is our answer? What is our message to *ALL* the American people?

Our answer is a policy of Openness. For young and old . . . rich and poor . . . black and white . . . Independents and deserted Democrats . . . we must create new vistas in American politics. We are the party of positive principles, not pessimistic posturing . . . the party of answers and solutions, not the disseminators of doubt and despair . . . the party of reason, responsibility and restraint, not those who promise the American people more rule and less reason . . . more freedom and less responsibility . . . more spending and a weaker dollar.

In the final analysis, we oppose government without consent—the increasing encroachment of government in our lives and futures—as well as irresponsible government action on the local level.

It is neither responsible nor compassionate to spend a city into bankruptcy. It is neither responsible nor compassionate to erode the value of peoples' hard-earned money through inflation by piling government program on program on program and financing them through continual budget deficits. This is not compassion. This is irresponsible hypocrisy.

In meetings like this, the Republican Party must resolve to return responsibility to government. To do this, it must regain its strength: on the local level, in our state capitals and on Capitol Hill in the Congress of the United States.

Time after time, a ruined party has been rebuilt. Again and again, an unbeatable majority has been beaten. With good candidates, with sound principles, with real leadership, the Republican Party will make a fight of it in 1976.

I will fight by vetoing all irresponsible legislation that is passed by the Congress. The legislation that I have vetoed so far will save the taxpayers—between now and the end of calendar 1976—more than $6 billion. The pessimists will tell you that is not positive action; that is negative action. I happen to believe that a cut of $6 billion in taxpayer bills is positive action.

I have promised to cut taxes and, more important, spending. I have offered the country a comprehensive energy program—including the Energy Independence Authority that not only will help free us from foreign energy sources but create jobs and assist economic recovery.

The Republican Party must be the party of perseverance and

progress in 1976—not the party of Opposition. No one asks that Americans speak with one voice, but it is no solution to argue indefinitely about what is wrong with America. We must make sure that the persistent raising of doubt does not, in fact, become an objective—an end rather than a means. It is time to recognize that we need *answers* as well as questions about the future of our country.

The answers must come from many Americans. They must come from citizens who care about our country and care about where we are going. And we in the Republican Party must care about them—their ideas, their hopes and fears, their solutions.

I have said many times in the past that mine would be an open, candid administration. Let me say that now of the Republican Party. Let us have an open, candid party—not of left, right or center. Let us look to a fresh start—with the fresh air of open discussion, fresh ideas, and fresh faces.

We are not only a party of principles, we are a party of people. Principles live only insofar as they are supported by the people. We must bring people and principles together across our land. This is the answer to the pessimists and the doom-pushers of today: people and principles.

Americans are a people of principle. Americans care. The Republican Party has not and will not abandon America to the critics and the cop-outs. The Republican Party will unite the American people and the principles that made our Nation great . . . and together we will celebrate the victory of the United States.

END

FOR IMMEDIATE RELEASE   OCTOBER 30, 1975
OFFICE OF THE WHITE HOUSE PRESS SECRETARY
(Milwaukee, Wisconsin)

THE WHITE HOUSE
REMARKS OF THE PRESIDENT
AT UIHLEIN HALL
PERFORMING ARTS CENTER

9:22 P.M. CST   (as delivered)

Bill, former Governor Warren Knowles, Congressman Bill Steiger, Congressman Bob Kasten, Chairman George Parker, Senator Krueger, Representative Shabaz, National Committeeman Ody Fish, Finance Chairman Bill Messinger, Dinner Chairman Frank Ferguson, former Lieutenant Governor Jack Olson, First Vice Chairman Alice Read, Second Vice Chairman Curtis McKay, Dorothy McDonald, Reed Coleman, distinguished guests, ladies and gentlemen:

That concludes my speech. Thank you very much. (Laughter)

Let me thank George Parker, most affectionately known as the State's pen. (Laughter) I enjoyed the fact that George met me at the airport along with Ody Fish, but most importantly it is great to be back in Milwaukee again, particularly on the day before a favorite American event, Halloween. (Laughter) In fact, on the way in from the airport I asked Ody Fish if there was any special way people in Milwaukee and, particularly, Wisconsin celebrated trick or treat. Ody said, "Well, for the treat we pretty much give out the traditional items like candy, apples, popcorn, things like that." I said here in Wisconsin do you have any special treats—or tricks I should say. He said, "Mr. President, only when the Democrats in the Legislature work on the State budget." (Laughter)

Ody said this is one year Wisconsin Republicans could have used Houdini. (Laughter) He was an expert on getting through locked doors. (Laughter)

I commend everyone in the Republican Party, particularly the Republican State Legislators, for the battle you have fought this year with the Democrats against secrecy and openness in Government—congratulations.

Since this is our Bicentennial year, let's remember that the

345

history of the United States and the Republican Party are closely linked, no history of America can be written without that of our Republican Party. We have over one hundred years of sound principle and good people and we should be darn proud of it.

You here in Wisconsin know better than anyone, for much of the groundwork of the Republican Party was laid right here in Ripon in 1884. Of course I better mention Jackson, Michigan for some very obvious reasons. (Laughter) But tonight I want to talk with you not only of our common heritage but our common journey into the future.

Not only of the proud principles of our Nation's past, but of those upon which we must build in the future.

There is an increasing expression in America today that beliefs and values of our past are no longer relevant to our present nor to our future. Some suggest that America has seen its best days, that our decline has started, that the quality of life in America is sliding downhill, that our economy is on the skids, that the values most of us hold high are out, and the new counter-culture is in.

To that I say, nonsense, with emphasis. And to those who would write a self-fulfilling prophesy of doom for this country, I say you are out of step with the vast majority of Americans, Americans who believe in this country and in themselves and they are proud of our country and they are proud of themselves and their families.

Let me make certain there is no misunderstanding. I did not take the sacred oath of President to preside over the decline and fall of the United States of America. I totally reject the scenarios of pessimism. I have no sympathy with those who have a self-destruct attitude for this great country.

Instead, I look to the future of America, a future which will be built upon a proud past. I look to a Nation that was not only able to conquer the challenges, but provides its citizens with unmatched personal fulfillment by the year 2000.

Only a short 25 years from now, I see America, whose citizens reside in a community of peace with other nations, share the still highest standard of living in the world, live longer because killer diseases have been conquered and the quality of life enhanced, and enjoy opportunities and housing and education and jobs limited only by their personal initiatives and long-range objectives; experience, individual liberties and freedoms which have not only been secured, but expanded, whose citizens share a national will and spirit which is still climbing as this Nation moves well into its third century.

346

To make this vision come true, we must return Government to sound, responsible Republican principles, and we will. We must elect to your State and local offices and to the Congress responsible and responsive Republican candidates who believe as we do and who share our collective objectives.

The battle lines for 1976 are being drawn between these opposing forces, between those who believe in fiscal responsibility and those who believe every problem will go away if we just throw enough tax money at it.

Between those who believe a strong national defense is the best insurance of peace, and those who would spend your tax money instead for controversial social experiments.

Between those who believe in local control over local problems and those who believe Uncle Sam should help solve all problems individually and collectively.

Between those who believe that American business should be unshackled from Government over-regulation so it can expand the economy and create jobs and those who believe Federal paper shufflers know what is best for America and for its business community.

Between those who believe in the expansion of individual freedom and liberty and those who believe in big Government and that it should direct peoples' lives.

That is a fundamental issue.

Let me emphasize 1976 is more than an election year. It is also a year of decision for all Republicans. It is the Republican Party's golden opportunity to prove to all that it has the strength to survive setbacks, the resolution to rouse the Nation's greatness and the will to win elections. We can do it, and we will do it.

But, to make this proof secure, we Republicans must make some practical changes in our political ways; not in principles, but in approaches.

We must discard the attitude of exclusiveness that has kept the Republican Party's door closed while we make speeches about keeping it open. We must invite into our ranks all who care about the great country in which we live and all who share our goals enough to work through the Republican Party to achieve them.

We must build, step by step, a party that works year round and not just at election time. Most important, we must emphasize our differences with Democrats rather than with each other. We must concentrate on winning elections instead of arguments.

As we look toward 1976—and what a year to have before us—the apathy and the cynicism which have overtaken some Americans must be overcome by offering candidates of outstanding ability and rock-hard integrity.

We must develop programs that are forward looking and problem-solving, and we must elect a Congress that will carry them out, and we will.

In Bill Steiger and Bob Kasten you have quality, but we need a lot more quantity from Wisconsin. Isn't that right?

I proposed to the 94th Congress—that is the one in session now, or I guess it is in session (Laughter)—some people say it has been more out of session than in, but I wouldn't allege that, but I proposed to the 94th Congress a permanent annual cut in your Federal tax bill of $28 billion and a corresponding cut in the growth of Federal spending of the same amount.

All I get so far from this Democrat-dominated, ''can't do'' Congress is it can't be done. I say it can, it will and it must be done this year. If this Congress isn't capable of doing the job, let's elect a Republican Congress that can and will.

America's vitality, its prosperity have been sapped by the irresponsible spending of this Congress, which is controlled two-to-one by the Democrats, and a previous Congress, which has been controlled by Democrats for 38 out of the last 42 years.

I might add parenthetically, for 33 out of those 38 years, there have been deficits which have run up the cost of living and run down the value of the dollars that you earn by the sweat of your brow.

Under the Democratic spenders, the Federal budget for the first time in our history topped $100 billion in 1962. It doubled to $200 billion eight years later, and will more than double again to $423 billion in this coming fiscal year unless we get some action.

Let me emphasize, the $28 billion reduction in taxes which I proposed must be accompanied by equally substantial cuts in the growth of Federal spending. This means the spending ceiling must be $395 billion. That is adequate to meet our needs both at home and abroad, and we must get that ceiling, period. We will keep a scorecard on those that don't vote for it.

You know that under the laws . . . Democratic Congresses have already written and piled high in statute books without a single new appropriation or program . . . and despite everything I can do as President by vetoing further increases, our Federal expenditures will increase next year by $50 billion. That is just growth.

I was in California the other day, and the growth in the Federal budget in 12 months is five times the annual budget of the State of California. Something is wrong. The Democrats in Congress don't like my vetoes, but these vetoes have already saved taxpayers some $6-1/2 billion. I will go on vetoing unwise, unnecessary spending bills again and again and again and again.

I will do it as long as it saves you money, but more importantly, it saves our Nation's future, and that is the crux of the battle we are facing at the present time.

What concerns me most is what I see as Government without consent, the increasing encroachment of Government in our lives and in our future, the irresponsible Government action on the local as well as the national level.

Let's make sure we understand each other. It is neither responsible nor compassionate to spend a city or a nation into bankruptcy.

I am going to say this quietly—(Laughter)—I can assure you this President will never allow the doors of the United States Treasury to be flung open to every city with a hole in its pocket.

I suspect some of you know I spoke to this problem yesterday. (Laughter) I said that if the Federal Government goes on spending more than it has, providing more benefits and services than it can pay for, then a day of reckoning will ultimately come to Washington and to our entire country just as it has to New York City. And tonight let me ask each of you and all of you collectively that same ominous question I asked in Washington a little over 24 hours ago.

When that day of reckoning comes, who will bail out the United States? Believe me, it is neither responsible nor compassionate to erode the value of people's hard-earned money through inflation by piling Government spending on spending, program on program without the revenues to pay for them. This is not compassion, this is pure and simple irresponsibility.

I know it, you know it and 214 million Americans know it through the length and the breadth of this great country and by this time next year we should make darned sure every responsible voter knows who did it and who didn't do it.

The message of the Republican Party and what it stands for must be carried to all of the American people. We must let people know that this is the party of openness, the Republican Party, an open party that insists on open Government. And that is precisely what you are doing here in Wisconsin and I congratulate your legislative leaders. For the young and old, rich and poor, black and white, independent and discerning, and, yes, deserted Democrats, for all of these Americans and more we have something in this great party to offer them.

We are the party of principles, not pessimism. The party of answers and solutions, not the disseminators of doubts and despair. The party of reason, responsibility and restraint, not the party that purveys promises which can't be kept or programs which can't be achieved. Responsibility, that is the key word, one we acquaint with Republicanism and we have a record on this point that Republicans can stand on with pride. But we are not only a party of principles, we are a party of people and this magnificent demonstration here tonight proves it without any question. You can be missionaries in every one of the 71 counties in the great State of Wisconsin. You can say with conviction that principles can be converted into action only when they are supported by a majority of the people.

We must bring people and principles together across our land in Wisconsin and 49 other States. That is the answer to the pessimists, the doom pushers of today. We believe in people and we believe in principles.

The Republican Party's goal is to unite the American people in the principles that made our Nation great over a period of almost 200 years.

In the first 100 years of our Nation's history, we developed a form of Government that provided more liberty, more opportunities for more people than any Nation in the history of mankind. In the second hundred years of our Nation's history we developed an industrial and agricultural capacity unmatched in the history of this great globe.

In our third century we must dedicate ourselves to expanding the opportunity for freedom and liberty, individually, yes, and the Republican Party can be the mechanism for that.

In 1976 together we can celebrate a great victory with those principles and those people, a joint victory. Not merely for the Party, believe me. But for the people of the United States.

Thank you very much.

END   (AT 9:47 P.M. CST)

PRESIDENTIAL REMARKS, PEARL HARBOR, HAWAII

Two versions of these remarks follow. The first was written by the author; it was not used. The second version, as delivered by President Ford, was written by Hartmann and Friedman.

The President ultimately gave a "Gold Star Mother" speech at the suggestion of John Marsh. The author recommended against it. This was the first speech Mr. Ford would give after visiting Japan and China. The author asked: what would the Chinese think when the President rattled his sword after such a visit? And the Japanese? Why remind them of Pearl Harbor? Was it not extraordinary for an American president to visit these Far Eastern powers and then turn around and sound the trumpets of defense?

The author found it incongruous and said so to his superiors. But they were thinking of the Republican Right. And so the excuse of the "Gold Star Mothers" was used. To the author this exemplified the difference between a congressman and a president—it was Mr. Ford operating at his congressional best.—JJC

Nov. 19, 1975
Author's First Draft

PRESIDENTIAL REMARKS, USS ARIZONA MEMORIAL, PEARL HARBOR, HAWAII, SUNDAY, DECEMBER 7, 1975.

We meet here today at this crossroads of the Pacific to recall the past and to rededicate ourselves to the future.

On this solemn occasion, we honor the heroic sacrifices of those Americans who fell here at Pearl Harbor 34 years ago today.

We remember not only the past but the promise of the future—that these sacrifices and our country's efforts, to this day, may bring lasting peace to the Pacific and all of Asia.

Today marks a rendezvous not only with the past and future but with the old and new. It is a time of historic significance.

I return to the United States from a journey to Asia—to the Peoples' Republic of China, Indonesia and the Philippines.

We are building across the Pacific a new bridge of understanding between the old nations of Asia and the still young country of America. Between the ageless cultural and intellectual civilization of Asia and the young culture and civilization of America. Between the younger institutions of Asia—socially and industrially—and the

351

world's oldest republic and its most industrialized society which is America.

Asia is old and yet young. American is young and yet old.

My mission to Asia was not to cross the Pacific in miles or in hours but to span the centuries and civilizations that have kept our peoples so apart and our societies so distant for so long.

My mission to Asia was to reconcile the old and manifest the new. That aim is one and the same—to find and demonstrate harmony in diversity. That we have more in common than we do in contrast. And that which one continent has in contrast to the other complements both.

I am here today at this historic hour to rededicate the United States to the cause of lasting peace in the Pacific and all of Asia:

We seek not hostility but harmony. We seek not confrontation but cooperation. We seek not bitter rivalry but a balance of power and interests in Asia. We seek to restrict none but expect all to restrain *themselves*. We seek not the end of old revolutions but the beginning of new evolutions. We seek less our self-interest than others' self-reliance. We seek the territory of none but the eventual trust of all. We seek lasting peace but not at any price.

Let it be known and understood that while we pledge peace, we will retain our full power in the Pacific. We will resist the violent. Without security from external threat, we cannot enjoy tranquility within our own land.

Four of the world's major powers—Japan, the Peoples' Republic of China, the Soviet Union and the United States—share the greatest responsibility for peace in Asia. No misunderstanding must become too big for these nations because the world has become too small for any miscalculation.

The cornerstone of lasting peace in the Asia-Pacific area must be the balance of power and interests. There is no reason why all nations of the area cannot attain such equilibrium and stability. There is every reason for all of us to seek them.

The history of the Pacific and Asia is not so old that we cannot begin a new chapter. There is, indeed, no more solemn or sacred a place from which the American people can pledge a renewed effort for mutual understanding and trust in the Pacific.

We make that pledge at this Memorial here today—to construct a stronger and longer-range relationship with Asia—a relationship based on reason, responsibility and restraint.

Pearl Harbor remarks

Nowhere does the world offer so many people such challenges than the developing nations of Asia, striving to offer half the globe's population a better life.

We can meet this challenge of millions, literally billions of people, through common commitment in Asia:

A common commitment to greater industrial and technological development. A common commitment to increased food production in all Asian lands. A common commitment to the increased . development of natural resources. A common commitment to the freer trade of goods and the exchange of ideas and cultural achievements. A common commitment to free and fair competition in all fields of human endeavor in Asia.

These are the new bridges of a new Asia. These are the hopes of a new and better world. This is what men and women of all nations . . . all ideologies . . . all races . . . and all classes . . .. have striven and died to attain *not* only in terms of centuries but for *civilizations*.

We, the people of the United States, reach out today across the Pacific Ocean and extend the hand of friendship and fraternity to all the peoples of Asia, with whom we share a common destiny. We reach for a new future for all of us and, in so doing, join in a common journey of Asia and America toward peace and progress.

This must be the conclusion of the centuries and of history. This must be the conclusion of civilization itself.

November 19, 1975
Author's Second Draft

PRESIDENTIAL REMARKS, USS ARIZONA MEMORIAL, PEARL HARBOR, HAWAII, SUNDAY, DECEMBER 7, 1975

We meet here today at this crossroads of the Pacific to recall the past and to rededicate ourselves to the future.

On this solemn occasion, we honor the heroic sacrifices of Americans at Pearl Habor 34 years ago today. We memorialize our martyrs with reverence and gratitude.

We remember not only the past but the promise of the future—that these sacrifices and our country's efforts may bring lasting peace to the Pacific and to all the world.

Today marks an historic rendezvous not only with the past and the future but with the old and the new.

I return to the United States from a journey to Asia—to the Peoples' Republic of China, Indonesia and the Philippines.

We are building across the Pacific a new bridge of understanding between the nations of Asia and the United States. It would span the ageless civilization of Asia and the new civilization of America.

Asia is old and yet young. America is young and yet old.

My mission to Asia was not to cross the Pacific in miles or in hours but to traverse the centuries and civilizations that have kept our peoples so apart and our societies so distant for so long.

My mission to Asia was to seek harmony in diversity—to demonstrate that we have more in common than we have in contrast.

I am here today at this historic hour to rededicate the United States to peace in the Pacific and all of Asia.

We seek not confrontation but cooperation. We seek the territory of none but the trust at all. We seek lasting peace—but not at any price.

Let it be known and understood that while we pledge peace, we will retain our full power in the Pacific. Without security from external threat, we cannot enjoy tranquility within our own land.

Four of the world's major powers—Japan, the Peoples' Republic of China, the Soviet Union and the United States—share the greatest responsibility for peace in Asia. No misunderstanding must become too big for these nations to overcome. The world has become too small for miscalculation.

The cornerstone of lasting peace in the Asia-Pacific area is the balance of power and interests. All nations of the area can attain such equilibrium and stability. There is every reason to seek these aims.

The history of the Pacific and Asia is not so old that we cannot begin a new chapter. There is no more solemn or sacred a place than this Memorial from which the American people can pledge a renewed effort for mutual understanding and trust in the Pacific.

We make that pledge today—to construct a stronger and longer-range relationship with Asia—a relationship based on reason, restraint, responsibility and respect.

Nowhere does the world offer so many people such challenges than the developing nations of Asia, striving as they are to offer half the globe's population a better life.

354

Pearl Harbor remarks

Nations and peoples can meet this challenge through common commitment in Asia:

A common commitment to greater industrial and technological development. A common commitment to increased food production in all Asian lands. A common commitment to the increased development of natural resources. And a common commitment to the freer trade of goods and the freer exchange of ideas and of cultural achievements.

These are the new bridges of a new Asia. These are the hopes of a new and better world.

We, the people of the United States, reach out today across the Pacific Ocean and extend the hand of friendship and fraternity to all the peoples of Asia, with whom we share a common destiny. We reach for a new future for all. In so doing, we join in a common journey of Asia and America toward peace and progress.

OFFICE OF THE WHITE HOUSE PRESS SECRETARY
(Honolulu, Hawaii)

THE WHITE HOUSE

REMARKS OF THE PRESIDENT
AT THE
U.S.S. ARIZONA MEMORIAL

8:01 A.M. (Honolulu time)

(as delivered)

Admiral Gayler, distinguished guests:

We who remember Pearl Harbor will always remember. For us it is a moment etched in time, a moment of shock and mixed feelings and particularly disbelief, a moment of shame and a moment of sorrow, of anguish and of anger, an end to irresolutions, a summons to action, the start of a total commitment that comes but rarely to men and to nations.

Whoever watched the Pacific churned by winds of wars comes to this hallowed place with feelings overcoming words. Our shipmates who rest in honor here, our comrades in arms who sleep beneath the waves and on the islands that surround us need no eulogy beyond the eternal gratitude of the land that they loved.

On this Sunday morning in December, we remember them and in all the history of war there is a recurrent question, why do young men have to die? Why not save instead of spend our bravest and our best? Could they not live for their country, work for their country, achieve for their country? Can't we have living heroes, patriots and raise our monuments to lives well lived rather than memorials to lives snuffed out in the black smoke of battle?

I believe we can and will build a safer and saner world. If I did not believe it, then I and hundreds of thousands like me learned nothing in the Pacific during World War Two. If I didn't believe it I would not have supported America's bipartisan policy of peace through strength for more than a quarter of a century of severe challenges, trials that are far from finished here today.

If I didn't believe it, I would not have journeyed 27,000 miles around the Pacific as President to talk peace and mutually beneficial ties with the leaders of Japan, the Republic Korea, the Soviet Union, the People's Republic of China, Indonesia and the Philippines.

The one billion six hundred million people of these nations and of the United States make up more than half of the whole human family. If a majority of people want peace, why cannot the world have peace? If a majority want to live in friendship, why cannot we all live in friendship?

There may be uncertainties, but surely it is worth a try. Here in Hawaii with its diversity and its harmony, such a goal seems neither impractical nor impossible. The crossroads of the Pacific can become the crossroads of old and new civilizations, the lives of all lands can be preserved and prosper in the Pacific.

We who remember Pearl Harbor will never drop our guard nor unilaterally dismantle our defenses, but we Americans must and will use our moral leadership and our material strength to bring the Pacific community and the world little by little year by year closer and closer to real and reliable peace.

We will hold our course for a peaceful Pacific, remembering that vigilance, the price of liberty, must be paid and repaid by every generation. We will keep faith with our past as we work to build a better world for our children and our grandchildren.

I believe they will see peace come through and thank us as we thank those fallen heroes we honor here today. Their duty is done. Let us do ours.

Thank you and aloha.

END

(AT 8:07 A.M. Honolulu time)

The Ford White House Staff

White House Staff Organization Chart

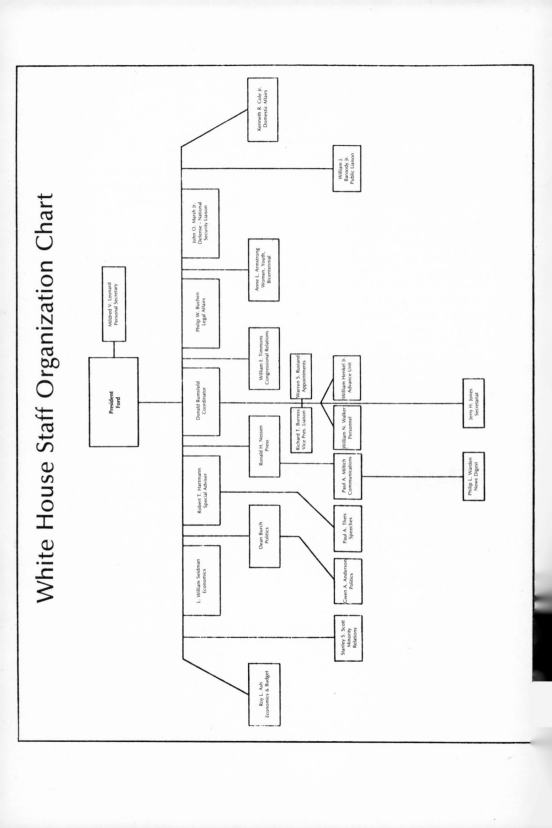

The White House Staff

Counsel to the President . . . . PHILIP W. BUCHEN.
Counselor to the President . . . . ROBERT T. HARTMANN.
    Office of Counselor: Neta C. Messersmith, Gail A. Raiman, Joann
    L. Wilson.
Secretary of State and Assistant
    to the President . . . . HENRY A. KISSINGER.
Counselor to the President . . . . JOHN O. MARSH, JR.
Assistant to the President . . . . DONALD H. RUMSFELD.
Director of the Office of Management and Budget. . . JAMES T. LYNN.
Press Secretary to the President . . . . RONALD H. NESSEN.
Assistant to the President for Economic Affairs . . . . . L. WILLIAM SEIDMAN.
Assistant to the President for Domestic Affairs . . . . . JAMES M. CANNON.
Assistant to the President for Public Liaison . . . . WILLIAM J. BAROODY, JR.
Assistant to the President for Legislative Affairs . . . . MAX L. FRIEDERSDORF.
Counsel to the President . . . . RODERICK M. HILLS.
Deputy Assistant to the President . . . . RICHARD B. CHENEY.
Deputy Press Secretary to the President . . . . WILLIAM I. GREENER, JR.
Deputy Press Secretary to the President . . . . JOHN W. HUSHEN.
Deputy Assistant to the President for National Security
    Affairs . . . . LT. GEN. BRENT SCOWCROFT,
                                            USAF.
Counsel to the President . . . . WILLIAM E. CASSELMAN II.
Special Consultant to the President . . . . ROBERT A. GOLDWIN.
Deputy Press Secretary to the President . . . . GERALD L. WARREN.
Deputy Assistant to the President for Legislative
    Affairs (Senate) . . . . WILLIAM T. KENDALL.
Deputy Assistant to the President for Legislative
    Affairs (House) . . . . VERNON C. LOEN.
Secretary to the Cabinet . . . . JAMES E. CONNOR.
Special Assistant to the President for Hispanic
    Affairs . . . . FERNANDO E. C. DEBACA.
Staff Secretary to the President . . . . JERRY H. JONES.
Special Assistant to the President for Consumer
    Affairs . . . . VIRGINIA H. KNAUER.
Military Assistant to the President . . . . CAPT. LELAND S.
                                            KOLLMORGEN, USN.
Associate Counsel to the President . . . . KENNETH A. LAZARUS.
Associate Counsel to the President . . . . JAMES A. WILDEROTTER.
Special Assistant to the President for Women . . . . . . PATRICIA S. LINDH.
Special Assistant to the President for Human
    Resources . . . . THEODORE C. MARRS.

Special Assistant to the President for Minority
    Affairs .... STANLEY S. SCOTT.
Executive Editor, Editorial Office .... PAUL A. THEIS.
    Editorial Department: Aram Bakshian, Jr., Judy Beth Berg-Hansen, Margaret
    Ann Bocek, Becky Bovelsky, Maureen W. Brown, Patricia Byrne, John
    Casserly, John Coyne, Lynda M. Durfee, Roland L. Elliott, Mary Alice
    Fenton, Cheryl Ford, Milton Friedman, Susan J. Gregory, Joann Reed
    Hamberger, Margaret Hartford, Eliska Hasek, Brenda L. Hicks, Anne
    Higgins, James H. Holmes, Claudia Korte, Earl M. Kulp, Jill McAulay,
    Caron A. McConnon, Judith D. Morton, Elizabeth A. Nolan, Robert Orben,
    Edith Perruso, Patricia A. Petrone, Gerald J. Popeo, Frances Kaye Pullen,
    Teresa B. Rhodes, Shirley Rock, Martha G. Stevenson, Pat Strunk, Agnes
    Waldron, Jo Walker, Kathryn Wooten, Ann B. Yarjan
Special Assistant to the President for Labor-
    Management Negotiations .... W. J. USERY.
Director, Presidential Personnel Office .... WILLIAM N. WALKER.
Assistant Press Secretary to the President .... MARGARETA E. WHITE.
Deputy Executive Assistant to the Counselor to the
    President .... GWEN A. ANDERSON.
Special Assistant for Legislative Affairs (House) .... DOUGLAS P. BENNETT.
Executive Assistant to the Counselor to the President JOHN T. CALKINS.
Director, Advance Office .... BYRON M. CAVANEY, JR.
Assistant Press Secretary (Domestic Affairs) .... JOHN G. CARLSON.
Assistant Press Secretary to the President .... THOMAS P. DeCAIR.
Associate Counsel .... DUDLEY H. CHAPMAN.
Personal Secretary to the President .... DOROTHY E. DOWNTON.
Director, Correspondence Office .... ROLAND L. ELLIOTT.
Director, Office of White House Visitors .... MICHAEL J. FARRELL.
Director, Office of Presidential Messages .... ELISKA A. HASEK.
Deputy Staff Secretary to the President .... DAVID C. HOOPES.
Personal Photographer to the President .... DAVID HUME KENNERLY.
Personal Assistant to the President .... MILDRED V. LEONARD.
Special Assistant for Legislative Affairs (House) .... CHARLES LEPPERT, JR.
Special Assistant for Legislative Affairs (Senate).... PATRICK E. O'DONNELL.
Aide to the President .... TERRENCE O'DONNELL.
Assistant Press Secretary .... JOHN W. ROBERTS.
Executive Assistant to the Counselor to the President RUSSELL A. ROURKE.
Director, Scheduling Office .... WARREN S. RUSTAND.
Assistant Press Secretary (Foreign Affairs) .... EDWARD J. SAVAGE.
Assistant Press Secretary .... LARRY M. SPEAKES.
Director, Research Office .... AGNES M. WALDRON.
Deputy Director, Office of Public Liaison .... DONALD A. WEBSTER.
Deputy Director, Presidential Personnel Office ..... M. ALAN WOODS.
Social Secretary .... NANCY RUWE.
Press Secretary to the First Lady .... SHELIA RABB WEIDENFELD.
Physician to the President .... REAR ADM. WILLIAM M.
                                                LUKASH, MC, USN.

White House Staff

Chief Executive Clerk .... Robert D. Linder.
Chief Usher .... Rex W. Scouten.

This Office serves the President in the performance of the many detailed activities incident to his immediate office.

The staff of the President facilitates and maintains communication with the Congress, the individual Members of the Congress, the heads of executive departments and agencies, the press and other information media, and the general public.

The various Assistants to the President are personal aides and assist the President in such matters as he may direct.

References

CHAPTER 1

David C. Whitney, *Founders of Freedom in America, Lives of the Men Who Signed the Constitution of the United States and So Helped to Establish the United States of America* (Chicago: J.G. Ferguson Publ. Co., 1965), p. 142.

CHAPTER 2

John C. Fitzpatrick, ed., *The Writings of George Washington*, Vol. III, George Washington Bicentennial Edition (Washington, D.C., Gov't Printing Office, n.d.), p. 295.

CHAPTER 3

Lewis Copeland, ed., *The World's Great Speeches from Pericles to Roosevelt* (New York: Garden City Publ. Co., 1942), p. 261.

CHAPTER 4

L.H. Butterfield, ed., *The Adams Papers/Diary and Autobiography of John Adams, Diary 1771–1781*, Vol. II (Cambridge, Mass.: Atheneum, Harvard University Press, Belknap, 1964), p. 156.

CHAPTER 5

Dwight D. Eisenhower, *The White House Years, A Personal Account, 1953–1956, Mandate for Change* (Garden City, N.Y.: Doubleday and Co., 1963), p. 296.

CHAPTER 6

Harry S Truman, *Memoirs, Years of Decisions*, Vol. I (Garden City, N.Y.: Doubleday and Co., 1955), pp. 239–330.

CHAPTER 7

Harry S Truman, *Memoirs, Years of Trial and Hope*, Vol. II (Garden City, N.Y.: Doubleday and Co., 1956), p. 196.

CHAPTER 8

Arthur M. Schlesinger, *A Thousand Days: John F. Kennedy in the White House* (Boston: Houghton, Mifflin Co., 1965), p. 719.

CHAPTER 9

Saul K. Padover, ed., *Thomas Jefferson on Democracy* (New York: Mentor Books, New American Library, 1946), p. 93.

CHAPTER 10

Frank Kingdon, ed., *As FDR Said, A Treasury of His Speeches, Conversations, and Writings* (New York: Duell, Sloan and Pearce, 1950), p. 108.

CHAPTER 11

Harry S Truman, *Memoirs, Years of Trial and Hope*, Vol. II (Garden City, N.Y.: Doubleday and Co., 1956), p. 196.

CHAPTER 12

J. G. Randall, *Midstream: Lincoln the President* (New York: Dodd, Mead and Co., 1953), p. 132.

CHAPTER 13

Dwight D. Eisenhower, *The White House Years, A Personal Account, 1956–1961, Waging Peace* (Garden City, N.Y.: Doubleday and Co., 1965), p. 631.

CHAPTER 14

Henry F. Pringle, *Theodore Roosevelt* (New York: Harcourt, Brace and World, 1956), p. 242.

CHAPTER 15

Emmet J. Hughes, *The Living Presidency* (New York: Penguin Books, 1974), p. 55. Contributed by Nelson A. Rockefeller.

CHAPTER 16

Frank Kingdon, *As FDR Said, A Treasury of His Speeches, Conversations, and Writings* (New York: Duell, Sloan and Pearce, 1950), p. 69.

CHAPTER 17

Harry S Truman, *Memoirs, Years of Decisions*, Vol. I (Garden City, N.Y.: Doubleday and Co., 1955), pp. 545, 546.

Index

Boyd, Forrest, 123
Breslin, Jimmy, 89, 263
Brezhnev, Leonid I., 3, 126, 127
Brock, William E., III, 176, 217
Broder, David S., 153, 174, 268
Brooke, Edward W., 78
Brown, Maureen, 292
Buchen, Philip W., 101, 125, 202,
    209–10; mentioned: 4, 57, 88, 100,
    153, 226, 237, 268
Buckley, James L., 97
Buckley, William F., 70
Burch, Dean, 87, 116
Burns, Arthur F., 168, 186, 191, 192,
    211, 212, 261
Bush, George, 176, 222, 226, 229, 230
Business Council, 16, 17, 18, 21, 32
Butler, Pat, 103, 133, 150, 157, 196,
    239–40, 243, 244, 265, 273, 280, 284,
    285, 286, 289–90, 291, 294
Butler, Paul, 194, 197
Butterfield, Alexander, 122
Butz, Earl L., 280
Byrnes, John, 268

Calhoun, John C., 149, 158–59, 238
Calkins, John T. (Jack), 100, 193, 194,
    195, 200, 229, 266, 272–73, 281–82,
    285
Callaway, Howard (Bo), 98, 99, 116,
    119–20, 125–26, 145, 148–49, 175–
    76, 177, 189, 216, 229, 236, 268, 279
Cannon, James M. (Jim), 80, 96, 113,
    123, 125, 128, 247, 282
Capone, Al, 196
Capovilla, Loris, Msgr., 82
Carlson, John, 222
Carter, James E., Jr., 113
Case, Clifford P., 134
Casselman, Bill, 55, 202
Casserly, John J., 2, 9, 22, 49, 69, 78,
    294
Cavanaugh, James H., 248–49
Cavaney, Red, 238
CBS News, 74, 77, 138, 235
Census Bureau, 87, 108

Central Intelligence Agency (CIA),
    96–97, 101, 112, 122, 177, 202, 230,
    247, 273
Chapman, Dudley H., 55
Cheney, Richard B. (Dick), 46, 47, 125,
    126, 135, 174–75, 176, 191, 223, 228,
    239, 243–44, 258–60, 279, 287;
    mentioned: 100, 113, 133, 157, 232,
    249, 262, 270, 281
Chicago Tribune, 201, 264
Christian, George, 104
Christian Science Monitor, 53, 186
Clarke, Ed, 140–43
Clifford, Clark, 19
Clift, Dennis, 131–32
Colby, William E. (Bill), 222, 223,
    226–27, 228, 230, 235, 237
Colson, Charles (Chuck), 10, 86
Columbus Dispatch, 206
Committee to Re-elect the President, 87
Congressional Quarterly, 144, 145
Connally, John B., 46–47, 106, 228
Connor, James E. (Jim), 96, 124, 157,
    279
Considine, Bob, 172–74
Considine, Millie (and Considine
    children), 173, 174
Coolidge, Calvin, 194
Cotton, Norris, 69
Coyne, John, 243, 246
Culp, Earl 243

Daughters of the American Revolution,
    69
Davis, Jan, 273, 280
DeCair, Tom, 217
Democratic Party Study Group, 29
Democrats, 33, 36, 43, 50, 62, 72,
    124–25, 230
Derwinski, Ed, 130, 132
Detroit, 28, 91
Devereaux, Kemp, 108
Dirksen, Everett, 135
Domestic Council, White House, 51,
    123, 169, 177, 186
Douglass, Robert, 87

Index

Index

Roman Catholic Church, 82
Romilly, George, 190
Romney, George, 98
Roosevelt, Mrs. Eleanor, 200
Roosevelt, Franklin Delano: quoted, 107,
   255; mentioned: 65
Roosevelt, Theodore: quoted, 199
Rosenberger, Theresa, 179, 241, 246
Rosenman, Sam, 19
Rousek, Bob, 133, 141, 157, 197
Rumsfeld, Donald: feuds with, 42,
   73, 75, 112–13, 119, 145, 148,
   156–58, 159, 160, 166, 169–70, 174,
   176–77, 201, 202, 208, 226, 228, 230,
   236, 268; personality & style,
   20, 40–41, 55, 75, 88, 101, 112, 120,
   124, 149, 150, 157, 158, 159–60,
   176–77, 207–8, 226, 228, 230, 231,
   267, 270; planning, 19, 22, 40–41, 48,
   54–55, 101, 130, 157, 208; and staff,
   4, 17, 19, 22, 30, 40–41, 42, 48,
   54–55, 75, 100–101, 119–20, 124,
   126, 130, 149, 150, 156–57, 159–60,
   166, 170, 174, 178, 179, 186, 207–8,
   225–26, 245, 267, 268; mentioned:
   57, 74, 123, 125, 152, 172, 181
Rustand, Warren, 64, 69, 84, 160, 164

Sadat, President, 223
Safire, Bill, 203, 293
San Diego Union, 103
Sanford, Terry, 113
Scali, John, 111
Schieffer, Bob, 74
Schleede, Glen, 51–52
Schlesinger, James, 203, 222, 223, 226,
   227, 228, 229, 230, 231, 235, 236,
   237, 239, 245, 260
Schor, Toots, 174
Scientology Ministers, National Council
   of, 123
Scott, Stan, 149, 159
Scowcroft, General Brent, 80, 100, 126,
   134, 165, 218, 222, 227
Scranton, William, 87, 268, 279
Secret Service, U.S., 57, 157, 167, 180,
   190

Seidman, L. William: personality &
   style, 16, 17, 22, 56, 60–61, 88, 116,
   117, 147, 161, 162–63, 195, 206, 210,
   237, 268; policies, 16, 17, 21, 22,
   60–61, 71, 112, 117, 161, 162–63,
   186, 206, 253; mentioned: 3, 4
Shapp, Milton, 113
Shriver, Sargent, 113
Sigma Delta Chi, Society of Professional
   Journalists, 206
Simon, William, 16, 17, 38, 100, 101,
   146, 170, 186, 191–92; mentioned:
   2, 21, 22, 168, 169, 190, 195, 211,
   236, 253–54, 261
Smith, Doug, 257–58, 272, 281–82, 290
Smith, Red, 173
Social Security Administration, 33
Socolow, Sandy, 4–5
Solzhenitsyn, Alexander, 126–27, 128,
   148
Sorensen, Theodore (Ted), 19, 195
Spaulding, Aaron, 244
Spencer, Stuart, 189
Stanford University, 166
State Department, U.S., 33, 187
Steponkus, Bill, 192–93
Stockmeyer, Steve, 192
Syracuse University, 214

Taff, Paul, 10
Theis, Paul: 2, 192–97, 203–5, 213–14;
   personality & style, 10, 27, 75, 139,
   175, 178, 179, 201, 232, 233, 235–36,
   238–39, 240–41, 252, 257, 265–66,
   269, 271–72, 283; policies, 32, 50,
   75–76, 90, 91–92, 110, 118–19, 121,
   131, 132, 133, 154, 162, 178–79, 187,
   188, 201, 202, 233, 236, 240, 243,
   257, 265, 266, 280, 284; politics,
   86–87, 96, 108, 179, 205; speeches, 3,
   16, 18, 27, 28, 29, 46, 49–50, 69, 71,
   79, 93, 114–15, 121, 131–32, 140,
   154, 161, 162, 177–79, 218, 219, 222,
   233, 239, 240–41, 242–44; mentioned:
   46, 51, 52, 76, 79, 83, 88, 186, 191,
   212, 232, 286, 292

373